Go girl!

**Raising Healthy,
Confident and
Successful Girls
through Sports**

DISCARD

by **HANNAH STORM**

with **MARK JENKINS**

SOURCEBOOKS, INC.
NAPERVILLE, ILLINOIS

This publication is designed to provide accurate and authoritative information in regard
to the subject matter covered. It is sold with the understanding that the publisher is not
engaged in rendering legal, accounting, or other professional service. If legal advice or
other expert assistance is required, the services of a competent professional person
should be sought.—From a Declaration of Principles Jointly Adopted by a Committee of
the American Bar Association and a Committee of Publishers and Associations

Trademarks: All brand names used in this book are trademarks, registered trademarks, or
trade names of their respective holders. Sourcebooks, Inc. is not associated with any
product or vendor in this book.

Published by Sourcebooks, Inc.
P.O. Box 4410, Naperville, Illinois 60567-4410
(630) 961-3900
Fax: (630) 961-2168
www.sourcebooks.com

Library of Congress Cataloging-in-Publication Data
Storm, Hannah.
Go girl!: raising healthy, confident and successul girls through sports / by Hannah
Storm and Mark Jenkins
        p. cm.
Includes bibliographical references.
        ISBN 1-57071-928-4 (pbk.)—ISBN 1-57071-972-1
1. Sports for girls. I. Title: Raising healthy, confident and successful girls through
sports. II. Jenkins, Mark, 1962- III. Title.

GV709 .S76 2002
796'.082--dc21

                                                          2002003855

Printed and bound in the United States of America
            LB 10 9 8 7 6 5 4 3 2 1

For Hannah Beth, Ellery, Riley, and their wonderful dad

Acknowledgments

No book is ever a solo effort. I would like to thank all the experts who gave of their time to talk to me about how to make girls' sports experiences positive and fun. My gratitude also goes out to Carol Mann, Deborah Werksman, and Peter Lynch at Sourcebooks, Howard Schatz, Rhonda Barrymore, all my friends at the Boys and Girls Club of Greenwich, and finally to my family, whose love and support make all the difference.

Table of Contents

Introduction

● ● ●

What are your dreams for your daughter? I know mine. I have three daughters, and I want each one of them to have the deep sense of security and self-confidence that comes from being loved and nurtured right from the start. I want my daughters to follow their dreams, have happy relationships, and fulfill their greatest potential. But how do I instill the sense of self in my daughters that will allow them to do that? I know that, in addition to the love and nurturing I give them, I need to expose them to all the positive things that life has to offer. When parents think of what is fun, challenging, and educational for girls, we tend to focus on activities like art, dance, or music. *But what about sports?*

More and more studies are showing that one of the most effective ways to raise joyful, healthy, and successful daughters is to encourage them to be physically active from a young age. It is essential to get them to participate in sports when they're old enough, and especially important to keep them involved throughout their teen years.

Even though I work in sports, I still found I needed help as a "sports parent." I was unsure of the answers to questions like, *When should I buy my oldest daughter her first bike? How early should I start my daughters in swimming lessons, or put them on a soccer team?* I looked for a resource that would help me find the right sports programs and information for my daughters. When I found that no such resource was available, I decided to create one myself by writing this book. I talked to the top experts in their fields, both to be able to answer countless questions for myself and also to pass on this information to other parents like you. Throughout the book, you will find quotes and advice from these experts that were gathered from interviews and research into their work.

You may already be eager to get your daughters involved in sports, or your children may be asking for more sports activities. Perhaps you played sports as a child and are active now, or maybe you weren't athletic as a child and don't love exercise now. Wherever you are on that spectrum, you'll want your daughters to enjoy the lifelong benefits that sports and physical activity offer: fun, fitness, and healthy competition, to be sure, but also personal development, identity, and values.

As a sports journalist, I've seen the benefits of sports for girls up close and personal. One of the most exciting things I have discovered in writing this book is the broad scope of these benefits. Sports benefit our daughters in so many ways—physically and academically as well as emotionally and socially. These are benefits that researchers have discovered after studying some of the millions of girls and young women who have played sports thanks to legislation passed in 1972 that forced public schools to give girls the same access to sports programs that boys had traditionally enjoyed. This legislation is known as Title IX of the Educational Assistance Act—"Title IX" for short—and is heralded as a watershed event in girls' and women's sports.

When I became aware of the huge advantages that sports and physical activity could offer my daughters, I became doubly interested in making sure they get the opportunities to participate in athletics. One of the most effective ways to do this is to give them the skills early on to succeed in sports—what one expert I spoke to calls the "alphabet of movement." Of course, it's important not only to teach our daughters such skills, but also to create an environment in which our daughters' success in sports is as valued as our sons'.

Some challenges come with participation in sports. That's why in these pages you'll find important information about teaching sportsmanship,

What Is Title IX and What Does It Mean in Athletics?

Title IX of the Education Assistance Act of 1972 is the federal law that prohibits sex discrimination in schools and other educational programs that receive federal funds. It applies to all aspects of educational opportunities, but is especially well known for its success in opening the door to athletics for women and girls. Because almost all public elementary schools and secondary schools, and most colleges and universities, receive some sort of federal funding, their athletics programs are covered by Title IX.

Title IX requires schools to:

- offer male and female students equal opportunities to play sports;
- treat male and female athletes equitably; and
- give male and female athletes equal shares of athletic scholarship money.

preventing and treating injuries, practicing good sports nutrition, and working with coaches. I have also provided information on fitness, an important topic distinct from sports participation, and a section on individual sports so that you can find the right activities to offer your daughter.

There's so much we need to know! But by using the sound advice I got from top experts, you can be assured that you're doing your very best to help your daughter feel healthy, happy, and ready to take on the world!

chapter 1

Why Girls Need Sports

● ● ●

There's no doubt about it: *sports are good for girls.* You need only to watch TV or read the newspapers to be aware of the growing body of evidence attesting to the importance of girls playing a wide variety of sports. Scarcely a week goes by without news of another major study extolling the virtues of sports and physical activity for girls. A blue-ribbon committee formed by the President's Council on Physical Fitness and Sports examined the results of dozens of these studies and released them in a landmark 1997 publication called *Report on Physical Activity and Sports in the Lives of Young Girls: Physical and Mental Health Dimensions from an Interdisciplinary Approach.* The bibliography in this report ran for pages and pages!

The depth and breadth of this information made me even more determined that my daughters get the opportunity to become athletes—girls who are as likely to play basketball as take figure-skating lessons, and who are more interested in being at the local Boys & Girls Club than at home on the couch. My conclusions can be summed up by legendary former U.S. Surgeon General Dr. C. Everett Coop, who said, when I asked him about sports for girls, "The health and social benefits to girls of participating in sports programs are self-evident in the present and incalculable in the future." I believe that it is essential that we create a *sports-positive* environment for girls. To do that, we need to understand how vital sports are for our daughters. So, before we address how to get our daughters into sports and keep them involved, let's take close look at the benefits of physical activity for girls.

Three Forms of Fitness

The benefits of sports for girls can be divided into three main areas of "fitness," what I classify as *health fitness*, *academic fitness*, and *emotional/psychological fitness*.

Health Fitness

Vigorous physical activity benefits kids of both sexes, and bodes well for good health into adulthood, but it is becoming increasingly clear that sports and exercise have special benefits for girls, including reduced risk of some chronic illnesses later in life, improved body composition (the ratio of fat to muscle), a stronger immune system, decreased menstrual discomfort, and stronger bones.

Reduced Risk of Certain Chronic Illnesses in Later Life

Being active as a child reduces the risk of certain deadly diseases in adulthood. Heart disease, hypertension, and diabetes are all seen less frequently in women who were active as girls, as are endometrial and breast cancer. Girls who play sports begin menstruating a little later than girls who are inactive. This is believed to have something to do with lower fat levels in girls who are active, and studies have shown that for every year a girl's menstruation is delayed, the risk of her contracting breast cancer as a woman is reduced by 5–15 percent.

Improved Muscle-to-Fat Ratio/Body Composition

Approximately twice as many kids are overweight today as compared to the 1960s. The states of being overweight or obese are defined in chapter 11. Being overweight or obese is a risk factor for a host of killer illnesses, most importantly heart disease, hypertension, diabetes, and certain cancers. Kids become overweight because they expend fewer calories than they consume. Not exercising enough is particularly prevalent among adolescent girls who, at this self-conscious time in their development, are too often taught to believe that sports are "unladylike." Not surprisingly, kids who play sports and are physically active are much less likely to be overweight than those who are "couch potatoes." And, a healthy body composition contributes to better lifelong health overall.

Stronger Immune System
Moderate exercise strengthens a child's immune system by increasing the levels of various disease-fighting substances in the body, including interferon and interleuken-1. Being in shape can help a person combat diseases ranging from the common cold and flu to cancer.

Less Menstrual Discomfort
Exercising several times a week has been shown to decrease menstrual complaints in girls: their periods are more regular and they have lighter flow, less cramping and discomfort, and shorter duration of flow.

Stronger Bones and Lower Chance of Developing Osteoporosis Later in Life
By increasing the strength and thickness of their bones when they're young, exercise helps young women avoid osteoporosis in later life. In addition to "weight-bearing" exercise (anything you do on your feet) such as running, walking, and aerobic dance, strength training with weights is extremely effective at building bone strength. Because strength training is now thought to be so important for young girls, you may want to find a strength-training program for your daughter or design one yourself. We'll talk more about strength training in chapter 9.

Academic Fitness
Modern scientific evidence reinforces the age-old belief that a healthy body is a prerequisite to a healthy mind. Or, put more simply, if you want to help your daughter excel in school, *get her into sports!*

Numerous studies have examined the effect of sports participation on girls' academic performance, and the results are stunning. Here's how young female athletes compare to girls who don't play sports:

- They have higher grade point averages.
- They score better on their SATs.
- They have a lower risk of dropping out of school.
- They have a better chance of getting into, staying in, and performing well in college.

Girls who play high-school sports significantly outperform nonathletic girls in academic subjects such as science and math that tend to be dominated by boys. Because experts believe that the male dominance in these subjects is psychological and has nothing to do with intelligence, this suggests that participating in sports gives girls the confidence to participate on a more equal footing in the classroom with boys. In addition, exercise may actually make our brains work better! Experiments have shown that physically fit rats are smarter at figuring out mazes than their overweight peers.

Emotional/Psychological Fitness

The physical benefits of playing sports are almost a given; what I find really exciting is the fact that physical activity has a profound effect on the emotional and psychological health of girls.

Exercise has repeatedly been shown to improve how girls feel about themselves in areas such as self-esteem, self-concept, self-confidence, and perceptions of competence. Girls who are active also tend to be more optimistic, which has a direct bearing on motivation, and therefore achievement. According to the Women's Sports Foundation, 80 percent of female Fortune 500 executives identified themselves as former "tomboys."

Experts believe that it is not just enhanced fitness that improves girls' emotional and psychological health (although this is certainly a factor), but also the very act of participating in sports that is empowering.

With improved self-esteem comes benefits that all of us parents can appreciate: a lower risk of sexual behavior and pregnancy, as well as reduced drug and alcohol abuse. Girls who are athletes are also less likely to smoke or to have eating disorders.

In addition, physically active girls are less likely to be victims of anxiety and depression, two conditions that are sadly on the rise among teenage girls in our society (girls are *twice* as likely as boys to suffer from anxiety and depression). In fact, exercise is such an effective preventive measure against developing emotional problems that it is increasingly being used by therapists to treat patients, and doctors routinely prescribe exercise to combat depression. The prestigious International Society of Sports Psychology finds a positive relationship between physical activity and mental health, concluding that exercise can help with anxiety, mild depression, and stress reduction, both short- and long-term.

The emotional and psychological rewards of participating in sports for girls include better self-image, higher confidence, increased energy, less tension, and a stronger ability to deal with challenges life might throw their way.

Why Sports Build Emotional/Psychological Fitness

Numerous theories have been advanced to explain why sports enhance emotional/psychological health in athletes, especially girls. It's likely that the answers lie in a combination of the following biological and psychosocial factors.

Supporters of the biology school of thought contend that exercise releases certain chemicals in our brains—serotonin, for one—that give us a natural "high" that also works as an antidepressant. Other scientists point to the stress-relieving effect on the body that occurs when it gets warmer during exercise. Some experts believe that moving the body simply reverses the natural inclination of the depressed person to be still, and in so doing counteracts feeling depressed.

From a psychological standpoint, there is evidence that sports and athletics provide girls with a sense of self-control and competence, and a channel for emotional release. Sports also give girls opportunities to positively interact with their peers and coaches, who can be strong adult role models and reinforce parental support.

Sports and "The Complete Girl"

"Sports and physical activity are not a separate component of a girl's life," says Dr. Barbara Moore, president of *Shape Up America!*, the health and fitness organization founded by former U.S. Surgeon General C. Everett Coop. "They permeate every aspect of her existence, from her health to her academic performance to her popularity among peers." As we've seen, sports and physical activity have a *positive* impact in these areas that make up "the complete girl." That is why I believe it is so important that we encourage and give girls the opportunity to play sports and exercise.

I grew up in an era when sports for girls were not encouraged. Most parents didn't think much about whether their daughters were physically active. Luckily for me, both of my parents were good athletes and my father was a team sports executive, so they actively encouraged me to play sports. In grade school, I played a little soccer and softball. Later, I discovered my talent for high jumping, and joined the high-school track team. I was also our school mascot (a wildcat!) and ran our pep rallies. I certainly wasn't an elite athlete, but I had fun, and the fact that my sports experience was so positive explains why I continue to be physically active as an adult. Even with three kids, I still try to stay physically fit by making time to hit the treadmill and lift a few weights a couple of times a week. I also believe that the qualities I learned in sports, especially discipline and teamwork, have helped me in my competitive, high-pressure job.

Because I believe so strongly in the benefits of sports, I was dismayed to learn that girls drop out of sports in numbers disproportionately higher than boys. It's not sports themselves that can turn girls off, but rather factors such as peer pressure, lack of parental support, negative cultural images, and the way that some sports programs put too much emphasis on winning. We will address these issues later in the book.

Now that we know what extraordinary benefits are available to girls who play sports and are physically active, the remainder of this book will help you make sure your daughter has every opportunity to experience these benefits!

chapter 2

Baby in Motion
Nurturing Your Pre-athlete (Birth to Two Years)

One of the great joys of being a mother is marveling at the simple things that babies learn to do—who can ever forget their baby's first smile or first steps? Also parents naturally worry about our daughters' development: *Shouldn't my baby be walking by now? Why isn't she crawling yet?* The seasoned pediatrician's answer is always the same—"Relax, every baby is different." In fact, anyone who has more than one child can attest to that! I had one daughter who held her head up and looked me right in the eye the day she was born, and another daughter who didn't walk until she was seventeen months old.

Some little girls may seem physically gifted from the start, and others may seem happier sitting still and watching the world go by. It is very important as parents not to stereotype our daughters as "athletic" or "not athletic" at an early age. *All* girls need to be physically active in some way. You should know that even top researchers who've devoted their lives to helping young children improve their movement skills agree that there's little a parent can do to accelerate their baby's acquisition of large movement skills.

"Early on, movement skills are 'hardwired,'" says Linda Bunker, a professor at the University of Virginia's Curry School of Education, who has been studying motor learning and sports performance for over three decades. "In

When Concerns about Movement-Skill Development Are Justified

Many parents with concerns that their toddler is developing slowly are just being impatient or comparing their child to another youngster who's an early developer. For these parents, things almost always work out just fine. But certainly there are situations where concern *is* justified. A good guideline is the "30-percent rule," which holds that developing movement skills *more than 30 percent later than average* may be cause for concern. For example, since most children walk between twelve and fifteen months, a child who shows no inclination of walking by seventeen months old may benefit from a visit to the pediatrician, or in some cases, a specialist.

You may also benefit from speaking with other people who see a lot of children. It was my daughter's nursery-school teachers who confirmed that my daughter had more difficulty doing some things that her peers found easy. We discovered that she had muscle weakness on one side of her body, which has been helped immensely with occupational therapy.

other words, until kids are about two years old there's almost nothing you can do to hurry along skills such as sitting, crawling, or walking."

Poring over growth/development charts and worrying about when your daughter lifts her head or starts running around the yard is a surefire recipe for sleepless nights—and is completely unnecessary.

It's also important to make the point that there's really no relationship between early movement-skill development and future athletic success: the baby who reaches those "honey-get-the-videocam" milestones early on is not necessarily destined for Olympic gold, the same way that the tot who learns to walk relatively late is not doomed to warm the bench.

That said, almost every expert I spoke to when writing this book emphasized that what we *can* do is provide our babies with the freedom to learn these skills at their own pace.

"The most important thing you can do at this stage is to give your daughter opportunities to investigate the world around her," says Linda

Bunker, who also happens to be one of the country's leading advocates for girls' participation in sports. "The more a baby sees, touches, tastes, hears, and smells, the more she develops neural pathways that allow her to process information better as she matures."

Legendary child movement-skill development expert Dr. Vern Seefeldt of Michigan State University, who is the founder of the prestigious Institute for the Study of Youth Sports, puts it this way: "Don't pressure her to crawl or walk, just provide her with an environment conducive to trying out these things."

Dr. Seefeldt points out that physical exploration helps develop a baby's brain, "so that each time a child acquires a new skill—lifting her head, for

Infant Fitness Programs: Unnecessary—and Potentially Dangerous

Blame our "overachiever" society for the fact that intensive infant fitness programs are on the rise. Promoters claim that participation in these programs helps very young kids get a head start on fitness and movement skills. However, most child-development experts believe that these programs are at best useless and at worst harmful.

Experts familiar with infant development believe that because movement-skill development occurs primarily as a result of natural curiosity, structured exercise programs do no good at all. They may even take away from time we parents should be spending with our infants in touching, holding, face-to-face contact, and minimally structured playing situations.

Not only that, but infants don't have the strength or reflexes necessary to protect themselves from outside forces, and when parents force their baby's body into extreme positions, as these exercise programs often recommend, they may unknowingly injure their soft, still-unformed bones.

The American Academy of Pediatrics is quite forthright on the subject, stating that "structured infant exercise programs [should] not be promoted as being therapeutically beneficial for the development of healthy infants."

example—she receives new stimuli from the world around her that encourage her to take on more complex tasks."

According to every expert I spoke with about helping our daughters develop their movement skills, the bottom line is this: we have to give our children the freedom to explore, but not overprotect them. An overprotective parent is often the culprit when a child is taking too long to reach a movement-skill milestone. A not-uncommon example is parents who are concerned because their baby isn't rolling over. When the pediatrician asks if they ever put her on the floor, they say never. Within a few days of being put on the floor, *presto!* The baby girl rolls over! I see many parents (especially when it's their first child) who carry their infants constantly. This isn't helpful for our daughters' motor-skill development—we need to give them freedom to move around. Like many, I was overprotective of my first child. Whenever she fell, I immediately rushed to her side, and I constantly warned her to "be careful." This can make our firstborns overly cautious. We have to give our children the *chance* to learn how to walk. That includes learning to get up after they fall! We want to do for our children, but when it comes to developing movement skills, babies need to do for themselves—and in their own time.

What can we do to help our daughters develop their movement skills on their own? Here are some specifics:

- Before she learns to sit up, place items such as a "crib gym" within her reach so she can practice her hand-eye coordination. My personal favorite is a product called Gymini, made by Tiny Love and available in any children's store. Once she is rolling over and sitting up by herself, give your daughter other toys to hold and play with, such as balls, unbreakable mirrors, and blocks.
- Before you know it, she's on her feet—usually within six to ten months after birth. Hold her hands as she pushes up to a standing position or bounces to a song on your stereo.
- When she's up and walking, it's play time! Offer her low-tech, push-and-pull toys or even an old-fashioned hobbyhorse. Even though our daughters will teach themselves to walk and run without us cheerleading them on, they'll be all the more motivated when we encourage them and join in the fun!

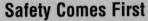

Safety Comes First

It's extremely important to give our baby daughters the opportunity to explore their world. However, this has to be balanced with safety considerations. You want to prevent your child from getting into unsafe cabinets or falling downstairs. Make sure to secure gates at the top and bottom of stairways and be aware that you usually need a more secure type of gate (one that is actually attached to the wall) for the top of the stairs. Childproof as large an area as possible to allow her room to move around safely, keeping in mind not to make it overly restrictive. Remember that unless she's in her crib, you always need to keep an eye on an infant who's "on the loose."

Do We Treat Our Female Babies Differently Than Our Boys?

I'll never forget a gift that I received when my first daughter was born. Amidst all the teddy bears and baby dolls, one friend brought a little stuffed football to my hospital room. When the baby pressed it, it said "Go! Go! Go!" followed by the sound of a crowd cheering. It was one of my favorite presents, and hers too, but admittedly it was unusual. Had I not been a sportscaster, I doubt my baby girl would have received a football toy.

Typically, baby boys get balls and trucks and baby girls get dolls and clothes, because the girls are seen as more delicate than the boys. However, at this stage in their very young lives, there are few differences between the way boys and girls develop physically. In some respects, girls are more advanced. Studies have shown that up to the age of five, girls have movement skills that are measurably *superior* to those of boys'. In general areas such as balance, agility, accuracy of movements, and overall coordination of these skills, girls perform better than boys. However, girls eventually fall behind in their movement-skill development because they tend not to receive sufficient encouragement from parents and other adults, and therefore boys overtake them.

Often, differences in the way we socialize girls and boys begin in the crib. As Linda Bunker puts it, "It's as if in some respects parents are

Gymboree Play Tips

Featured in this section are fun activities you can do with your baby, created by Gymboree Play and Music and reprinted with the permission of Gymboree. These play tips were created to support different aspects of your child's development. Remember, all activities should be performed under the direct supervision of an adult.

Activities for Age 0–6 months

Bolster/Cushion

Fold a towel or blanket in half lengthwise. Roll it tightly, jelly-roll style, and secure with masking tape at each end. Place infant's chest on bolster with arms over edge. This strengthens neck muscles and gives your baby a new angle on the world.

Beach Ball

Lay infant atop a large beach ball on tummy with head turned slightly to the side. With your hand on baby's back, gently rock the ball back and forth and side to side for a strength- and balance-building experience.

Bubbles

Place your infant on a blanket or propped up on a bolster. Gently surround her in a shower of bubbles. Watch her changing responses as visual skills develop.

Blankets

A sturdy blanket makes a soothing "hammock" and stimulates an infant's sense of balance. With your baby face-up in center of blanket, have two adults face each other, and gently sway blanket side to side, then lift up and down.

Scarves

Use a variety of scarves to stimulate your infant's sense of touch. Gently rub baby's arms, legs, and head with the scarf. Lightly cover baby with scarf and pull it up and down the length of baby's body.

Activities for Age 6–12 months

Bolster/Cushion

Fold a towel or blanket in half lengthwise. Roll it tightly, jelly-roll style, and secure with masking tape at each end. With baby on her back, slowly roll bolster from baby's toes to chest for a soothing full-body massage.

Beach Ball

Play a game of "Baby Soccer": hold your child by the torso and gently swing her forward so that her feet "kick" the ball. This game can be played facing a wall, or another player.

Bubbles

Blow and catch a single bubble on a wand. Hold it out for baby to watch as you move it across her field of vision. Encourage baby to reach out and "pop" the bubble.

Blankets

As your baby watches, place a toy under a blanket. Ask her to find the toy, testing her ability to hold mental images. The blanket also makes a useful prop in a game of peek-a-boo.

Scarves

Place a scarf over your head and invite your baby to pull it off. This game reinforces her understanding that objects and people continue to exist even when out of sight—an important milestone.

Activities for Age 10–18 months

Bolster/Cushion

Scatter sofa cushions on a carpeted surface for your child to crawl on. Stack two or three cushions to support your pre-walker in a standing and cruising position.

Beach Ball

Ball play helps children understand cause and effect. Slightly deflate a beach ball making it easy for small hands to catch. Sit opposite child and roll ball back and forth. Challenge your early walker to walk while holding the ball.

Bubbles

Cover a coffee table or other favorite cruising spot with a tablecloth. Blow bubbles so that they land on the table for your child to pop. Watch as your child's eye-hand coordination and accuracy improve.

Blankets

With another adult, hold a blanket or mini-parachute above your child's head. For a test of balance, raise and lower it gently while your child stands underneath. Walk in a circle holding the blanket overhead singing "Ring around the Rosy" or other circle songs.

Scarves

Fill an empty container with several scarves and watch your child enjoy pulling them out, stuffing them in, and dumping and filling the container, over and over again.

Activities for Age 14–24 months

Bolster/Cushion

Scatter sofa cushions to create an obstacle course for your toddler to walk on and around. Invite your child to follow you as you walk through it.

Beach Ball

Build eye-hand coordination with a game of catch. Using a slightly deflated beach ball, kneel two to three feet in front of your child as you throw and catch the ball together.

Bubbles

Cover a table with a blanket or sheet to create a bubble fort. Crawl inside with your child and blow bubbles for her to catch.

Blankets

Challenge your child's ability to balance while in motion. Seat her on a blanket, placed on a carpeted floor. Pull her around the house on the blanket. Take care rounding corners and furniture on your indoor expedition.

Scarves

Give your toddler a scarf to hold in each hand. Play music and encourage her to dance and wave the scarves. Challenge listening skills by "freeze dancing"—stopping all movement when the music is unexpectedly turned off.

subconsciously preparing their boys for the rough-and-tumble of sports, while girls are being groomed for more demure activities." When baby girls cry, for example, they are picked up more quickly, held longer, and spoken to in a gentler, more soothing voice than baby boys are. In a study done at a hospital where infant girls were deliberately mislabeled as boys on their diapers, and vice versa, visitors invited to play with these babies treated them in different ways depending on whether they thought the babies were boys or girls. As one observer put it, "girls were handled like porcelain dolls while the visitors gently roughhoused with the boys."

There are many ways parents reveal different images and expectations of their infant children depending on whether they are boys or girls:

- Parents tend to describe their daughters as smaller, softer, and cuter than their sons, regardless of what they look like.
- Sons are generally described as stronger, more coordinated, and more alert than daughters.
- Parents tend to describe newborn girls as finer featured, less strong, and more delicate than newborn boys.
- Fathers engage in more active play with their sons than with their daughters, and are more likely to cuddle with their daughters than their sons.

Professor Susan Greendorfer of the University of Illinois is an expert in the field of how parental behavior impacts girls' participation in sports. "Certain messages about gender and definitions of masculinity and femininity are transmitted through everyday practices," says Greendorfer. "Something as simple as the contents and décor of a child's room can tell us a lot about how kids are socialized—and what their attitudes are toward physical activity." As she points out, long-term studies show that attitudes have not changed much in the last twenty years. Greendorfer points to two studies of children's rooms—one done shortly after passage of Title IX in 1975 and the follow-up done fifteen years later. In both studies, boys' rooms were more sports- and action-oriented, while girls' rooms were more family-oriented. Boys' rooms tended to contain more vehicles, machines, and sports equipment than girls' rooms, which were more likely to feature dolls, stuffed animals, and patterned decorations. Says Greendorfer, "How their rooms look send strong messages to our daughters about what girls are, what they do, and what they should be compared to boys."

There are no easy answers here, but this is an issue for parents of baby daughters to keep in mind. We will revisit this subject throughout this book when it comes under the more ominous label of "gender stereotyping." Meantime, it's important for us all to be aware that, deliberately or not, we may be treating our baby daughters differently than our sons, and we should avoid doing so lest we be putting them at a disadvantage later on.

chapter 3

Planting the Seed Early

How to Introduce Movement Skills into Young Lives (Two to Five Years)

The time in our children's lives between the ages of two and five is crucial when it comes to acquiring fundamental movement skills. Learning these skills early can set the stage for a successful sports experience later on and inspire a lifelong passion for physical activity. Conversely, kids who don't acquire these skills at a young age can be at a major disadvantage when they get into sports. Experts have identified a set of fundamental movement skills that are key to future sports success, and we'll look at these later in this chapter. However, many parents are *overly* eager to place their kids in organized sports when they're very young—so let's look at that issue first.

The Value of Sports Environments

Children shouldn't play team sports until they're about six years old. That's a sound guideline from the American Academy of Pediatrics (AAP). The reason is that before the age of six, children really don't understand the concept of teamwork (in psychological terms, they're "egocentric").

However, the AAP acknowledges that children develop at different rates, and your daughter may be ready a little before that age. On the other hand, she may not be ready for team sports until age seven or older. Take

Movement-Skill Milestones

Here are some of the movement-skill milestones you can expect your child to reach between the ages of two and five:

- **At Two Years...** She can walk and run confidently. She can go up and down stairs, pausing with both feet on each stair before going onto the next one, and perhaps needing to hold onto the banister. She can catch a big ball when you gently lob it at her, can jump in place on both feet, and is ready to start learning to ride a tricycle.
- **At Three Years...** She can now ride a tricycle, kick a large ball, and throw a small ball underhand. She boldly goes up and down stairs by herself. She runs, jumps, and hops.
- **At Four Years...** With her balance improving even more, she can hop on one foot and walk downstairs unassisted using the right foot and then the left. She can dodge you as you reach for her in a game of tag. She can throw a ball overhand.
- **At Five Years...** Watch out! Now she can run like the wind with her arms swinging in opposition to her feet the way they are supposed to. She can also skate, skip, and jump rope. Those stairs? She goes up and down them faster than you!

the quiz on page 41 to see if your child is ready for organized team sports. Remember, young kids have many years ahead of them when they can play sports, so there's no need to push them into soccer or T-ball before they are ready. If your daughter does try sports early on and doesn't like them, there's always next year.

Now what about classes in swimming, dance, gymnastics, or figure skating? There are tumbling, gymnastics, and dance classes for kids as soon as they can walk. Swimming classes shouldn't start until age five, while skating classes can begin as young as three years old. The three-to-five-year-old age range is typical for starting your daughter on figure skating. Institute for the Study of Youth Sports founder and movement-skills development expert Dr. Seefeldt maintains that it's fine for a child to participate in such

activities so long as the emphasis is on the joy of movement and participation, not competition or teaching exact technique.

One of the most important things we can do is put our kids in a variety
of sports-positive environments where they can enjoy themselves and at
the same time start learning skills they can use later. For example, kids love
skating rinks, and letting your daughter tentatively glide around on the ice
while holding a chair, or your hands, can sow the seeds of a love for skating that may evolve into a lifelong interest in figure skating or hockey. The
same goes with kicking a ball back and forth in the backyard (soccer),
throwing a ball around the park (softball), and tumbling at a Gymboree
class (gymnastics). These activities can help our kids develop the kinds of
fundamental movement skills that we'll address later, such as throwing,
kicking, running, jumping, catching, striking, hopping, and skipping.

If you're athletic yourself, it's tempting, as soon as your daughter takes
her first steps, to imagine her as an athlete. However, you shouldn't rush
your child into any particular activity. Often this happens when parents
have had strong experiences in particular sports. I fell into this trap once.
Based on how much I had enjoyed ice skating in grade school, I bought
my four-year-old daughter a tiny pair of skates and went to considerable
lengths to find her a coach. She wasn't the least bit interested, and much
preferred running around the rink facility than being out on the ice! I
should have bought *myself* a pair of skates and taken a spin!

In general, as far as organized leagues go, competition at this stage is
counterproductive—play isn't about winning or losing. Young kids tend
not to be adventurous when they think there's something at stake. These
inhibitions restrict their willingness to try new things, which is precisely
what we're trying to encourage at this stage.

Learning Fundamental Movement Skills

Sometimes it is challenging, but I try as often as possible to make sure that
my girls are moving around and learning to use their bodies. Kids aged two
to five years old benefit from being placed in active environments so they
can start to learn fundamental movement skills. Dr. Vern Seefeldt has done
extensive studies of movement skills and their relationship to sports, and
what he has found out—not surprisingly—is that young kids with strong

Other Activities

- Hopscotch—This age-old schoolyard game can easily be set up on a patio or in a driveway using sidewalk chalk, and encourages jumping and balance.
- Frisbee—Every child enjoys running to catch a Frisbee and spinning around to toss it. Be sure to throw the Frisbee to your daughter softly and encourage her to throw it as high and far as she can.
- Wiffleball—Using a ball full of holes and a plastic bat, your daughter gets practice at swinging, striking, and catching.
- T-ball—Many communities offer T-ball leagues for young children. The game is easy enough for this age group and encourages running, throwing, striking, and catching.
- Swimming—A two- or three-year-old will enjoy splashing in a pool, using her arms and legs while you hold her horizontally (face up) in the water. By age four to five, your daughter may be ready for swimming lessons. Children at this age must always be supervised while in the water—never leave your child alone in a pool.
- Tag—What could be more fun than running around in the yard or park, playing this simple game? Kids love variations like "freeze tag" or "animal freeze tag."
- Kickball—Kickball is an informal name for several different games played by children. In one version, kids chase and kick a semi-soft soccer ball or basketball across the yard aiming at one or multiple "goals." Another version of kickball is actually a variation of baseball in which a large rubber baller is rolled, instead of pitched, to the "batter," who puts the ball into play by kicking it. No matter what version they play, the important things is that kickball can be played in teams or unstructured groups, and encourages leg strength, kicking, and aim.
- Dancing—Children love to dance; all you have to do is move the furniture out of the way and put on some music. Classical music allows for long stretching movements; rock and roll will encourage more jumping around.

- Basketball—Fisher Price makes a kid-sized basket you can place in your backyard. Its height is adjustable so you can challenge your daughter as her aim gets better.
- Bike Riding—Even small children can ride, tricycle, or big-wheel on a patio or up and down the sidewalk. They enjoy moving around under their own locomotion, and will be developing their leg strength at the same time. Be sure to have your child wear a helmet.

fundamental movement skills perform better when they start sports. In addition, having strong fundamental movement skills helps kids *stick with sports*. That's because the better our daughters perform in sports, the more valued they will feel, and therefore the stronger the impetus will be for them to continue participating.

Dr. Seefeldt has divided these fundamental movement skills into three different categories: "locomotor," "non-locomotor," and "projection/reception of objects." In layman's terms, we can define them as "moving around," "moving your body while stationary," and "throwing/catching/kicking." Dr. Seefeldt calls these skills "the alphabet of movement" because, as he puts it, "the same way you couldn't spell if you didn't know the letter alphabet, you can't be expected to know how to move to your fullest potential if you don't know the 'alphabet of movement.'"

These are the skills he identified:

Moving around	Moving around while stationary	Throwing/catching/ kicking
Walk	Swing	Catch
Run	Sway	Throw
Leap	Rock	Kick
Jump	Stretch	Punt (a kick in which the ball is dropped from the hands and kicked before it touches the ground)

Gallop	Curl	Strike (to hit an object, such as a ball, with an implement such as a bat, stick, or racket)
Slide	Twist	Trap (to stop an airborne ball against the ground using one's feet)
Hop	Turn	Dribble with the feet, as in soccer
Skip	Bend	Roll (sideways as well as forward body rolls)
Roll	Push	
Stop	Lift	
Start	Pull	
Bounce	Hang	
Fall		
Dodge		

Again, helping our kids to start to acquire these skills early on is so important because it makes them successful in sports at a young age and thereby sets them up for a lifetime of sports and physical activity. In addition, children who are physically unskilled may be excluded from group activities and games. Dr. Seefeldt recommends that we encourage our kids to start learning these fundamental movement skills as early as eighteen months old, and certainly as soon as they start walking. Some skills you

Don't Push Too Hard

Children benefit from activities that they are comfortable with; trying to rush them can make them feel intimidated and may turn them off a particular activity. Let's say your daughter can climb the ladder of a playground slide but is uncomfortable with clambering over the top and sliding down. It's OK to offer help and give her a hand if she accepts it. But if she just wants to climb down the way she came, that's fine, too—she'll get around to making the slide soon enough. Kids progress at their own pace. The less we push, the more likely they'll try again until they succeed.

can start early—you can start teaching a child to catch and throw early on simply by having her hand you a ball and then passing it back to her. More challenging skills—such as punting and hanging—will be beyond the abilities of the average toddler, but you should be keenly looking for the time when your daughter is ready to begin learning them—as determined by her receptiveness and ability. Don't be afraid of giving her the opportunity to learn a more advanced skill even if you think it's too early. Just be willing to back off if she's not yet ready.

Parents should understand that there is a relatively brief window of opportunity to acquire these fundamental movement skills. If a child hasn't learned these skills by age nine, the opportunity is lost (when children get past a certain age, the brain receptors that let them learn new things start to close up). This doesn't mean that if a girl hasn't learned these skills by age nine she will never be able to participate in health-fitness activities such as jogging or weight lifting. But her ability to participate in movement-skill-dependent activities will be severely compromised. This applies to the long-term, too. For example, it would be a considerable challenge for an adolescent or woman who had never learned certain fundamental movement skills as a young child to take up a sport like tennis. Tennis requires you to be able to run, leap, gallop, stop, start, and dodge (locomotor); stretch, curl, twist, turn, and bend (non-locomotor); and catch, throw, and strike (projection/reception). The majority of the professional athletes that I have known excelled in a variety of sports when they were young. The fundamental movement skills we've referred to can be likened to a set of "tools" we can draw upon when faced with a sports "task"—the more tools we have, the easier it will be to accomplish the task.

Understanding How Fundamental Movement Skills Develop

I've noticed by watching my kids and their friends that they don't suddenly master a skill such as running or throwing. Like all fundamental movement skills, running and throwing are the end result of the stage-by-stage refinement of these skills.

Also, most fundamental movement skills don't exist in isolation. They are related to other skills. For instance, children only learn to skip after they learn to run, and they learn to run only after learning to walk.

Water Safety for Pre-School Kids

Drowning is one of the leading causes of death in young children, and is *the* number-one cause of child death in the Sun Belt states where pools are more common. The most common drowning scenario in this age group is when a child wanders away from adult supervision and either falls into a pool or enters the pool deliberately. The American Academy of Pediatrics therefore recommends that you *do not* install a pool in your backyard until all of your children are five years old.

If you have a young child and you already live in a home that has a swimming pool, or if you are visiting a friend or relative where there is a swimming pool, you need to ensure that the following potentially life-saving guidelines are observed:

- Never allow a young child in the water without an adult.
- Do not use flotation devices as substitutes for supervision.
- Always watch your child carefully when she is near a pool or any other body of water—whether it is the ocean or a hot tub.
- Remove items such as toys or tricycles from the pool area, as they can attract a child when you're not looking.
- Don't leave water in an inflatable pool, and better yet, put - inflatable pools away when they're not in use.
- Be sure that gates and doors leading to the pool are firmly closed.

The American Academy of Pediatrics discourages swimming lessons for children below four years of age because they give parents a false sense of security. For parents who insist on entering their children in swimming programs, the AAP recommends that you choose a program that doesn't allow young participants to put their head underwater, and to make sure the program allows you to be closely involved.

Your child is probably ready for unrestricted swimming lessons when she's five years old. However, because a child has completed a swimming program doesn't mean she can be in the water unsupervised. Cases of children panicking and drowning close to safety are common. Anytime a child is in the water, she needs to be watched at all times!

It isn't possible to keep an eye on your child every moment of the day. For this reason, if you have a swimming pool you need to erect a protective barrier around it. The Consumer Products Safety Commission (CPSC) offers these recommendations:

- Fences and walls should be at least four feet high and installed completely around the pool. Fence gates should be self-closing and self-latching. The latch should be out of a small child's reach.
- If your house forms one side of the barrier to the pool, then doors leading from the house to the pool should be protected with alarms that produce a sound when a door is unexpectedly opened.
- A power safety cover—a motor-powered barrier that can be placed over the water area—can be used when the pool is not in use.
- For above-ground pools, steps and ladders to the pool should be secured and locked or removed when the pool is not in use.
- Pool alarms can be used as an added precaution. Underwater pool alarms generally perform better and can be used in conjunction with pool covers. The CPSC advises that consumers use remote alarm receivers so the alarm can be heard inside the house or in other places away from the pool area.

Anyone who doesn't yet know CPR should take a course, but this is extra important if you have a swimming pool. CPR can save a child's life after a near-drowning. Babysitters and other caretakers, such as grandparents and other siblings, should also know CPR. Finally, keep rescue equipment by the pool and be sure a portable phone is poolside with emergency numbers posted.

This is significant because children need to adapt these skills in order to play sports. Take, for example, kicking a soccer ball correctly. It's more complex than one might think, as I discovered when I tried to teach it to my daughters. To kick a soccer ball, you have to run toward the ball, skip at the last moment to put the right distance between yourself and the ball while at the same time raising your kicking leg backward, and then, finally, strike the ball with the instep of your foot and follow through with your leg. This is no easy task for a child unless she has mastered several fundamental movement skills.

The lesson we need to learn from this is two-fold: 1) in order to completely master a particular fundamental movement skill, a child needs to progress successfully through a sequence of learning stages; and 2) because usually "one skill leads to another," it may be necessary for a child to first master a simple skill before moving on to learn a more sophisticated one.

What does all this mean to us as parents? We have to make it possible for our daughters to learn these skills. But how? For the most part, this involves providing our girls with an environment that is conducive to developing their movement skills. We need to encourage free-play situations in which our kids can be active and use their bodies in as many ways as possible. If you think your daughter is not participating in enough unstructured play, you will need to initiate play situations yourself. Watching videos is fine in moderation, but I find I sometimes have to pry my girls off the couch to get them outside and playing. One of my girls would much prefer to use her active imagination playing with her dinosaurs in the house than being physically active outside. I usually incorporate a game she likes, such as Duck, Duck, Goose or Hide and Seek, into our outdoor activities to get her running around. In bad weather, I might stick in a yoga video (a good one for children is called *Yoga Kids* and can be found or ordered at a video store or on the Internet) or put on music and dance around the play room. When I get moving, I can usually get my daughters moving, too.

Playing catch and roughhousing are two ways to work on a variety of fundamental movement skills. It's especially important that as parents we also take the time to help our daughters develop those skills that fall under the heading of "projection and reception of objects"—which mostly involve throwing, catching, and kicking skills. Women tend not to have strong projection and reception skills, not because women are "naturally uncoordinated," but because they weren't encouraged to develop these skills while they were growing up. That's why it's important that you work with your daughter on overarm throwing and catching, and kicking, punting, and trapping. An activity as straightforward as throwing and catching a Frisbee in the park can do wonders for developing these skills, and so can

Teaching Your Daughter to Ride a Bike

Teaching your daughter to ride a bike may be one of the first sports skills you share. Most three- to four-year-olds are developmentally ready to learn to ride a bike, especially if they've mastered the "art" of tricycle riding. A 12" bike with training wheels is the most common and conservative choice. Remember that children should always wear a helmet, whether or not there are training wheels on the bike.

Remember to adjust the training wheels so there's only one wheel touching the ground at a time. The bike will tip a little bit, allowing your daughter to develop the sense of balance that she needs on the two main wheels. Also, having training wheels that are the same level as the back wheel reduces the effectiveness of the brake pads on the back wheel.

As your daughter gradually gets the hang of riding her bike, raise the training wheels slightly every week or so. The day will eventually come when she's so good at balancing that the training wheels won't be serving any purpose. That's the day you can remove them!

Another way that your daughter can learn to ride her bike requires more of your time, a lot of your sweat, and maybe even a bruised shin or two on your part, but she will learn to ride her bike faster and it is also a good way for the two of you to bond.

Using this method, training wheels are not used. What you do is hold your daughter's shoulders and run along beside her as she pedals. Don't hold any part of the bike, because if you're holding the bike, she won't get a sense of learning to balance. As you run along beside her, holding her by the shoulders, you can "right" her when she begins to lean to one side. Plus, she'll learn when she starts to lean that it's time to straighten up when her shoulders touch your hands. Remember, this can be quite a workout for you! The place to teach your daughter to ride her bike using this method is a wide-open space such as a parking lot, park, or sports field.

If you want, you can combine the two methods described above. You can do this by starting her off with the assisted method, then attaching the training wheels to her bike but with a lot of "tip."

Most kids learn to ride a bike unassisted by age six or seven, though it's not unusual for there to be a couple of years leeway either way.

Making Your Own "Play Dough"—A Great Way to Improve Fine Motor Skills

This fun activity is beneficial for kids who have to work on their fine motor skills, and will also help out kids whose fine motor skills are well developed. One of my daughters has low muscle tone in her fingers and hands, and so we do special fine motor-skill activities at home to improve this common problem. One of our favorites is making our own "play dough"—which isn't as hard as you might think. The ingredients are: 2 cups of flour, 1 cup of salt, 4 teaspoons of cream of tartar, 2 tablespoons of oil, and 2 cups of water. Add whatever food colorings your daughter wants (we also like to add glitter to ours for extra fun) and both of you can start mixing the whole mess with your hands. Soon enough, you'll have play dough, and will have done a terrific workout for your daughter's little hands!

tossing around a tennis ball in the swimming pool. Upper-arm strength is also sometimes neglected in girls. A good way for your daughter to improve arm and shoulder strength is to climb, hang from, and swing on a jungle gym. If you can't afford a full-size jungle gym or don't have a backyard where you can put one, plastic indoor jungle gyms are a good alternative and can be found at any toy store.

Improving Fine Motor Skills

Fine motor skills are those that involve using the hands and fingers in a precise, controlled way to accomplish a specific task. Although not essential for sports, they are certainly needed for daily activities ranging from tying a shoelace to opening a tube of toothpaste to holding a pencil.

Obstacles to Learning

Kids have traditionally learned fundamental movement skills in unstructured play situations, as was certainly the case when I was a child. Unfortunately, many children now don't have the opportunity to learn fundamental movement skills because opportunities for free play have declined dramatically. Whereas once kids ran around their neighborhoods using their bodies to climb trees and squeeze themselves under hedges, today they are more likely to be sitting inside watching television or playing video games on the computer.

Because of the decline of free play, many kids enter organized sports quite unprepared in terms of strength, flexibility, and movement skills. Also, these skills are not traditionally prized in girls, which places them at a disadvantage. Parents actually tend to work less on developing movement skills with their daughters, although it's not hard to do so and can be great fun. It's good for parents' health, too, as most adults don't get enough exercise either! Even if you're not athletic, I encourage you to be more physically active with your daughters and to enjoy yourself!

Be a Cheerleader As Well As a Coach

Most of all, what our daughters need from us at this age is enthusiasm and encouragement. "Parents tend to think they treat their sons and daughters the same where it comes to playing," says Susan Greendorfer, Professor Emerita at the University of Illinois' Center for the Study of Youth in Sport, and a world-renowned expert in the relationship between family behavior and sports participation by girls. "But on the whole this isn't the case." As Greendorfer points out, studies repeatedly show that in a sports play environment—even one as elementary as playing catch in the backyard—adults tend to give boys more encouragement than girls. Later on, many girls who perform as well as or better than boys in tests of

"Playing Nice": The First Step toward Being a Good Sport

It's possible to teach kids how to be good sports even before they start playing organized sports. Here are some fundamentals for "playing nice":

- Never take a toy that isn't yours.
- Wait your turn.
- Don't push or hit.
- Don't throw anything that could hurt someone.

sports-related skills such as hopping, skipping, or throwing, actually rate themselves *lower*. This isn't girls' natural modesty at play. Girls undervalue their athletic abilities because they haven't received as much positive reinforcement as young kids compared to boys. The fact that many girls undervalue their athletic abilities hurts them as they get older because one of the main reasons that girls quit sports is that they don't consider themselves skilled enough. On the other hand, the girl who hears the words, "Great throw!" a lot when growing up is more likely to believe she can throw the ball well.

Therefore, although we live in a society in which sports are increasingly recognized as beneficial for girls, we nevertheless continue to face a dual problem involving reality and perception. The *reality* is that many girls may not be learning fundamental movement skills because parents and educators don't think they are important for girls to learn. As for *perception*, even when they have had the opportunity to develop fundamental movement skills, many girls may not have confidence in their ability in this area because they don't receive enough positive reinforcement when they demonstrate their ability.

Fortunately, the solution to this problem is simple—as parents we need to be with our girls more often in active environments and praise them lavishly for their efforts and successes! I know that I have become extra-conscious about praising my daughters when they try hard in sports and perform athletic skills well, and I hope you will, too.

Fun Fitness/Motor-Skill Activities

This section contains fun activities that you and your daughter can do together to help build her strength and endurance (you'll probably get a workout, too!). They will also help her learn and refine many of the fundamental movement skills identified earlier. By encouraging her to participate, you will be conveying to her the importance of taking the time to become fit and strong.

Some of the activities may be a challenge for your child, but with practice they will get easier. Many of these games are also great activities for when she has a friend over to play, and siblings of all ages can join in the fun!

President's Council on Physical Fitness and Sports Fun Fitness Activities

These activities were created specifically for young children by experts at the President's Council on Physical Fitness and Sports, and you should feel free to adapt them to accommodate your daughter's needs.

Over Hill and Dale

Sit on the floor with your legs apart and let your daughter walk around you, stepping over your legs. Variations: bend your knees to make a bridge she can crawl under. Let her roll a ball over and under your legs.

Twister

Your daughter holds a pole with both hands and steps through the triangular gap formed by the arms and pole. Without letting go of the stick, she should then step foot-by-foot backward and forward. This might be a little difficult, but your daughter might enjoy trying it.

Pogo the Stick

Hold a pole just above floor height and have your daughter jump over. Gradually increase the height of the pole and the distance from your child. We use a broom in our house for this!

Jump the River

Use a towel to form the "river." Your child stands on the banks of one side and tries to jump across without "falling in." Change the width of the river as she gets better at this.

Simon Says

Simon says, "Touch your knee to your chin." Simon says, "Touch your elbow to your foot." Choose body parts that involve stretching of the joints.

Wall Push-Ups

Your daughter stands an arm's length away from a wall with her legs together. She places her hands on the wall slightly wider apart than her shoulders. She leans forward and touches her nose to the wall and then pushes back to the starting position. Be sure she keeps her body straight and her heels on the floor. Challenge her to see how many she can do.

Jumping Beans

Hold your daughter's hands. Start bouncing on your toes and encourage her to do the same until you are both jumping up and down. Stop, rest, then start again. Variation: hop on one foot, then the other.

Beanbag Walk

Place a beanbag (or a soft toy) on your child's head and ask her to walk from place to place without it falling off of her head. She can make it easier if she holds it to her head. Variations: place the beanbag on a different body part (the back of her hand or shoulder, for example). Have her walk around or under obstacles.

Row, Row, Row Your Boat

Sit with your legs apart and your daughter sitting opposite you with her legs between yours. Grasp your child's hands. Your daughter leans back as if "rowing" a boat then pulls to an upright position as it is your turn to lean back. Repeat. Sing "Row, Row, Row Your Boat."

Wheelbarrow

Your daughter lies on the ground face down. Grasp her ankles and lift her upward. Ask her to push herself up until her arms are straight. Lifting her head, she walks forward on her hands as you hold her legs up. Her back should remain straight.

Tiptoe Walk

Your daughter walks around on her toes. Variations: she can place a beanbag or soft toy on her head or swing her arms.

Standing Statues

Ask your daughter, "Can you balance on one foot for a count of 'four alligators'?" (one alligator, two alligators...) Variations: count more alligators. Balance in different positions.

Balance and Grab

Place five items in an unbreakable dish near another container (such as a pail). Your daughter stands on one foot in front of the dish and container. She transfers objects from the dish to the container while maintaining her balance. Variations: change the distance between the dish and the container.

Inch Worm

Your daughter bends over and places both her hands on the floor. She keeps her feet stationary while her hands walk forward as far as possible. Then her hands stay stationary while her feet walk forward as close as possible to her hands.

Egg Roll

Your daughter sits on the floor with her knees bent and her legs spread apart. Holding her feet with her hands, she rolls to the right, then to the left, then comes back to the starting position. She should keep hold of her feet throughout the exercise.

Somersault

Teach your child to roll forwards and backwards. She needs to make sure her chin is tucked to her chest and her shoulders take the brunt of her weight. Practice on pillows, a mattress, or a trampoline.

Uppity, Uppity, Down, Down

Standing at the bottom of the stairs with your daughter, repeat the phrase, "Uppity, uppity, down, down," and together step *up* with your right foot then step *up* with your left foot, then step *down* with your right foot then step *down* with your left foot.

Hang Ball

Your daughter sits on the floor holding a ball tightly between her legs with her hands above her head. Lift her by her arms while she tries to keep the ball from dropping.

Catch

Stand with your daughter two to three yards away from you. Bounce a ball so that you can both catch it without moving your feet. ("Gertie" balls are great for indoor play and can be found at most toy stores.) If your daughter has difficulty catching the ball, use a balloon (it travels more slowly).

Toss

Make a paper airplane with your daughter and practice throwing it. Variations: throw a ball made of scrunched-up newspaper or rolled socks. Have her throw the objects up a flight of stairs, seeing how far up she can throw them. (Or go outside so she can throw rocks into a lake or stream.)

chapter 4

The Formative Years
(Six to Eleven Years)

In this chapter, we will answer a series of common questions parents have when their daughters are ready to start sports: *Which sport is right for my child? Should my daughter play sports with boys? Should I let my child quit her sports program?* We will also look at issues that arise for girls in this age range when the adults involved in the program overemphasize winning, or playing just isn't fun anymore. Along the way, we will review suggestions for how girls can overcome the kinds of gender-stereotyping that work against them and I'll explain how it's possible to redefine winning in sports to make it more fun for the kids who participate. And, finally, we'll take a look at the role that physical education should play in the health of our daughters.

Gender Identity and Sports

"Society's conceptions of gender strongly affect the way our daughters feel about physical activity," says Professor Susan Greendorfer of the University of Illinois' Center for the Study of Youth in Sport. "Whether or not girls participate in a particular activity—sports and exercise included—usually depends on whether they consider it 'gender appropriate.'"

Girls start learning society's conventions about gender very early in childhood from signals deliberately or unknowingly given to them by their parents and other adults in their lives. By age three, they are definitely aware of what behavior is and is not expected of little boys and girls. They also learn that it is "wrong" to engage in behaviors that are associated with the other gender.

One of the things that society teaches kids about gender is that boys and girls are not just different from each other, but in many respects *opposite* (girls are "sugar and spice and everything nice" while boys are "snakes and snails and puppy dogs' tails"). If boys are one thing, the feeling is, then girls are another. This is known as "gender opposition."

Establishing "gender identification" is extremely important for a child. To secure their sense of gender, girls usually go along with, and indeed defend, what they understand to be the definitions of masculinity and femininity.

Gender opposition characterizes how our children express themselves physically. Girls learn to use small gestures and movements and limit the amount of space they use around themselves—crossing the legs and arms are examples of this "ladylike" behavior. Of course, sports require much more extreme and vigorous use of the body. Traditionally, it was accepted that such uses of the body were "masculine," and girls would often decline to participate in boys' games and play. In any case, girls who did cross the playground to roughhouse with the boys and show physical prowess were customarily rebuked or ostracized.

Adults also reinforce these notions of gender identification. For example, in coed T-ball where the players are just five and six years old, coaches and the boy participants tend to convey the impression to girls that these are "male" activities and girls don't "belong." The roots of this extend all the way back to the Olympics in ancient Greece, where women were not only prohibited from participating in the events, they couldn't even watch!

"It's not surprising that many girls choose to avoid sports altogether in the belief that it compromises their femininity," says girls' sports expert Professor Linda Bunker of the University of Virginia, "while others restrict themselves to pursuits that may be considered more graceful or artistic—

such as gymnastics, figure skating, swimming, and diving." Many girls shy away from sports considered more appropriate for boys, those that are, in the words of the President's Council on Physical Fitness and Sport's 1997 *Report on Physical Activity and Sport in the Lives of Young Girls*, "aggressive, competitive, territorial, strength-focused team sports that involve a great deal of body contact."

To encourage our daughters to continue participating in sports, we need to show them that we value their status as young female athletes. One of the most important ways we can do this is by eliminating gender stereotypes in sports and physical activity. Here are some guidelines on how to do this:

- **Don't** characterize activities as either "girls' sports" or "boys' sports," as this can suggest to girls that their opportunities are limited by their gender.
- **Do** emphasize to girls that they can succeed in any sport they want.
- **Don't** tolerate discrimination. When you see girls being shortchanged in the sports environment, make your feelings plain.
- **Do** encourage boys and girls to reconsider their attitudes toward gender, and in particular, their negative preconceptions of girls' activities.
- **Don't** just pay lip service to efforts to dispel stereotypes.
- **Do** practice what you preach. Dads should play sports with girls; moms can learn to coach soccer and officiate volleyball and basketball.

We must also avoid gender-typed language. I was appalled when I heard a fellow broadcaster insult the performance of a male athlete who was struggling in the playoffs by saying that the ballplayer "played like a girl." What made it even worse was the fact that the comment got a lot of attention and was repeated many times, but it was never criticized. I fear that language such as this can be internalized by girls, and is a strong discouragement to their desire to play sports.

Some young children may be resistant to change or dispel stereotypes. However, parents can provide them with nonsexist information that they will increasingly rely on as they mature. Children who are in fifth and sixth grade may be ready to resist and challenge gender stereotyping.

It is important to sensitize ourselves to gender issues in sports, to seek out programs that are treating girls fairly, and to advocate on behalf of our daughters when they are not. There are also plenty of everyday things we can do to make our daughters believe that sports participation by girls isn't just acceptable, but *desirable*.

It's very important to attend our girls' games, and if we can't be there, to explain why not. If you can't attend a game, ask a close friend to go in your place, and if possible, videotape the action. Even though you can't be there, let your daughter know that you're thinking about her by leaving a good-luck note in her bag.

If possible, drive your daughter to and from games and practices and talk to her about her sports experiences during these journeys. She will come to treasure these times because they are all about her. However, avoid last-minute coaching tips, as these can add unneeded stress for your daughter.

Make game day a special one for your daughter and your family. No matter who wins or loses, enjoy this time together. Bring a picnic to eat at the field or make arrangements to go out for a meal afterwards. Never complain about the time an event takes or the disruption it causes to the family schedule, as that can make your daughter feel guilty about her participation

You can take photos of your daughter in action and display the results around your home. You and the other parents on the team may want to make large lapel buttons with photos of your kids on them and wear them to games to show your pride.

Whenever it's possible, we should buy our daughters good equipment so that they don't have to make do with hand-me-downs. If our daughters are serious about trying out for a new sport or activity, let's support them by making sure they get the proper equipment and coaching. Of course, financial considerations sometimes hamper us. It's important to be honest with our daughters about such matters, making it clear to them that the reason we won't pay for a particular item is because we can't afford it, not because we don't value their participation in a particular sport. Make birthdays and holidays the times to give her in-line skates, a new soccer ball, or her favorite female athlete's jersey.

We also owe it to our daughters to learn the rules of the sports they are playing. That way we'll know why the referee is blowing his or her whistle and we'll be able to talk knowledgeably with our girls about the game afterwards.

Remember to keep working on the fundamental movement skills of throwing, catching, kicking, and striking. The girl who learns these skills by age nine is much more likely to become an accomplished athlete. Focus on those movement skills that girls tend to get shortchanged on—especially throwing and catching. We can work on these skills by being active with our daughters—taking them to the park to throw a ball around, playing tag, playing tennis with them at a local court, or shooting hoops with them in the driveway.

Although many girls don't have the same opportunities to play sports as boys do, it's way off the mark to say that girls are naturally "unathletic," a comment I recently heard to my dismay from a respected political figure. Although girls' activities have traditionally been different from boys' (jumping rope, swinging on monkey bars, playing hopscotch, performing complex dance routines), these still require coordination, strength, and focus. Numerous studies of young children's movement skills have shown girls actually to be *more advanced* in areas such as balance and agility. However, this situation soon reverses itself because, in general, boys receive more encouragement than girls to practice their movement skills.

"The fact is that girls have the ability to excel in all kinds of physical activity," says Professor Greendorfer. "The problem is that they are shortchanged on the right opportunities."

Although the situation is gradually changing, most of the sports figures children see in the media are male. It's important for us to expose our daughters to women's sports events on television, as well as publications such as *Sports Illustrated for Kids,* that do not have a strong gender bias. We can also buy inspirational books about female athletes, and read the sports pages together to follow the performances of top female athletes such as Venus and Serena Williams, Mia Hamm, Marion Jones, Lisa Leslie, and Juli Inkster.

You can also make a concerted effort to watch women's sports on television. Expose your daughter to potential role models while showing her that there's more to sports on TV than Monday Night Football. Take her to professional and collegiate women's sports events whenever possible. Even a girl who's not an athlete will be inspired by the passion and talent showcased at your local high school, college, or in the WNBA, WUSA, and professional golf and tennis tournaments.

Planning physically active vacations with our daughters, such as hiking, climbing, and rafting, will teach them that it's not just boys and men who can handle the "rough stuff." Even if you go on a beach vacation, you can always sneak in some tennis, or during summer break look for a one- or two-week kid's camp that can expose your daughter to a new sport. Scan your local newspaper pages for weekend charity walks or "fun runs," which can be a rewarding way to spend some active time with your kids.

One of the most important things we can do, whenever possible, is to play sports with our daughters. My husband is a golfer and we let our kids play on the practice greens from the time they began to walk. Now they are comfortable around the game, and just being there has sparked their interest. Whatever sport is your favorite, just think of all the fun quality time this will give you as you teach your daughter how to play! Parents and kids can learn to forge strong bonds while participating together in any number of sports, from tennis to skiing to fishing.

And finally, we need to be good sports role models for our daughters. Studies show that when dads participate in a sport, this increases the likelihood that their children will play sports by 11 percent, and when moms play sports or are physically active, the participation rate increases 22 percent—even more reason to carve some time into your day for a workout!

According to Professor Greendorfer, "the strongest predictor of whether an adult woman exercises or plays sports is whether she was born into a family where being physically active was part of the 'family culture'— whether it was talked about or not." Since I've taken my girls with me to the gym from the beginning, they see me being physically active and they know this is an important part of our lives.

Is My Child Ready for Organized Team Sports?

There is no reason to push your child into team sports, but by the time she reaches six years old, you may want to begin to see if she is ready. The American Academy of Pediatrics (AAP) recommends that children do not start playing organized team sports until they are six years old. However, you know your child best. Some kids get frustrated when asked to try even simple skills, or maybe they have difficulty following coaching. How do you know when your daughter is ready for organized team sports? Reply to these true-or-false statements.

My daughter:

1. Prefers playing alone to playing with other children. T_ F_
2. Will try new ways to do familiar tasks. T_ F_
3. Has difficulty taking turns. T_ F_
4. Doesn't generally need me to repeat directions. T_ F_
5. Gets mad when told she's doing something incorrectly. T_ F_
6. Doesn't usually mind sharing toys. T_ F_
7. Has not developed the motor skills of other children her age. T_ F_
8. Has expressed an interest in playing organized team sports. T_ F_
9. Is shy around adults other than relatives. T_ F_
10. Can focus on a task for more than ten minutes at a time. T_ F_

If you answered true to most of the even-numbered questions and false to the odd-numbered ones, your daughter may be ready to start organized sports.

Toward a New Definition of "Winning"

Think about it: when we were kids and played games like freeze tag and hide-and-go-seek, there really wasn't any scoring and no one ever came out as the "winner." Yet we could play these games for hours and hours, stopping only when our parents would track us down and call us home for dinner.

The fact is that when children play, they aren't really interested in coming out on top. Instead, it is adults who have imposed the concept of winning into children's play activities, with the undesirable result being that it sometimes makes play less enjoyable for the participants.

In a national study of girls aged ten to eighteen, winning was not even given as one of the top ten reasons they played sports, and for boys it was only number seven! Furthermore, when these same kids were asked what they would change about youth sports, they overwhelmingly stated they wanted to see less emphasis on winning. It's true that children become more competitive as they get older, but among kids aged six to eleven, it's more important to be participating than winning. Indeed, several studies have shown that kids would prefer to play on a losing team than have to sit on the bench for a team that wins all the time.

More and more sports programs now claim that they de-emphasize winning. However, there is usually a significant gap between what the adults involved say and what they do. Even when the officials who run the program decline to keep scores or win-loss records, you'll find that other adults on the scene—coaches and parents especially—are only too eager to keep track. Many adults have forgotten about play for play's sake, which is what most kids believe in. For many of the parents, coaches, or officials, there has to be something at stake, and they mistakenly believe that kids feel the same way.

The problem is that adults tend to define sports in very adult terms—winning equals success and losing equals failure. This is a problem because focusing on winning severely narrows the scope for enjoyment in children's sports.

We actually need to change our definition of winning so that it is based on how much effort the participants put in, not whether they win or lose.

Dr. Michael Clark, a professor at Michigan State University's Institute for the Study of Youth Sport, suggests a specific four-step approach to doing this by balancing the competition, having players set individual goals, then measuring success according to these goals and celebrating effort.

Create Balanced Competition So Outcomes Are in Doubt

Young athletes generally want the competition to be fair and the outcome to be in question. Otherwise, they spend most of the time complaining about how unbalanced the teams are and how unfair the game is. It is usually only adults who want to win by lopsided scores; young athletes want fairness to be the dominating feature of the event. If a game *is* one-sided, it is better for teams to exchange players to make the teams more even, rather than keeping the teams as they are just because, from the adult perspective, "that's the way it's supposed to be." Kids are motivated by vigorous competition where their effort really matters!

Help Players Set Achievable, Individual Goals

It is important to establish meaningful and attainable goals in any activity, and sports are no exception. Young athletes need to have well-established goals to strive for, and they need to be closely involved in establishing these goals. Individual goals are more meaningful to players than team or group goals, because they let each athlete know exactly what needs to be accomplished. Coaches should have young athletes set goals, and parents can help, too. It's also important that these goals not be set in stone, as Dr. Clark points out. "There has to be some 'wiggle room,'" he says. "Rather than saying, 'I'm going to make all the free throws I take,' you should encourage your daughter to try to make 70 percent of free throws in practice and 65 percent in games." Goals, of course, should depend on age and experience, and can include, for example, a goal of reaching base at least twice in a baseball game, or getting in at least three-quarters of first serves in a tennis match.

Concludes Dr. Clark, "The idea is to get goals stated positively, make them attainable, have the individual athlete be responsible for her personal success, and to reevaluate her progress regularly."

Teach Athletes to Measure Their Success in Terms of Achieving These Goals

With individual goals clearly defined, young athletes can be evaluated according to their progress toward achieving these goals. In this way, the goals are the yardstick by which we measure effort: did your daughter make the kind of effort in each practice and competition that moved her closer to achieving her goals? If a player puts in effort to achieve her goals, then her performance is a success, no matter what the score of the game or competition.

Celebrate with Individual Rewards for Reaching These Goals

When our young athlete reaches her previously set goal, we should acknowledge and honor her achievement. This is a way to motivate our athletes, and demonstrate the importance of goals. Pointing toward the research of sports psychologists, Dr. Clark discourages material rewards such as trophies, T-shirts, and money. "These have been found to create problems in the long-term because athletes begin to see these rewards as the reason for playing," he says. High-fives and pats on the back are as desirable to children as material prizes. Always tell your daughter how proud of her you are. Dr. Clark and other experts say it's important to make participation in sports its own reward!

We redefine the traditional concept of the term "winning" when we recognize that *not every child can be the best athlete on the team*, but *every child can make the best effort*. This redefinition of winning can be positively applied to many life situations, but it is especially effective in helping young athletes have enjoyable sports experiences. Because girls are known to become especially discouraged at the overemphasis on traditional concepts of winning in sports, this new definition of winning may have special implications for young female athletes.

Using our new definition of winning, parents should ask questions, such as "Did you try your hardest?" and "Did you do something better than you previously could?" instead of "Did you win?" or "How many points did you score?" Even when the scoreboard is not in their favor, young athletes can reply "yes" to these more appropriate questions.

"What happens when we define winning in terms of effort rather than outcome," says Dr. Clark, "is we make youth sports more humane, meaningful, and satisfying." It also makes sports more enjoyable. And making sports more fun is the key to keeping all kids involved in sports.

Which Sport?

Another way to ensure that our daughters have an enjoyable sports experience is to get them into the right sports program. The quality of the sports programs our daughters are enrolled in and the adult leadership in these programs is much more important than the sport itself. According to Dr. Angela Smith, president of the American College of Sports Medicine, "It doesn't matter whether it's karate, ballet, or soccer, our girls' enjoyment will depend largely on the philosophy of the program and the attitude of the coach/instructor." Therefore, we should spend as much time looking into how the different programs in our area are run and who's in charge as we do analyzing which sport matches our child's personality.

Before enrolling a child in a sports program, a parent should go try to see it in operation and talk to the coaches, administrators, and other

What to Look For When Choosing a Sports Program for Your Daughter

- The kids are having fun.
- All the kids get to play at practices and in games.
- Good sportsmanship is part of the program.
- The coaches are organized and responsive to your questions.
- The coaches allow for rest and water breaks during practices, and end the practice if the kids seem tired.
- The coaches treat the players with respect and treat all the players equally.
- Equipment is well maintained and there is enough of it for every child.
- The other children's skill levels and age groups would be a good match for your daughter.

parents. It is not a bad idea to take our daughters along with us to gauge their reactions. Ideally, we should do this the year before starting a child in team sports. It's important to have a contingency plan in case a sport doesn't work out, such as a backup sport or another option.

A more appropriate question than "Which sport?" is "Which sports?" It's a much better idea for our children to play two or three sports over the course of a year than to specialize in just one. There are several reasons why. On the positive side, playing a variety of sports exposes a girl to different groups of kids and widens her circle of friends. It also gives her the chance to work on a number of different sports skills. Conversely, pushing a girl to specialize in one sport can cause burnout. She may decide later that she doesn't like the sport she's been specializing in, but she's lost the opportunity to learn other sports skills with her peers. The burnout rate in young athletes who specialize in one sport is extremely high, and a child who is forced into one sport at the expense of all others may get turned off sports for life. Also, specializing in just one sport may be physically hazardous because it exposes the same joints to repetitive stress—the wrists and back in gymnastics, for example, or the elbow and shoulder in tennis.

So-called "overuse" injuries, such as tendonitis and stress fractures, were unknown in kids until the advent of youth sports specialization, but they are now quite common. Dr. Lyle Micheli, cofounder of the United States' first sports-medicine clinic for young athletes, recommends that children not specialize in one sport. "Kids should be encouraged to participate in whatever sport is in season," says Dr. Micheli. "Playing the same sport year-in, year-out is a surefire recipe for injury."

When choosing a sports program to join, there are, of course, practical considerations, among them cost and convenience. There may not be figure-skating programs anywhere near where you live, or they may be too expensive. Meanwhile, soccer and basketball programs may be relatively affordable and plentiful in your area, making the decision for you quite easy.

One of the most important challenges when helping our daughters choose a sport is keeping our own preferences out of the equation. We are key participants in the decision-making process, but the choice of which sport to play ultimately belongs to our daughters. No matter *how* much a parent might want their daughter to become a star golfer, they shouldn't pressure her to fulfill their ambitions. It's fine to share your passion for a sport, but it's also important to know when to stop if she's not interested.

Even before it's time to choose a sport, we should discuss the issue with our daughters to find out what they are interested in. You may discover in your daughter's case that since all her friends are signing up for soccer, that's what she wants to play. And being with friends is as good a reason as any for a child to dedicate herself to playing a particular sport for the time being.

Should Girls Play Sports with Boys?

Until they reach puberty, boys and girls are the same size and weight, so there's no reason why they shouldn't play sports together. Girls generally reach puberty between the ages of ten and twelve years old, around two years earlier than boys do. After puberty, boys gain an advantage in strength and size due to hormonal changes. At this point, commonsense factors such as safety and fairness dictate that boys and girls should no longer compete against each other in most sports.

However, even before puberty many girls prefer not to play sports with boys. A frequent reason for girls quitting sports is that the boys in the program are too aggressive or are dominating the action. My daughter played in our local soccer program, which featured just two girls on each team. She didn't enjoy it because she never got to touch the ball. As a parent, I found the situation frustrating, but was told that there were not enough girls interested in playing to make up all-girl teams.

Most experts believe that the ideal situation for girls is to play on an all-girls' sports team that is as well resourced as the boys'. All-girls' sports programs offer opportunities for fun, friendship, success, and positive self-esteem that girls may not experience on boys' teams. "Girls playing on girls' teams is best for the young female athletes themselves and for girls' and women's sports as a whole," says Joy Griffin, president of the National Association for Girls and Women in Sports.

Although in general girls prefer to play with and compete against other girls, under certain circumstances girls may challenge for the right to participate in boys' sports programs. The two most common reasons for this are: 1) there is no opportunity for girls in a certain sport in a particular area, and 2) the girls' team or league in a particular area is not as well resourced as the boys' equivalent.

When there is no girls' team or girls' program in a certain sport in a particular area, the law is clear: girls should be allowed to play with the boys. The situation is less straightforward when the girls' teams or girls' programs are not as well resourced as the boys' are. In such cases, a talented young female athlete may wish to play on a boys' team so that she can take advantage of a more competitive environment. It's important to support girls who wish to pursue this goal, at the same time keeping in mind that playing on a girls' team—even one with fewer resources—can still be an exciting, challenging, and fulfilling experience. The decision to allow girls to play with boys if they are good enough is an important one, but we need to recognize it as only a short-term option. Our long-term goal should be to make sure that girls' sports programs are as well funded and well supported as boys' are.

Should You Let Your Child Quit Sports?

It's not uncommon for a child to say she wants to quit the sport she is playing. Before we allow a child to drop out, we should try to find out

Water Safety for School-Age Children (Age 5–12)

Kids love being in the water, and swimming can provide an enormous amount of healthy fun for our youngsters. Safety needs to be a priority, though. Even kids who've had swimming lessons can get into trouble in the water, whether it's in a pool, lake, river, or ocean. Therefore, never let your child swim unless she is being supervised by an adult.

Kids naturally try to push boundaries, so it's important that the following water-safety rules be emphasized:

- A child should be taught never to swim by herself.
- A child should never dive into water unless given permission by an adult who knows how deep it is.
- No one should ever swim in areas where there is traffic—whether in the form of jet-skiers, boats, or surfers.
- It is not advisable to swim when lightning is visible or when a lightning storm has been forecast.
- Your child should always wear an appropriate-sized, UL-certified lifevest when sailing, motor-boating, fishing, water-skiing, or jet-skiing.
- Teach your child never to hold anyone under the water for any reason.
- Emphasize to your child that she should not call for help if she's just kidding around.
- And finally, teach your child what to do if she gets into distress: she should stay calm and float or tread water until help comes.

why, and help her work through the problem. Her reasons for quitting may be quite straightforward: she doesn't like her coach or some of her teammates, or she may not be getting to play as much as she wants. Many parents I talk to lament that their daughter insists the "in crowd" is involved in a different sport. Thus, a talented cross-country runner may quit her sport because the "cool kids" are playing soccer. If this is what she truly wants to do, encourage her to return to her sport next season, or see if there's a way to fit both into her schedule in a moderate way. As long as she's not quitting to avoid a problem that you feel should be addressed, a change of programs is OK, but if there is a problem that can be solved, you'll want to encourage her to stick with it.

"Our daughters need to know that it's not OK to quit sports the first time anything goes wrong," says Dr. Martha Ewing, a renowned sports psychologist specializing in young athletes. "Unfortunately, kids learn quitting behaviors from their parents—there's a real tendency in this day and age not to persevere when things go against us." We need to explain to our daughters that quitting is a wasted opportunity for them to learn sports skills and be with friends, says Dr. Ewing. Also, if a child has beaten out other kids for a spot on the team, then quitting means wasting an opportunity for another child.

As in the case of so many problems our daughters encounter, such "crises" may soon be forgotten. The younger she is, the more likely this will happen. But if you find yourself in a situation where the stress is ongoing, it's a good idea to talk to her coach about the problem. If the problem is unresolvable, you should think about looking for another program. One thing you might consider is going along and watching a practice and asking yourself, "Would *I* want to be involved in this program?"

It's important for you to make sure that you're not confusing what's right for your daughter with *your* desire for her to continue playing sports. According to Dr. Ewing, many parents push their daughters so hard to succeed in sports that the activity is no longer enjoyable for the child, and the child wants to quit. When the child expresses a desire to drop out of the program, the parents become indignant. In fact, it's perfectly understandable for that child to not want to continue in what, for her, has become more work than fun.

What Should We Expect from School PE Programs?

We mustn't forget that our schools have an important role to play in keeping our kids fit and teaching them basic sports skills. In recent years, schools have relinquished some of this responsibility—in part because of budget cuts and the resulting attitude that physical education (PE) is expendable when compared to subjects like math and geography. This is regrettable, as what could be more important than our children's health?

The American Alliance for Health, Physical Education, Recreation, and Dance (AAHPERD), is trying to reverse this trend. Dr. Joanne Owens-Nausler is president of AAHPERD, and is one of the most dynamic health-fitness advocates on the scene. Dr. Owens-Nausler insists that parents need to expect more from their schools' PE programs. "If your child couldn't spell, you'd demand to see their English teacher, wouldn't you?" she asks. "Yet parents have an incredibly nonchalant attitude toward their children's competency in PE—the fact that many kids don't learn anything in PE doesn't seem to faze parents." Dr. Owens-Nausler also points out that parents don't seem to care if their children say they hate PE. "If our kids can't stand PE," she says, "we need to find out why and do something about it." If the classes are too big or the teacher doesn't know what he or she is doing, advises Owens-Nausler, we need to raise that issue with the principal.

In 1997, the Centers for Disease Control and the Council for Children issued recommendations for school PE programs, calling for physical and health education for all children by trained teachers using appropriate equipment and promoting exercise and sports as lifelong fun and healthy activities. These recommendations are reprinted in the following section.

Center for Disease Control and Council for Children School PE Guidelines

1. Schools should promote enjoyable, lifelong physical activity in PE programs that include:
   - comprehensive, preferably daily, physical education for children in grades kindergarten through 12;
   - comprehensive health education for children in grades kindergarten through 12; commitment of adequate resources, including program funding, personnel, safe equipment, and facilities;
   - the use of trained physical-education specialists and teachers for physical- and health-education classes; and
   - physical-activity instruction and programs that meet the needs and interests of all students, including those with illness, injury, and developmental disability, as well as those who are obese, sedentary, or not interested in traditional team or competitive sports.

2. Schools should provide safe settings for sports and exercise, including adult supervision, teaching, instruction in safe methods of physical-activity training, safe facilities, and the appropriate use of protective equipment.

3. PE programs should emphasize the fact that sports and exercise are fun.

4. PE classes should help students develop the knowledge, attitudes, motor skills, behavioral skills, and confidence needed to maintain physically active lifestyles.

5. Schools should provide afterschool physical-activity programs that address the needs and interests of all students.

6. Schools should include parents and guardians in physical-activity instruction and extracurricular programs. They should encourage parents and guardians to support their children's participation in sports, and also recognize their own powerful influence as role models for active lifestyles.

7. School personnel should promote enjoyable, lifelong physical activity among girls.

8. School administrations should regularly evaluate their physical-activity programs, including classroom instruction, the nature and level of student activity, and the adequacy and safety of athletic facilities.

9. Schools should establish relationships with community recreation and youth-sports programs and agencies to coordinate and complement physical-activity programs.

When Sports Stress Is Serious

Most children's complaints about sports quickly pass. However, sometimes the problems can be more serious, especially among elite athletes. Any child with the characteristic symptoms associated with stress or depression should be withdrawn from sports if these problems seem to be caused by the program. Stress symptoms include vomiting, loss of appetite, or headache, and depression symptoms include excessive sleeping, lethargy, or being withdrawn.

There should also be a strong *education* component in physical education. Even young kids can be taught the basics of health fitness and why it's important to exercise. A physical education curriculum should teach children what fitness is and how to get fit. The best curriculum I've seen for kids K–6 is one created by The Children's Health Market called "The Great Body Shop" (www.thegreatbodyshop.net).

After distributing a large and colorfully illustrated "Great Body Shop" pamphlet, teachers ask the students to describe the activities that the kids pictured on the cover are engaged in (dancing, playing baseball, bike riding, swimming). Once it is established that what the kids in the pictures are doing is exercising, the teachers move on to discussing, in kid-friendly terms, the benefits of exercise. Lesson one explains the four components of fitness—strength, flexibility, endurance, and low body fat. Students go on to learn which sports they can do to get fit and keep fit, and get a homework assignment that involves being active. To enhance what they have learned in lesson one, the students do five "reinforcement activities":

1. finding their pulse;
2. using math skills to compare their active and resting heart rates;
3. a kickball relay race to learn about endurance;
4. identifying the forms of play that their school provides; and
5. learning to recognize the role that exercise plays in relieving stress and venting anger.

Throughout the Great Body Shop curriculum, we see innovative, fun ways to teach kids about the importance of being active. If your child's school doesn't have a well-thought-out and comprehensive program such as the Great Body Shop, you might want to lobby your principal and school board to adopt it or one like it!

chapter 5

Stickin' with It

Keeping Pre-teen and Teenage Girls
Interested in Sports
(Eleven to Seventeen Years)

● ● ●

Before I began writing this book, I assumed, like most people, that girls' sports were in great shape. I have witnessed the increase of women's sports on TV and the formation of women's professional sports leagues. I was the first play-by-play announcer for the WNBA and learned to appreciate the opportunities that women now have in basketball. Before the formation of that league, many players who were highly skilled in college had to go overseas to make a living, playing hoops in Italy, Japan, or Turkey, far away from family and friends. With more pro women's sports leagues forming, the women's World Cup soccer championship a hit with Americans, and female Olympic gold medal winners a hot commodity, women's sports seem to be growing in popularity. In spite of all this opportunity and exposure for women's sports, I was surprised to learn that, starting in their early teens, girls actually begin *leaving* sports in great numbers, just at the time when sports can provide them with self-esteem and a boost in their academics. The reasons for the high dropout rate are complex. This chapter will help you understand what may be behind your own daughter's requests to drop out, and what you can do, as a parent, to support her.

"Adolescent girls are like saplings in a hurricane. They are young and vulnerable trees that the winds blow with gale strength." This is how Mary Pipher, author of *Reviving Ophelia* and an expert in adolescent psychotherapy, describes the challenges of female adolescence, when girls generally experience sharp declines in self-esteem, academic performance, and body image. All of us who went through adolescence can attest to the fact that it wasn't always easy and presented its own set of challenges—both for daughters and their parents!

Sports can help girls withstand squalls at any point in their young lives, but at no time does our daughters' involvement in athletics and exercise help them more than during the stormy years of adolescence. "The teen years are when playing sports pays special dividends," says Angela Smith, president of the American College of Sports Medicine, "and conversely, when the disadvantages of 'couch potato-ism' become apparent."

Sports participation is so very important for adolescent girls because it enhances their health, their academic performance, and their psychological and emotional fitness.

Adolescent girls who exercise and/or play sports are healthier and less susceptible to chronic conditions such as obesity, osteoporosis, heart disease, diabetes, and certain forms of cancer—including ovarian and breast cancer. They also have lower dropout rates, do better academically in high school and college, feel more popular among classmates, are more involved in extracurricular activities, and are more likely to aspire to community leadership. They also have better self-confidence, higher self-esteem, and a more positive body image, which is critical because girls who view their bodies as useful and powerful are less likely to abuse their bodies. This is particularly important since a number of contemporary disorders such as anorexia, bulimia, and drug abuse begin in adolescence.

Mental Health and Adolescent Girls: Why Exercise Is So Important

Being physically active is beneficial for everyone's mental health, and especially that of adolescent girls. It improves self-esteem and self-confidence and reduces the risk of anxiety and depression.

Adolescence is a time of great physical, mental, and emotional change for our daughters. These changes can profoundly alter how they feel about themselves, their social standing, and their relationships with friends and family. There is the potential for emotional distress, anxiety disorders, and clinical depression. While most girls have effective coping strategies and weather adolescence in the end, it is important for us as parents to be aware of and on the lookout for signs that our daughter is in distress and needs our help. Thankfully, sports participation appears not only to decrease the incidence of anxiety disorders and depression in adolescent girls, but also to help a girl whose mental health has been negatively impacted.

It is estimated that as many as 20 percent of adolescent girls suffer from serious depression—twice the percentage of boys. Unfortunately, symptoms of depression are too often dismissed as "part of growing up."

Adolescent depression is similar to adult depression, with symptoms that include recurring feelings of negative self-worth, sadness, sleep and appetite changes, tearfulness, difficulty functioning at school or work due to lack of concentration, and thoughts of suicide (there has been a significant increase in suicide by adolescents of both sexes over the last thirty years).

Clinical psychologist Mary Pipher has written powerfully in her bestselling book *Reviving Ophelia* about depression in adolescent girls:

> It makes some adolescent girls sluggish and apathetic, others angry and hate-filled. Some girls manifest their depression by starving themselves or carving their bodies. Some withdraw and go deep within themselves and some swallow pills. Others drink heavily or are promiscuous. Whatever the outward form of the depression, the inward form is the grieving for the lost self, the authentic girl who has disappeared with adolescence.

Traditional treatments for adult depression—usually "talk" therapy and antidepressant drugs—are not always effective ways to manage depression in adolescent girls. But there is increasing evidence that what *does* work to treat depression in girls in this age group is sports and physical activity. Numerous studies have proven a beneficial relationship between physical activity and the mental health of adolescent girls, and there is a huge amount of anecdotal evidence that such a relationship exists.

Continued participation in sports and physical activity, then, is not just good preventive medicine for mental health—it is also effective therapy for those who have begun having trouble coping with adolescence. That's because exercise creates responses that directly counteract the symptoms of depression. Exercise doesn't just improve mood and self-esteem, but also increases energy levels and enhances sleep and eating patterns.

When we understand the profoundly beneficial relationship between sports and physical activity on the one hand and female adolescent mental health on the other, three things become clear:

- If our daughters have already been playing sports and been physically active, it's critical that they stay involved in adolescence.
- If our adolescent daughters don't play sports or exercise, we must encourage them to do so.
- If we have adolescent daughters who are suffering from mild or serious depression, we should get them involved in a sports and/or exercise programs, or take them to a therapist who may prescribe such therapy.

Why Adolescent Girls Drop Out of Sports

It appears that a girl's desires to drop sports are often based on pressures to conform to society's conceptions of "appropriate" female behavior. The tendency for girls to want to drop out of sports is even stronger in adolescence, when the desire to reinforce gender identity becomes particularly acute. Thus, adolescent girls frequently shed their assertive, playful, tomboyish selves and become deferential and insecure. They may begin to avoid behavior that is strong, physical, and athletic.

Another reason that we see so many adolescent girls dropping out of sports is because they don't receive enough positive messages about their participation in vigorous sports. Unlike their male peers, whose social status is enhanced by their prowess on the sports field, girls are often valued according to their attractiveness and appeal to boys. What a girl *looks like* tends to be much more important than what she *achieves*. This continues to be an issue that transcends sports—you only have to pick up a teen magazine or watch music videos to realize that popular culture constantly reinforces these messages. As a result, being pretty and being able to attract

Road Runners Club of America Run Smart Safety Tips

Many girls take up running for fitness when they are in their teens. The following safety tips for girls and women who run are from the Road Runners Club of America. Pass them on to your daughter.

- Carry identification or write your name, phone number, and blood type on the inside sole of your running shoe. Include medical information.
- Don't wear jewelry.
- Carry change for telephone calls.
- Run with a partner.
- Write down or leave word if you're running alone. Make sure your friends and family know which are your favorite routes.
- Run in familiar areas. In unfamiliar areas, it's a good idea to contact a local RRCA club or running store. You should also know the location of telephones and open businesses and stores.
- Always stay alert. The more aware you are, the less vulnerable you are.
- Avoid unpopulated areas, deserted streets, and overgrown trails. Especially avoid unlit areas at night. Run clear of parked cars or bushes.
- Do not wear headphones. Use your hearing to be aware of your surroundings.
- Ignore verbal harassment. Use discretion in acknowledging strangers. Look directly at others and be observant, but keep your distance and keep moving.
- Run against traffic so you can observe approaching automobiles.
- Wear reflective material if you must run before dawn or after dark.
- Use your intuition about suspicious persons or areas. React on your intuitions and avoid the person or area if you feel unsafe.
- Carry a whistle or other noisemaker.
- Call the police immediately if something happens to you or someone else, or if you notice anything out of the ordinary during your run.

the opposite sex become more important than areas like academics or sports performance. As a mother of three girls, one of my biggest concerns is that they maintain a positive self-image through their teenage years.

In addition, there are also fewer opportunities for girls to participate in sports than boys because many institutions still do not comply with laws that state that male and female athletes should receive equal benefits and services.

Despite a lack of positive reinforcement, and in some cases, opportunity, the fact that more adolescent girls than ever before are playing sports is testament to how enjoyable and fulfilling these kinds of physical activity can be. All the same, societal pressures to live up to gender roles are very real, and are the cause of many teen girls quitting sports every year. "Just because more girls than before are playing sports doesn't mean that *enough girls* play sports," says Dr. Angela Smith. Of particular concern is that girls are dropping out of team sports such as soccer, basketball, softball, field hockey, ice hockey, and lacrosse that are thought to improve their self-esteem and personal growth. How do we stop our older girls from dropping out of sports? This is the focus of the next section.

Keeping Adolescent Girls Involved in Sports

There is no single thing we can do to keep our daughters involved in sports through adolescence. This becomes a matter of direct parental support, ensuring that the athletic programs they're participating in are safe and enjoyable, and of course, making sure they have the *opportunities* to participate.

Parental and Peer Influences

Parents play a key role in keeping their daughters involved in sports. Above all, it's important to *value* our daughters' sports participation, to make them feel that sports are a good thing. Some specific things you can do to show your daughter that you value her participation in sports are:

- Attend all of her games. Don't be shy about taking the whole family to sporting events. Younger children can get inspired by their older siblings'—sisters' and brothers'—activities.

- Display in your home photographs of her in sports action.
- Buy her the best equipment that you can afford.
- Set aside time to attend women's sports events with her.
- Encourage her support of a particular sports team.
- Give her a subscription to a sports magazine.
- Read the newspaper sports pages with her and discuss their contents.
- Play sports with her and make it an important part of your parent-child bonding.

It's extremely important that we praise our daughters' effort and performance. Confidence creates a beneficial cycle. Girls who feel that they are developing as athletes are more likely to stay involved in sports, which in turn causes their skills to improve, which builds more confidence. Unfortunately, girls often do not receive the same encouragement as boys do, with the result being that girls undervalue their abilities. Girls who quit sports tend to rate their athletic abilities as being quite low. And of course, it doesn't help when they hear comments along the lines of, "Well, you're pretty good, for a girl."

We also need to help our daughters overcome the kinds of gender-typing that drive girls out of sports, or discourage them from participating in the first place. We should never use sexist language and phrases such as "throws like a girl" and "plays like a girl," nor should we discourage girls from playing certain sports because they are "unladylike." 'Along the same lines, we should sensitize ourselves to the gender makeup of the athletic programs in which our daughters participate, applauding those programs if the girls are being treated fairly, and lobbying on our girls' behalf if they are not.

Why Girls Play Sports: The Parent Factor

Studies show that adolescent girls are more likely to play sports when their parents:

- support and encourage their efforts;
- don't criticize their performance; and
- maintain realistic expectations of their performances.

We should also try to keep our daughters' teammates involved in the program. More so than boys, girls tend to play sports to be with their friends. I know my daughters are much more likely to participate in something if they know that at least one of their girlfriends will be there. Peer approval and acceptance is extremely important for adolescent girls. If your daughter's friends start dropping out of sports, she may follow suit. Parents need to communicate with one another about keeping their daughters involved in sports. If your daughter mentions to you that one of her friends is thinking about quitting the program, don't hesitate to call the parents of that girl and discuss the matter with them. Stress to the parents why you think it's important that their daughter stay involved, and ask if there's anything you can do to make a difference. Be up-front about the fact that the main reason for your concern is that you don't want your own daughter to quit. Consider getting *all* the parents together to discuss the issue of how to prevent the girls from dropping out of sports (volunteer your home as the meeting place, if necessary). Communicating with other parents may also be a great way to uncover and address any problems in the sports program itself.

Fun and Safety

Not having fun is one of the most common reasons girls drop out of sports. Making sports enjoyable is really the responsibility of the coach and program organizers. However, it is our responsibility to make sure our daughters are being coached by qualified personnel whose responsibilities include keeping the team members interested in playing. We take a much closer look at the role of the coach in chapter 7. According to Dr. Lyle Micheli, director of the Boston Children's Hospital Division of Sports Medicine, who is a longtime advocate of coaching certification, a trained coach should:

- Structure practice sessions so they include conditioning exercises and warm-up and cool-down periods to reduce the risk of injuries.
- Give ample rest periods and water breaks to prevent overheating.
- Prescribe preseason conditioning programs so athletes are fit and strong enough to play the sport.
- Not push kids to the point where they injure themselves.

- Discourage breaking rules of the game.
- Ensure the team has proper equipment and facilities.
- Enforce the wearing of protective equipment.
- Recognize early signs of pain and dysfunction.
- Perform first aid or CPR if an accident occurs.
- Discourage unsafe nutritional practices.
- Provide appropriate motivation.

Another reason girls quit sports—especially adolescent girls—is injuries. There is justifiable concern that girls get injured more often than boys in sports. Stress fractures are a type of sports injury seen much more frequently in young female athletes because they are caused by menstrual irregularities, a sometime byproduct of vigorous physical activity. Girls and women are more at risk than boys of sustaining disabling "ACL" (anterior cruciate ligament) knee injuries. As we see in chapter 12, there are many things we can do to help reduce our daughters' risk of injury.

Equal Opportunities

Of course, there is little point in having girls interested in playing sports if there are no opportunities available to them. I have been amazed at the inequality that still exists within sports programs for boys and girls. Thirty years after the passage of Title IX, many schools have not complied with the law that stipulates that male and female athletes receive equal equipment and facilities, coaching budgets, game and practice times, and transportation and travel allowances.

You might have noticed inequality at the school your daughter attends. Girls' basketball games may be scheduled for Thursday afternoons while the boys' games are always on Friday nights. Or the school may give preference to the boys' teams for use of the facilities. Or the athletic department has been saying for years that there just isn't enough money for the girls' soccer team to become varsity, even though they keep coming up with the money for boys' programs and equipment. Often, I have seen junior varsity teams not funded for girls, while they are for boys.

What are the options available to us when such inequities exist? Frankly, I don't think most of us would know where to start. Fortunately, the Women's Sports Foundation—the country's leading advocates for

Sports Careers for Women: A Growing Phenomenon

If your daughter is truly enjoying her sports participation, you can encourage her to think about pursuing a career in sports. There are many more opportunities now than there have ever been.

When I was in high school, I was involved in sports, but also drama and music. I didn't want to be an athlete; I wanted to be a performer. I enjoyed sports, I thought, what better job than to go into television and fulfill my desire to perform by talking about sports? It was a great idea, but there was one problem. At the time, there was no such thing as a female sportscaster—needless to say, it was an uphill battle to follow my dreams. The good news is, now there are many more opportunities for our daughters in different sports-related areas. There are now an estimated six million jobs available in the sports industry, more and more of which are available to women. So dramatic has the increase been in sports-related jobs for women that the *New York Times* recently devoted a cover story to this phenomenon. The article pointed out that the explosion in sports for young women has led to increased career opportunities for women in sports-related professions such as sports administration and special-events management.

The passage of Title IX legislation prohibiting sex discrimination in school hiring policies had much to do with the dramatic change in the sports-employment landscape, as did equal-opportunity laws in the workplace. Also, hiring decisions are now being made by people in their forties and fifties, who came of age in the heyday of Title IX and equal-opportunity legislation, and many of whom are sympathetic to the need for more equitable hiring policies.

Here are some possible career paths for your daughter.

Media

As the first woman ever to host the studio show of a major sport, I am gratified to turn on the TV and find female sportscasters in a variety of important roles. If your daughter is interested in broadcasting, you might also encourage her to go into radio. All the sportscasters I know (myself included) got their start that way. The explosion of the Internet has also created demand for female employees by sports-related websites seeking to develop a women's component to their sites. Traditional print media is also trying to tap into the needs of female consumers, and we have seen jobs for journalists created by the launches of publications for female athletes. There has also been a parallel increase in jobs in advertising sales, marketing, and public relations. Increasing coverage of women's sports is being seen on broadcast, cable, and satellite television, and there has been a growing need to find qualified women to work, not just in front of the camera, but also behind the scenes as producers and directors.

Front-Office Positions in Pro Sports Teams

The advent of pro women's soccer and basketball leagues, as well as pre-existing organizations such as the LPGA and WTA, has led to the creation of an enormous number of front-office management positions for women, from general manager to marketing representatives to media-relations jobs.

Sporting Good Manufacturing

Companies that make athletic apparel and footwear have had to make major changes to accommodate the fact that so many more girls and women are playing sports than ever before. They are now designing and manufacturing products specifically for women, and they're also hiring women to create and market these items. Seeing a niche develop, certain companies now manufacture only women's sporting goods, and these companies tend to be operated by women.

Coaching, Administration, and Officiating

There is a huge demand in high schools and colleges for women who are qualified to fill coaching, administration, and officiating positions. The professional organizations who service these groups—such as the National Association of Collegiate Women Athletic Administrators (NACWAA) and the Women's Basketball Coaches Association—are dedicated to recruiting more women and retaining women in sports careers.

Event Management

More careers are emerging in corporate sports-event management. As many companies want to create their own signature sports events geared toward female consumers—everything from ski races to golf outings to beach volleyball—there will need to be women available to manage these events.

Here are some hints for your daughter on getting into a sports career:

- Help her to identify what she is interested in, and what she really *likes* to do.
- She can get her foot in the door by volunteering for a summer or part-time internship. (I did this in college for school credit.)
- Look into what colleges offer degrees or courses in the field in which she's interested (in broadcasting, for example, it's important to be able to write well, so if your daughter's interested in this field, a good liberal arts education is a solid start).
- Help her find and join any organizations or associations related to her area of interest.
- Seek out a mentor for your daughter who will assist her in the process of achieving her career goals.
- Always encourage your daughter to follow her dreams, be persistent, and work hard!

For a list of organizations for sports-related professionals, refer to appendix 3.

female athletes—has come up with a step-by-step approach to achieving gender equality in athletics. Because I think this is such an important part of supporting our girls in sports participation, I've included their entire step-by-step advice in appendix 1.

The Elite Female Athlete: Choices and Challenges

Many a parent dreams that his or her daughter will become a top athlete and receive local, national, and even international acclaim. There is nothing wrong with such ambitions for your child, as long as they are realistic and not based on a desire on your part to experience success vicariously through your daughter. Faced with the decision of whether or not to enter your daughter into an elite sports program or a so-called "travel team," you should understand what may lie in store for her and your family. Many parents I know are torn when faced with these decisions—they want to do what's best for their daughter by encouraging her athletic talents and providing her with the best competition, but the reality is that elite sports can be very hard on the family. Being on travel teams, for instance, is costly both in terms of time and money. A family has little chance of quality time together when one parent is in another city or state at a game every weekend. You must evaluate what your priorities are, and what, truly, is the best situation for the overall development of your daughter and your family.

You need to be aware that, first of all, the chances of success for a girl who starts elite sports programs are by no means assured, and, in fact, the odds are definitely against her. The percentage of girls who receive college athletic scholarships alone is quite small (barely 1 percent), and the prospects of a professional career are even more remote.

Contrast this with the significant compromises parents and athletes must make for more intensive coaching, training, and competition. There are pressures on the family associated with long hours of practice, sibling rivalry, separation from family members, extensive travel, and financial demands (especially in gymnastics, swimming, figure skating, club soccer, tennis, and ice hockey programs). Keep in mind that many elite sports programs are run in a very authoritarian way and parents may lose much of their say when it comes to their daughters' participation. Elite sports programs also have to be much more hard nosed because they are by definition success oriented. Players who don't "measure up" are cut from the program, often to their great disappointment. In certain sports such as gymnastics and figure skating, a girl who matures early finds that her more womanly physique counts against her and she may be dismissed when these signs of maturity become evident.

Keeping Down the Cost of Sports Participation

As children's and youth sports have become more high-stakes and intensive, so too have the costs gotten higher and higher—for travel, equipment, instruction, and rental of practice venues. In many cases, schools have eliminated inexpensive but unglamorous intramural sports to focus on high-profile activities that will bring attention to the school, but which are more expensive for students to participate in. Faced with soaring costs associated with sports participation, what's a parent to do? Here are some suggestions.

Before enrolling your daughter in any particular sports program, figure out ahead of time what it will cost for her to participate. Add up all the obvious costs, from equipment to travel to specialized coaching camps. Also, question other parents to find out if there are hidden costs involved.

Once she's on a team, communicate with other parents if you have concerns about the program's costs. *Does the team really need new uniforms? Is it essential that the team participate in so many tournaments so far from home?* It's frequently the case that other parents are hesitant to raise such contentious issues, worrying that they will be regarded as complainers and that their kids may be discriminated against by the coach. Being part of a united group of team parents that addresses concerns such as costs is an important aspect of being a responsible sports parent.

Still, many parents feel a responsibility to help a child who shows athletic promise make the very most of it. To these parents, here is some advice from Dr. Robert Malina, Professor of Kinesiology at Michigan State University:

- Let your daughter participate in decisions about her athletic participation. Also, give her the opportunity to remove herself from a select program if she wants to. Listen to your daughter!

- Select a coach who not only challenges and improves your daughter's athletic abilities, but also keeps the activity fun.

- Some youngsters make such remarkable progress when they enter an elite program that their parents and/or coaches want to fast-track them in the sport. Adults need to recognize the problems associated with moving up too fast in a sport, from increased risk of injury to greater financial demands.

- Monitor the training environment. Observe coach behaviors and listen to the feedback given by the coach to the young athletes. Is it instructional, or demeaning and threatening? Are there pressures related to diet, weight regulation, weight training, and conditioning regimens that may be inappropriate for the child and potentially harmful? Do the young athletes have any say about when and how much they practice and compete? Participation should be fun and enjoyable for your daughter.

- Be careful of becoming over involved in your child's athletic training and aspirations. Ask yourself: is it your child's dream of sports success...or *yours*?
- Give strong consideration to potential lifestyle consequences for your daughter and your family.

Sibling Rivalry—What's a Sports Parent to Do?

Children compete incessantly for their parents' attention and approval. Experts say that this rivalry is even more intense when the siblings are the same gender and relatively close in age (born within three years of each other). Sports add another ingredient to this potentially volatile mix, especially when one child is clearly a more accomplished athlete than the other.

What can parents do to alleviate rivalries between athletic siblings? Rivalries will develop even when parents do their best to create a healthy, non-competitive environment, but here are some do's and don'ts for minimizing sports-related conflict:

DO

- Encourage a younger child to try sports other than the one her older sibling is playing.
- Go along to watch each child's games equally.
- Look for aspects to praise in the less-accomplished athlete.
- Offer praise for effort, not just achievement.
- Praise older kids for teaching or supporting younger siblings.
- Provide support and plenty of praise for non-sports activities such as reading or crafts.

DON'T EVER

- Play favorites.
- Compare your kids.
- Assign roles to your kids—"Wendy is the athlete, but Laura is a super-smart student."

My goal is not to turn my daughters into superstar athletes. What I want to do is provide them with the kind of athletic experience that will give them the confidence they need to weather their adolescence, and hook them on sports and physical activity for life. I believe this is a responsibility we should take as seriously as all the other aspects of parenting!

chapter 6

Teaching Your Young Athlete to Be a Good Sport

● ● ●

Throughout two decades of covering professional, collegiate, and even high-school sports, I have seen many examples of athletes being good and bad sports. Unfortunately, it is much easier to recall examples of bad sportsmanship. From my perspective, the biggest culprit, from the pros to the little leagues, is ego. Many athletes feel as if they are above the sport, the rules of the game, their teammates, and even their coaches, not to mention their opponents!

Psychologists tell us that children who learn positive values through sports tend to behave in socially responsible, ethical ways in other areas of their lives—at home, in school, and, later in life, in the work place. Sports are a powerful tool for building good character. I strongly believe this to be true. Unfortunately, we're all familiar with images of children denying to the referee that they committed a foul when it's obvious that they did, doing in-your-face victory dances when their team wins, or bawling their eyes out or kicking the goalposts when they lose. Children who are taught that it's OK to cheat, act obnoxiously, and embarrass their teammates or opponents will likely behave this way outside of sports.

Until recently, it was thought that boys were much more likely than girls to be poor sports. Girls, it was believed, tended to be less aggressive, more inclined toward cooperation, and therefore less likely to be poor sports. But with many more girls than ever before participating in sports, and increasing pressures on girls to win, examples of poor sportsmanship by girls are becoming more and more prevalent.

Our children won't miraculously become good sports when we sign them up for a sports program. Sadly, the most outrageous examples of poor sportsmanship are found in our youth leagues, where kids are not imitating their favorite sports heroes, but exhibiting bad habits and terrible manners learned from their own parents. All too often it is the parents themselves who are badly misbehaving. The first thing we need to do is to learn ourselves, and then teach our children, what it means to be a good sport.

What Is "Being a Good Sport"?

It is not easy to define what being a good sport means. I think you'll agree with my "Good Sport Code of Conduct."

Being a good sport means I will:
- Try my hardest
- Treat my opponents with respect
- Win without boasting or showing off
- Lose without complaining

This Good Sport Code of Conduct is a start. We should have our daughters learn the Code. We should talk with our daughter's coach about making it part of the team's pregame warm-up. And we should ask the program organizers to incorporate it, or something similar, into the program philosophy.

Talking to Kids about How to Be a Good Sport

You may want to have some general conversations with your daughter about being a good sport and then observe her behavior as she participates in a sports program. You can then address particular instances that arise and train your daughter to be a good sport in the same way that you teach her table manners.

You may find it necessary to have regular conversations about being a good sport with your daughter, and to talk to her about her teammates' behavior or opposing players' behavior. You can point out examples of being a good and bad sport and encourage your daughter to imitate the behavior you approve of. Keep in mind that children imitate or "try on" behavior they see in others, and be prepared to discuss with her what works and what doesn't. It can be as simple as saying, "I like the way that girl from the visiting team shook your hand at the end of the game," or "I like the way you left the field after you struck out. I could tell you were disappointed but you behaved like a good sport." Or, you may need to set aside time for discussion, particularly if you see your daughter imitating or joining in poor-sport behavior with her friends on the team.

Kids need guidance on how to behave appropriately in the organized-sports environment. I created the checklist below to help my daughters learn how to be good sports. It is followed by discussion points relating to each of the items in the checklist.

Being a Good Sport Checklist
1. Does she try her hardest?
2. Does she show respect to her opponent(s)?
3. Does she play by the rules?
4. Does she keep her cool?
5. Is she a team player?
6. Does she accept that everyone should get a chance to play?
7. Does she listen to her coach and do what he/she says?
8. Does she accept the decisions of the game officials?

1. A Good Sport Tries Her Hardest
In chapter 4, we discussed the importance of redefining winning so it emphasizes effort instead of outcome. That's why the first thing I emphasize in my checklist is the importance of trying your hardest. Trying your hardest means doing your best. There's nothing more your daughter can do than try her hardest. Any athlete who tries her hardest is a winner regardless of the score of the game or the outcome of the event. Trying your hardest is also a way to show respect to teammates, the coach, the game officials, the people who came to watch the competition, and the opposing team.

2. A Good Sport Shows Respect for Her Opponent

The "Golden Rule" applies to sports, too—so encourage your daughter to treat the opponent the way she would like to be treated. Remind her that they may be from a different team or a different town, but they're kids just like her. It's important that she be nice to her opponents before, during, and after the game. That means saying "Hi" if she sees them before the game or contest starts (and "Welcome" if they're from another town); being a good sport during the game; and sincerely thanking them for playing after the game finishes. It's not always an easy balance, but showing respect to the opponent means trying her hardest while the game is being played, and at the same time showing good manners. I think it is very important to shake hands with the opposing team or player after a game—it's a way of putting the competition into a proper perspective.

3. A Good Sport Plays by the Rules

"It's not cheating unless you get caught," is an awful expression, and one that certainly has no place in children's sports! Rules are necessary so a game can be played in an orderly and safe manner. If your daughter chooses to play a sport, she has an obligation to learn the rules of that sport and play the sport within those rules. If she doesn't play by the rules, she's more likely to be a cheat in school, at home, or at work later in life. In addition, she shouldn't leave it completely up to the referees to enforce the rules. Tell your daughter that, when possible, if she commits a foul that the referee or umpire doesn't see, she should raise her arm, stop play, and inform the game official of the foul.

I saw a great example of this at the U.S. Women's Open, the most prestigious women's golf tournament in the world. Stephanie Keever, a student at Stanford University and standout collegiate golfer, was in the position to become "low amateur" at the Open—a great honor. But in the third round, she brushed the sand with her club. No official saw her violation, but she called a penalty on herself, costing her two strokes. She ended up with a ten on the hole, effectively ending her chances. Even though the hole was disastrous for her score, she received great acclaim for exhibiting sportsmanship and abiding by the rules of the game.

4. A Good Sport Keeps Her Cool

If your daughter loses her cool in sports, she spoils the game for every-one—including herself. Complaining to game officials, blaming team-mates, and physically or verbally attacking an opponent(s)—these are all examples of losing your cool. To be a good sport, she'll need to channel the natural frustrations athletes sometimes feel in the heat of the moment into playing better. For example, tell your daughter that if she gets a bad pass from a teammate and the ball goes to someone on the opposing team, it doesn't make sense to stop and yell at the teammate—she should chase the ball and try to win it back! The same goes if she gets what she thinks is a poor call from a game official. I have seen countless athletes get dis-tracted or angry and then lose the game because they lost their concen-tration. And finally, if the coach takes her out of the game even when she wants to stay in, she shouldn't scowl at the coach and the player sent in to replace her, but instead wish that player "good luck," and use it as moti-vation the next time she gets a chance to play. Remind your daughter that losing her temper can be a huge distraction and usually spoils a person's performance.

5. A Good Sport Is a Team Player

If her sport is a team sport, your daughter should be encouraged to be a team player. She can cheer on her teammates during practices and games and offer them comfort and encouragement when they make mistakes. Being a team player also means not hogging the ball or in any other way trying to steal the limelight from the other players on her team. And it means helping out the coach and teammates when help is needed. Before the coach asks, she can offer to help set up or clear away equipment. No one player should receive special favorable treatment—in the same way, no player should consider herself "above" performing tasks for the team.

6. A Good Sport Accepts That Everyone Should Get a Chance to Play

Most children's sports programs have a policy that everyone gets to play—regardless of ability. If your daughter is one of the better players on the team, it's natural for her to get frustrated if she's taken out of the game to make way for someone who's not as skilled. However, it's important that at this stage *everyone* gets the chance to play. Ask her to imagine how it would feel if *she* were one of the less-skilled players and never got to play. It wouldn't be much fun, and she would never get the chance to improve! The more talented players should provide encouragement to those who are less skilled. Remember that children who are not very talented athletes sometimes blossom into great players later on if they get the chance to continue participating.

7. A Good Sport Listens to Her Coach and Does What He/She Says

If your daughter wants to be part of a team, she needs to do what the coach asks of her. Backtalking to the coach during practice or a game is rude and can distract her teammates. Sometimes, even coaches can make mistakes or do things she won't agree with, but that doesn't necessarily make them bad people. If she disagrees with her coach's tactics or decisions, encourage her to wait until she cools down and then voice her concerns privately and in a civil tone of voice.

8. A Good Sport Accepts the Decisions of the Game Officials

Like coaches, referees and umpires try their hardest and are officiating at games because they love children's sports. And because they are human like you and me, they can make mistakes. There is no point in arguing with a referee or umpire about a call. It simply wastes energy, because let's face it, how often does a game official actually reverse his or her decision? Your daughter is much better off channeling her frustrations into trying harder in the game instead of getting mad at the referee. There's an expression I like that sums up the whole issue: "The referee is always right, even when she's wrong." One final note: if it's not part of the duties of the captain of the team to thank the referee after the game, encourage your daughter to take it upon herself after the whistle blows to simply say, "Thanks, ref!"

Adults Need to Be Good Sports, Too

Who's at fault for the spiraling decline of sportsmanship? Many people would argue that the blame lies squarely at the feet of pro athletes, whose trash-talking, chest-thumping, and brawling is broadcast into our homes

The Effects of Out-of-Control Sports Parents on Young Athletes

Parents should value their daughters' sports participation. But sometimes they go too far. It's equally important to keep our support in perspective. Many parents' behavior can get out of control.

The effects of parental misconduct and abusive treatment by adults in the sports environment can be profound for the young athletes forced to endure such behavior. Under some circumstances, young athletes who have strong reactions to viewing violence or aggression can develop post-traumatic stress disorder. Children and adolescents who are treated abusively in the sports environment are more likely to engage in high-risk behaviors, including suicide and attempts at suicide, delinquency, inappropriate and unwanted sexual activity, and violence against others. Mistreatment of athletes in youth sports has also been linked to a variety of physical and emotional health conditions, including eating disorders.

all too often. To an extent, our kids tend to emulate the behaviors of their favorite athletes, and what happens in the big leagues eventually trickles down through the college ranks, high schools, and community sports played by six-year-old kids. However, it is much easier for these kinds of inappropriate behavior to permeate kids' sports when the children are not getting positive adult involvement.

Many of us parents and coaches are ignoring our own complicity in the decline of sportsmanship. There is not enough emphasis by adults on what constitutes appropriate behavior, and not enough disapproval when kids act like poor sports. Worse than that, coaches and parents themselves often behave appallingly! The first place children look for clues about how to behave is the example of adult role models around them.

Scarcely a week goes by without another report of outrageous conduct by adults involved in children's sports. There was the case of the Massachusetts youth hockey coach who was beaten into a fatal coma in front of his players by a parent, and another case where a hockey father killed another father in a fistfight. Other incidents involved a soccer coach in Florida who was charged with battery for head-butting a referee, and a New York father who was accused of beating up his son's hockey coach after a verbal argument. The National Association of Sports Officials reports that incidents of violence in youth sports are getting more frequent and more serious.

These are the worst sorts of adult misconduct that occur in children's sports. However, thousands of other unpleasant and inappropriate acts that don't make the news are committed every day by coaches and parents in front of young athletes. They include:

- Booing or taunting
- Using profanity or obscene gestures
- Verbally intimidating, threatening, or assaulting players, coaches, or officials

When adults act this way in the children's sports environment, why should we expect the athletes to behave any differently? Here are some guidelines I developed for how we parents should behave at children's sporting events.

Sports Parent Code of Spectator Conduct

- I will get my child to the game/event at the appointed time, not just in time for me to watch.
- If I think I am going to be late for my child's game, I will let her know ahead of time so she is not disappointed or worried about me. When I arrive I will not announce myself and distract her.
- I will learn the rules and techniques of the sport my child plays so I will be an educated spectator and afterwards will be able to discuss the game knowledgeably with her.
- I will treat every player/participant, parent, and coach on my child's team with respect.
- I will treat every player/participant, parent, and coach on the opposing team with respect.
- I will welcome player/participants, parents, and coaches of teams visiting from other towns as guests to my town.
- I will ask other spectators to act appropriately if I see them behaving otherwise.

- I will not question the judgment of coaches or game officials in such a way as to distract the players, coaches, or other spectators.
- If I disagree with a coach's decision, I will raise the matter civilly after the contest away from the other players and parents. I will never approach the coach when I feel my anger might compromise our discussion.
- I will never approach or confront a game official. If I have a problem with the officiating, I will ask my child's coach to bring the matter up with the official.
- I will always cheer, never jeer, and will acknowledge *effort* as well as *outcome* with my cheers. I will also applaud the other team's outstanding efforts.
- I will *never* use profanity in the youth-sports environment.
- I will not yell instruction at my child or her teammates. I will leave the coaching to the coaches.
- I will never smoke cigarettes, chew tobacco, or drink alcohol at my child's sports event.
- I will emphasize to my child the importance of being a good sport.

In children's sports, parental misconduct may be serious enough that players actually quit the program and sports altogether, which sets them up for all the problems associated with an inactive lifestyle.

Seminars for Sports Parents

Some children's sports programs are making it mandatory that all the parents attend a seminar to teach the importance of good behavior in the sports environment. The Parents Association for Youth Sports (PAYS) runs the most popular of these programs. This year alone, the program will be conducted in over four hundred cities nationwide.

A study that was conducted to gauge the impact of the program in Jupiter, Florida, found that 60 percent of the parents surveyed said they have witnessed a positive change in the overall behavior and attitudes of other parents since taking part in PAYS; 62 percent of the parents said they now feel empowered to stand up against negative acts that undermine their child's youth program; an overwhelming 93 percent said they supported the implementation of the PAYS program on a mandatory basis;

and 84 percent said they had a positive reaction to the meeting and thought it was beneficial.

In an article on the National Alliance for Youth Sports website, Steve Gompertz, the boys' basketball director for the Andover Athletic Association, which was the first organization in Minnesota to mandate PAYS, said "The vast majority of the parents involved in our programs haven't been a problem. But those few parents that are [a problem] can require a lot of our volunteers' attention and really take away from the experience we're trying to give these kids. We want to be proactive about this and not wait until it escalates into a crisis. The Association thinks this training will clarify expectations and set in motion a sort of peer pressure to behave appropriately."

To find out more about the PAYS program, visit the website for the National Association of Youth Sports at www.nays.org.

All around us is evidence that our society has replaced civility with crassness, bad manners, and lack of consideration for others. Children's sports may be one of the few places where we have a chance at reversing this trend. Being a good sport isn't some quaint and outdated notion. It is a trait that can help our daughters in all areas of their lives. We must revive the characteristic of being a good sport in our children so they can pass it on to their kids someday.

chapter 7

Who's in Charge?

The Importance of the Coach's Role to Your Daughter's Sports Experience

● ● ●

When we get together with my husband's family, invariably the subject of Ollie Mayfield comes up. Who is this person who has taken on almost legendary status in our family lore? He's my husband's high-school football coach! Twenty-five years after his high-school days, my husband and his family still tell stories of this great coach who, with a speech to the team here or a simple note to one of his players there, had a profound motivational impact on the kids who played for him. Through the years, Coach Mayfield took a team that was the laughingstock of Tucson, Arizona, instilled a fierce sense of school pride (my husband recalls Coach Mayfield walking the hallways of the school with a tape recorder blasting the school fight song!), and shaped them into a perennial state-playoff contender.

I hope your daughter will encounter a special coach like Coach Mayfield along the way, one whose positive influence is lasting. The quality of coaching is one of the most important factors in determining how beneficial your daughter's sports experiences are. This chapter will teach you what you can do to ensure that your precious daughter receives the best coaching possible...even if her coaches aren't as special and memorable as Ollie Mayfield was.

Coaches are a vital part of a young athlete's life. Today, children who play sports spend an average of eighty hours per season with their coaches, according to a survey by the National Youth Sports Coaches Association. As parents, we'll want to know who our daughters' coaches are, what they know about sports, and what their philosophy is toward girls having fun in sports. We shouldn't simply take it for granted that they know what they're doing.

"The lack of qualified coaches is the biggest crisis in youth sports," says Michelle Klein, Executive Director of the Boston-based National Youth Sports Safety Foundation. "The present situation puts our children at emotional and physical risk."

The vast majority of coaches are well-meaning and responsible. Most coaches are community-minded people (and parents themselves) who give freely of their time to help children reap the benefits of sports. And as education about youth sports increases, coaches will become better at recognizing and preventing the dangerous physical and psychological effects that sports can have on children.

Yet abuse does take place. A 1993 Minnesota Amateur Sports Commission study found the following incidences of mistreatment by coaches:

- 45.3 percent of boys and girls surveyed said they had been called names, yelled at, or insulted while participating in sports.
- 17.5 percent of the athletes surveyed said they had been hit, kicked, or slapped while participating in sports.
- 21 percent of athletes said they had been pressured to play while injured.
- 8.2 percent of athletes said they had been pressured to intentionally harm others while playing sports.
- 3.4 percent of athletes said they had been pressured into sex or sexual touching.
- 8 percent of all the athletes surveyed said they had been called names with sexual connotations while participating in sports.

Some specific examples of grossly inappropriate behavior by coaches include the following:

- In New York State, a Little League coach slammed an umpire to the ground over a disputed third-strike call against the coach's eleven-year-old child.

- In Iowa, a girls' softball coach was convicted of videotaping his players in the shower.
- In California, an eighteen-year-old soccer player died of heatstroke after being made to run in excessively hot temperatures.

Definitions of Coaching Abuse

Coaching abuse in children's sports can take several forms. The most common form of mistreatment is emotional abuse. "Ideological" abuse, physical abuse, sexual abuse, and sexual harassment also occur. Often it is difficult to know whether specific behavior is illegal or simply inappropriate. The following information will give you pause to think about what might constitute abuse in children's sports.

Emotional Abuse

It is common for emotionally abusive coaches to downplay the damaging effects of their behavior. "It's nothing serious," they might say. "I'm just trying to toughen them up." This is especially common when they consider that behavior necessary for instilling discipline. The effects of physical abuse are easy to see, but emotional abuse is just as hurtful. A child's self-esteem can be damaged if a coach yells things like:

- "That was a dumb play."
- "You're so clumsy."
- "You're an embarrassment to your team."
- "You're not worth the uniform you play in."

Negative statements are especially harmful to a girl when they demean her gender. Even semi-joking comments from a coach such as, "I *knew* I should have coached a boys' team," when a girl on the team makes a mistake, can erode a girl's confidence.

Children look up to coaches as important authority figures and take criticism from them very much to heart. Being shouted at or humiliated by coaches can be extremely hurtful for kids—especially when it's done in front of their teammates. When a coach speaks to his or her team in a disparaging way week in and week out, players may start to believe the things they're being told about themselves. Children who are continually subjected to negative comments may experience damage to their self-esteem.

Instead of being critical or demeaning, it is far more helpful for coaches to "accentuate the positive." They can do this by telling an athlete what she did *right* before correcting a mistake. It's also better for coaches to use a positive, encouraging tone of voice than one that is threatening or frightening. Above all, coaches need to establish a friendly, positive atmosphere in their program, an environment that is conducive to kids having a good time and learning new skills.

Ideological Abuse

Ideological abuse refers to a wrongheaded belief system that a coach may adopt to run his or her team. "Winning isn't everything, it's the only thing," and "Good guys finish last," are examples of ideologies that overly emphasize winning at the expense of having fun and being good sports. "No pain, no gain," is an ideology that minimizes an athlete's legitimate complaints of pain, which may cause overuse injury. Taking the fun out of sports, discouraging sportsmanship, and dismissing the athlete's complaints of pain may *all* be construed as abusive.

After signing up my oldest daughter for soccer, the first thing I did was ask about the person who coached her team. The person in charge told me that he was a first-time coach, but assured me, "He's very enthusiastic...he'll be great." So off we went in great anticipation of our first game. Well, the very first thing that the coach told the group of wide-eyed preschoolers to do was "huddle up and take a knee." (I had to explain to them exactly what that meant!) He then went on to say, "We're the best and we're out here today to beat the other team!" This was before they had even so much as done a drill or kicked a soccer ball! I was very taken aback, and then had to watch an interminable game in which the coach insisted on enforcing every little rule. My daughter never got near the ball, and dissolved into tears halfway though the ordeal. She has not been back to play soccer since. This coach's tough approach was inappropriate for the age group and soured the whole experience for my daughter.

Physical Abuse

Coaches who use physical contact as punishment are guilty of abuse. Even a light "clip around the ear" is unacceptable, as are the more obvious forms of abuse such as hitting or kicking a child, throwing equipment at her, or shaking her. Even if this happens just once to your daughter, it is imperative that you report the incident to the program administrators so they can sanction the coach. If a pattern of physical abuse comes to light, then dismissal of the coach is the only option.

Sexual Abuse

Sexual and/or romantic relationships between coaches and athletes represent an abuse of status and power and are completely unacceptable. Because a superior-subordinate relationship exists, the coach has to understand that players are not qualified to take responsibility for their role in an inappropriate relationship, even if it was the player who supposedly initiated it. It is always, always the coach's responsibility to make sure that no inappropriate relationship is allowed to develop. Behavior that constitutes sexual harassment may include:

- Inappropriate touching (fondling instead of a hug, a long kiss on the lips, suggestive stroking)
- Pressure for sexual favors
- Sexual jokes
- Talking about one's sex life or sex habits

An example of sexual harassment of a player by a coach might include the coach's insistence that player hug him or she won't "start" in the next game, or inquiries by the coach into the player's sex life.

How to Respond to Sexual Harassment: Help for Your Daughter

Your daughter needs to know what to do if she is ever sexually harassed. The first thing she needs to do is tell the harasser to stop. Through her actions and her words, she should make it very clear to the person harassing her that his or her behavior is unacceptable and unwelcome. Then she needs to report the situation to someone in a position of authority—the athletic director, principal, or a teacher. Accompany your daughter when she makes the report. In case the situation escalates, it's important that your daughter keeps a record of what happened. Specific are important—the who, what, where, and when of the harassment. Names of witnesses need to be recorded.

If you don't think the situation is being handled appropriately, you can help your daughter file a complaint with the Department of Education Office for Civil Rights. Information on how to do this can be found in the publication, "How to File a Complaint with the Office for Civil Rights" (www.ed.gov/offices/OCR/ocrpubs.html).

Why Coaching Abuse Exists

Very few coaches have any formal training. Only a small percentage of the 2.5 million coaches involved in children's sports programs in this country have had any instruction in how to coach children's sports. Although it's important to make the point that volunteer coaches are the backbone of our youth-sports programs and that they are well-meaning and dedicated, the fact is that most are underqualified. Just because a coach's heart is in the right place doesn't necessarily mean he or she knows what they're doing.

Think about it: we wouldn't dream of sending our child to a school with uncertified teachers, but parents have traditionally shown no qualms about allowing their children to be instructed in sports by people who often have no more qualification to coach sports other than the fact that they may have at one time played the sport and are willing to show up regularly. I know that I didn't give the subject much thought until I started writing this book.

Why are our standards so low? "The main reason is that the demand for qualified coaches far exceeds the supply," says Michelle Klein. "And if we want the positions filled, we can't afford to be choosy. To make matters worse, the turnover is extremely high." It's true that on average, the person who coaches children's sports does so for only three to five years—the duration of their own children's involvement.

Fortunately, serious coaching misconduct is rare. However, it is not uncommon to encounter the following: coaches who overemphasize winning at the expense of fun; who don't know the fundamentals of the sport they're coaching; who don't know basic first aid and how to use safety equipment; who verbally abuse their young charges; and who are insensitive to the kinds of gender-typing that can cause a girl to quit sports.

National Standards for Coaches

The situation has been able to continue in part because, until just a few years ago, there was no set of national standards we could apply to our children's coaches. That changed with the release in 1997 of the 124-page *National Standards for Athletic Coaches*, a set of guidelines created by the National Association for Sports and Physical Education (NASPE) in conjunction with the National Association for Girls and Women in Sport (NAGWS). The new national coaching standards are a master list of coaching competencies intended to give guidance to administrators, coaches, athletes, and parents regarding the skills and knowledge that coaches should have. Each competency is divided into five levels, from level-one "beginner coaches" to level-five "master coaches." However, the new national coaching standards are not part of a national certification program to train coaches. Also, they are not sport-specific, though they may serve as a model for sport-specific organizations that certify, educate, and train coaches.

The manual (available from the online store at the NASPE website at www.aahperd.org/naspe/publications-coachesstandards.html) should be required reading for anyone who is running a sports league. Sports-program organizers should make sure that the coaches in their programs meet these standards. There are a number of coach-training and certification programs, and the coaches in your child's program should be encouraged to get such education.

Coaching for the Coaches

The organizations listed below train and certify coaches for children's and youth sports. Visit their websites to find out more about what they offer. Urge the organizers of the sports program your daughter is involved in to offer training courses for the program's coaches, or to require that they have some coaching education.

National Association for Sport and Physical Education (NASPE)
www.aahperd.org/naspe/naspe_main.html
1900 Association Drive, Reston, VA 22091
703-476-3410

American Sport Education Program (ASEP)
www.asep.com
American Sport Education Program
1607 North Market Street
Champaign, IL 61825
1-800-747-5698 (toll free) or 217-351-2674

Program for Athletic Coaches' Education (PACE)
www.mhsaa.com/administration/pace.html
Youth Sports Institute of Michigan State University
213 IM Sports Circle Building, Department of Kinesiology
Michigan State University, East Lansing, MI 48824-1049
517-353-6689

Coaching Association of Canada (CAC)
www.coach.ca
141 Laurier Avenue West, Suite 300
Ottawa, Ontario K1P 5J3
613-235-5000

American Red Cross/US Olympic Committee Sport Safety Training
    Course for Coaches
USOC, One Olympic Plaza
Colorado Springs, CO 80909
719-632-5551

How Do We Evaluate the Coaches?

How do we know that our daughters' coaches know what they are doing? We can take some comfort if he or she has been trained and certified by a recognized program. Barring that, your daughter's coach—and certainly the organizers of the program in which she's enrolled—should have read the national standards and followed their recommendations.

Until it's compulsory that all children's and youth sports coaches are certified—a goal of organizations such as the American College of Sports Medicine (ACSM)—it's up to us as parents to evaluate our children's coaches. The following checklist was developed by the ACSM, and you can use it to help determine whether your daughter's coach is doing a good job.

My daughter's coach:

- Organizes practices so the kids aren't standing around for too long.
- Demonstrates solid knowledge of the sport he/she is coaching and the ability to teach new skills.
- Spends time talking to the players individually or in small groups.
- Pays attention to safety issues, including conditioning, equipment, and playing conditions.
- Never belittles a player, uses language that reinforces gender stereotypes ("you play like a girl"), screams, or uses an otherwise inappropriate tone of voice.
- Listens to the kids—and their parents.
- Adheres to league rules about playing times and position assignments.

Here is a summary of what the *National Standards for Athletic Coaches* stipulate that our children's coaches should be expected to know.

Safety

Coaches must insist on safe playing conditions and equipment, including:

- Playing fields free of potholes, glass, and other debris
- Padded posts
- Proper footwear
- Well-fitted protective equipment and padding
- Equipment sized for young athletes, including hockey sticks, baseball bats, tennis rackets, and skis
- Enforced wearing of safety equipment such as mouthguards, helmets, shinguards, and flotation jackets

It's also key that coaches know about other areas of injury prevention, including the prevention of overuse injuries and heat-induced injuries. A good coach will know that one of the most effective ways to prevent overuse injury is to ensure that all the athletes have a preseason sports physical. Heat injuries can be prevented by allowing frequent water breaks during hot weather, and not scheduling overly strenuous practices during hot weather.

Growth, Development, and Learning

The defining characteristic of children is change. Coaches need to understand that the physical changes that take place when children are growing also influence their learning and performance. They should understand the social and emotional changes that are taking place in the young athletes in their charge, and with this in mind, know that they sometimes have to be flexible.

Training, Conditioning, and Nutrition

Coaches should know the essentials of how the human body works. It is particularly important that they learn how growth in childhood makes the body more vulnerable to certain types of injuries, and also how sound nutritional practices are essential to the good health and performance of young athletes. These topics are covered later in chapters 8 and 12.

Skills, Strategies, and Tactics

Coaches should understand not just the sport they are coaching, but the tactics and strategies that are *appropriate* for the age group they are coaching. They should know how to run a practice so it is enjoyable and productive for the young participants.

When the Coach Isn't Up to Standard

What are your options if your daughter's coach doesn't measure up? You have several courses of action. You can start by talking to the coach. Is he or she aware of the problem, whether it is the abusive way he or she speaks to the kids or the fact that he or she doesn't know how to fasten a batting helmet? You could offer to help. After all, a rookie coach or one without strong organizational skills may be overwhelmed by everything there is to do, and your assistance may get things running more efficiently. If your concerns are unresolved, consider speaking with the person in charge of the program. Let that person know that a harmful situation exists and that you expect them to do something about it. If you feel the situation is serious enough, or has not improved, consider moving your daughter to another team or league. This is a last-ditch solution, but it may be the best one if you feel she is at risk.

National Youth Sports Coaches Association (NYCSA) Coach's Code of Ethics

- I will place the emotional and physical well-being of my players ahead of a personal desire to win.
- I will treat each player as an individual, remembering the large range of emotional and physical development for the same age group.
- I will do my best to provide a safe playing situation for my players.
- I will promise to review and practice basic first-aid principles needed to treat injuries of my players.
- I will do my best to organize practices that are fun and challenging for all my players.
- I will lead by example in demonstrating fair play and sportsmanship to all my players.
- I will provide a sports environment for my team that is free of drugs, tobacco, and alcohol, and I will refrain from their use at all youth sports events.
- I will be knowledgeable in the rules of each sport that I coach, and I will teach these rules to my players.
- I will use those coaching techniques appropriate for all of the skills that I teach.
- I will remember that I am a youth sports coach, and that the game is for children and not adults.

Reprinted by permission of the NYCSA.

If you are unhappy with the quality of the coaching in your daughter's sports program, you should also consider becoming a coach yourself!

Coaching Your Own Daughter

Coaching can be immensely fulfilling, but it can also be a challenge, especially if you're coaching your own child. It's important to know what you're getting into, so talk to some coaches before you take the plunge. It's also important that you want to coach for the right reasons. Some good reasons to want to coach: you sincerely want to help out, you want to enhance your daughter's sports experience, and you want to learn to do something that can bring enormous happiness to children. If you're being honest with yourself and find that your reason for wanting to coach is that you want to live vicariously through your daughter, get her more playing time, or boost your ego, rethink your decision.

Before you go any further, it's probably a good idea to talk to your daughter about your decision. She will probably be very excited that you will be coaching her, but it's important to explain to her that she will have to share your attention with the other players and that you will play no favorites. Above all, you need to explain to your daughter that she will be treated like all the other athletes. Once you get the go-ahead from your daughter, go for it!

The National Youth Sports Safety Foundation Golden Rules of Coaching

- If athletes are coached with criticism, they learn low self-esteem.
- If athletes are coached with hostility, they learn to fight.
- If athletes are coached with ridicule, they learn to withdraw.
- If athletes are coached with shame, they learn to feel guilty.
- If athletes are coached with patience, they learn to improve.
- If athletes are coached with encouragement, they learn confidence.
- If athletes are coached with praise, they learn to have faith.
- If athletes are coached with fairness, they learn justice.
- If athletes are coached with approval, they learn positive self-esteem.
- If athletes are coached with honesty, they learn to trust.
- If athletes are coached with modesty, they learn teamwork.

The following guidelines were developed by the National Youth Sports Safety Foundation. They were created by Susan E. Warren and Donna Volpe and are used with the permission of the National Youth Sports Safety Foundation, Inc.

The more you educate yourself about youth sports, the more fulfilling you will find it to be. Coaching requires that you wear several different hats—trainer, teacher, nutritionist, counselor, nurse, and mediator. Buy a good book or video on coaching principles, and join a coaching association such as the National Youth Sports Coaches Association, whose websites feature interesting and useful articles. You could even take a coaching course. Definitely obtain a copy of the *National Standards for Athletic Coaches*. Learning first aid and CPR are essential.

One of your first acts as team coach should be to hold a preseason meeting for players and parents. At this meeting, you should explain your goals for the season and what your philosophy is regarding issues such as playing time and position assignments. Make sure that your philosophy is in line with the league's position, and state that it is. If, for example, the league's rules state that all the players get equal playing time, be sure they do. During the meeting, announce that your daughter is on the team and that you will treat her like everyone else. It's also important that during the meeting you encourage the parents to come to you immediately with any constructive criticism; dissatisfaction that is allowed to fester usually ends up in major conflict or backbiting.

We talked earlier about the need not to play favorites with your daughter when you're her coach. It's equally important that you don't neglect your child or be overly hard on her in your efforts to prove to her teammates and their parents that you're being evenhanded.

Playing time and position assignments are hot-button issues for many parents, so it's a good idea to keep records. Write down which kids play what positions and for how long each game. Refer to these records often for inequities.

Just as important as the decision about whether to coach your daughter is deciding when to stop. Often, the parent-child relationship can get in the way of effective coaching. A good indication that this is happening is when a child starts to ignore her parent-coach's instruction, but is willing to listen to another adult—an assistant coach perhaps. It's difficult to know when to bow out. The best way to decide whether or not to continue coaching your daughter is simply to ask her honestly if she would feel more comfortable being coached by someone else.

Of course, being head coach isn't the only way you can help out the team and be able to spend more time with your daughter. There are other ways to volunteer. There is always demand for someone willing to perform jobs such as assistant coaching, record keeping, officiating, lining the fields, chaperoning trips, managing equipment, and scheduling.

Our daughters' coaches are essential to their enjoyment of their childhood sports experience. A bad coach can sour a girl on sports and turn her off physical activity for life. On the other hand, a qualified and nurturing coach can set the stage for a lifelong interest in sports and exercise. As parents, it's our duty to do as much as we can to make sure our daughters get the most beneficial coaching experience possible.

chapter 8

Nutritional Needs

● ● ●

One of my greatest concerns about my kids is one that I think is shared by all mothers: I worry about what my kids eat! Luckily, most children do manage to get the nutrients they need—but for a child in sports, these nutritional needs may be greater. Therefore, it is important to make sure that your young athlete is eating the foods she needs to be healthy.

In addition, eating healthy foods is not the only issue that needs to be faced. It's ironic—sports and physical activity are supposed to promote good health in our daughters, but sometimes playing sports can actually interfere with good nutrition. Frequent, lengthy practices and games can disrupt family meal times. The quest to succeed can promote fad diets and unwise weight-loss strategies. Young female athletes may be at a higher risk of "nutritional abuse" because of society's pressures on young women to be thin. Also, girls tend to make up the majority of participants in sports such as gymnastics, figure skating, and diving, where there is a strong emphasis on maintaining low body fat. At the same time, your daughter may be inundated by advertisements for special drinks and meal substitutes aimed at athletes. This chapter will discuss the basics of general nutrition and will also address issues of particular importance when your daughter is physically active.

What to Eat: The Food Guide Pyramid

The Food Guide Pyramid provided by the U.S. Department of Agriculture is an excellent guide to eating a balanced diet both for you and your daughter over three years old. If your daughter is younger than that, you'll want to consult the Food Guide Pyramid for Young Children, also provided by the U.S. Department of Agriculture and found on their website (www.usda.gov/cnpp/).

When you use the Food Guide Pyramid, you don't need to calculate exact amounts of protein, minerals, and so on that are needed every day. The Food Guide Pyramid is simple, systematic, and goes beyond the "basic food groups" once promoted by nutritionists and other health professionals. It is based on the USDA's research of what foods Americans eat and what nutrients are in those foods. It emphasizes complex carbohydrates, which are the most important source of fuel for physical activity. If you use the Food Guide Pyramid, you can feel confident that your family is getting enough calories, all the essential nutrients, and a diet low in fat.

To obtain a copy of a brochure that describes the Food Guide Pyramid in detail and shows you practical ways to eat healthily, log on to the USDA's Internet site (www.usda.gov/cnpp/) where you can also read about the Food Guide Pyramid and the Food Guide Pyramid for Young Children online.

Meanwhile, from guidelines provided by the experts who created it, here are the basics of using the food guide pyramid:

What to Eat: The Food Guide Pyramid in Brief

In order to use the Food Guide Pyramid, it is important to understand its structure. This section contains the USDA guidelines for following the Food Guide Pyramid.

The Food Guide Pyramid divides food into six groups. At the top of the pyramid are foods you should eat only sparingly. As the pyramid widens toward the bottom, the suggested number of servings increases. The foods toward the top of the pyramid *are not* more important or somehow better. Being higher on the pyramid simply means you should eat less of that type of food each day.

The recommended amount of daily servings reflects adult-size servings. Therefore, a serving size for a three-year-old might be a quarter or half of a serving for an adult. Also, keep in mind that daily serving recommendations are guidelines, and on some days kids may eat more or less of a certain food group.

Different foods within the lower five food groups have varying combinations of nutrients, so be sure to choose food combinations that utilize more than one group.

Bread, Cereal, Rice, and Pasta
6–11 servings daily (refer to page 100 for what counts as a serving)

The Bread, Cereal, Rice, and Pasta group is at the base of the pyramid, indicating that the majority of the daily recommended allowance for foods should be chosen from this section. Children should consume at least half of their daily calories from the Bread, Cereal, Rice, and Pasta food group. These foods are high in complex carbohydrates, which are the body's favorite fuel. Whole grains also add necessary bulk to the digestive tract to aid in elimination of wastes.

Vegetables
3–5 servings daily (refer to page 100 for what counts as a serving)

Vegetables provide many of the vitamins and minerals kids need to release energy from proteins, carbohydrates, and fats, plus build strong bodies, regulate heartbeat, and pass messages along the nerves. Since vegetables contain many different vitamins and minerals, it is important to have a variety of them in your child's diet. Vegetables also provide fiber to aid in the elimination of body wastes.

Be sure to scrub vegetables before cooking. Ideally, vegetables should be steamed, microwaved, or eaten raw. Occasional stir-frying is acceptable. Boiling vegetables is OK, but some of the vitamins and minerals will end up in the cooking water.

Fruit
2–4 servings daily (refer to page 100 for what counts as a serving)

Fruits are especially good sources of important vitamins like A and C. Vitamin A is important for healthy eyes, skin, and hair. Vitamin C helps your child's body absorb calcium and phosphorus and use them for healthy bones and teeth, along with muscle and nerve functions. Fruits also provide B vitamins, which help your child's body form red blood cells and aid the body in using proteins. This food group also adds minerals such as potassium (to keep cells healthy) and roughage for proper elimination of wastes from the body.

Be sure to scrub fruits before eating. It is best to eat fruits raw. Avoid peeling or slicing fruits until just before use.

Milk, Yogurt, and Cheese
2–3 servings daily (refer to page 100 for what counts as a serving)

This food group is an important source of vitamin A, vitamin D, calcium, and protein. Vitamin A is important for healthy eyes, skin, and hair. Vitamin D helps your child's body absorb calcium and phosphorus, important for healthy bones, teeth, muscles, and nerves. Protein, an important part of your child's diet, can be found in this food group.

Meat, Poultry, Fish, Beans, Eggs, and Nuts
2–3 servings daily (refer to page 100 for what counts as a serving)

Protein in the body is made from the building blocks called amino acids. Protein's main functions are to repair and maintain body tissues, produce hemoglobin to carry oxygen to the cells, and produce antibodies, enzymes, and hormones. Some of the amino acids in protein are produced by the body; others must be obtained in the diet.

Foods in this group also provide vitamin B–complex, and calcium and iron to help build strong bones and teeth and support muscle and nerve functions.

Fats, Oils, and Sweets

Fats and oils are essential nutrients to maintain body function, but should be used sparingly. Fats help the body absorb vitamins A, D, E, K, and beta-carotene. They help slow sugar's release into the bloodstream and are important for the formation of cell membranes.

Aim for fat intake of 30 percent or less of total daily food intake. Saturated fats (butter, beef fat) should be limited to 10 percent or less of the fat total. Unsaturated fats (safflower and corn oil) and monounsaturated fats (olive and peanut oil) are healthier choices. Fats shouldn't be restricted in children under age two. The developing brain and other organs of the young child need a certain amount of fat for proper development.

Sugars, which are simple carbohydrates, are easy to digest and are quickly absorbed into the bloodstream where they provide quick energy. Sugars provide some nutritive value, but they should be eaten sparingly because they are often accompanied by fats and don't provide vitamins and minerals.

Special Nutritional Needs of Young Athletes

You may be surprised to learn that athletes' nutritional needs are almost identical to nonathletes'. They require carbohydrates, fats, protein, vitamins, minerals, and fluids in quantities determined by their size and activity level. It is true that athletes need to eat *more* than their nonactive counterparts. It stands to reason—a girl who exercises regularly places significant demands on her body's reserves of fluid and energy. Just how much should a young female athlete be eating? You can figure this out in three steps.

Determine How Many Calories She Should Be Eating

It's difficult to say how many calories young female athletes need every day. A good ballpark figure is 2200 calories, but as Debra Wein, R.D., points out, a girl who is extremely active may require between six hundred and one thousand more calories than that. Nancy Clark, R.D., passes on a good guideline: "Eat when hungry, stop when content."

Recognizing Nutritional Quacks

The food-supplement industry has huge advertising and promotional budgets, and they often secure the services of celebrities to endorse their products. Many of these products promise muscle building and quick recovery. Some of the buzzwords we hear today are "creatine," "chromium," and "antioxidant." An old expression holds true here: "If it sounds too good to be true, it probably is." There really isn't anything in a pill, powder, or shake that's going to improve a young athlete's performance without potentially compromising her health. All the legitimate sports-medicine and fitness organizations have issued position statements against the use of non-medically prescribed nutritional supplements. Don't let your daughter purchase or use nutritional supplements to improve her sports performance unless they have been prescribed by a doctor or sports nutritionist. If your daughter is tempted to purchase a product she sees in a magazine or TV ad, urge her to look at the fine print. Usually there is a government-mandated disclaimer that says, basically, that there is no proof the product works.

Young female athletes are extremely vulnerable to misinformation from the food-supplement industry, whose goals are often to undermine confidence in conventional foods. "From the time of the ancient Greeks, athletes have believed there are superfoods that will make you jump higher, run faster, and shoot straighter," points out Debra Wein, R.D., a top sports nutritionist and member of the Massachusetts Governor's Council on Fitness and Sports. "It's not much different today. Just consider the TV and magazine ads for sports drinks, energy bars, and mineral supplements." Despite the countless myths and misconceptions about the relationship between nutrition and sports, young female athletes have virtually the same nutritional needs as everyone else—a balanced diet that is high in carbohydrates and low in protein. It is up to us to educate ourselves about sound nutrition practices and to pass this information on to our daughters. Otherwise, they may become susceptible to the often self-serving efforts of the nutritional quacks.

Athletes should know how to recognize bogus nutritional advice. Avoid any nutritional advice that:

- Offers lost of weight loss fast
- Suggests that weight loss is possible without exercise or other lifestyle changes
- Promotes nutritional supplements at the expense of whole food
- Relies on testimonials (especially from celebrities) and before-and-after photos
- Discourages the eating of entire food groups or demonizes nutritional elements such as sugars or carbohydrates
- Is described using superlatives such as "amazing," "unbelievable," or "miraculous," or is touted because it is "ancient," "Asian," or "European."

The food-supplement industry has almost limitless advertising and promotion budgets, so young female athletes should be on guard for these kinds of wild claims. If you do feel it would be beneficial to work with a nutritionist for your daughter, a qualified nutritionist should be a registered dietician and be credentialed by the American Dietetic Association.

Find Out the Number of Servings She Should Be Eating from the Food Guide Pyramid

	Younger or very inactive children About 1600 calories	Most active children and adolescents About 2200 calories	Very active children and adolescents About 2800 calories
Grain group	6 servings	9 servings	11 servings
Vegetable group	3 servings	4 servings	5 servings
Fruit group	2 servings	2 servings	4 servings
Milk group	3 servings	3 servings	3 servings
Meat group	5 oz	6 oz	7 oz

What Counts as a Serving
Bread, Cereal, Rice, and Pasta
1 serving =
- 1 slice of bread
- ½ cup cooked rice or pasta
- 1 ounce cold cereal
- ½ bagel
- ½ English muffin

Vegetable
1 serving =
- 1 cup of raw leafy vegetables
- ½ cup of other vegetables, cooked or chopped raw
- ¾ cup of vegetable juice

Fruit
1 serving =
- 1 medium apple, banana, orange
- ½ cup of chopped, cooked, or canned fruit
- ¾ cup of fruit juice

Milk, Yogurt, and Cheese
1 serving =
- 1 cup of milk or yogurt
- 1½ ounces of natural cheese
- 2 ounces of processed cheese

Meat, Poultry, Fish, Dry Beans, Eggs, and Nuts
1 serving =
- 2–3 ounces of cooked lean meat, poultry, or fish
- ½ cup of cooked dry beans or 1 egg counts as 1 ounce of lean meat
- 2 tablespoons of peanut butter or ⅓ cup of nuts count as 1 ounce of meat

Young female athletes have approximately the same nutritional needs as their male counterparts. These needs are identical until they reach puberty. Starting in adolescence, though, girls may have slightly different requirements. Specifically, girls may have an increased need for iron, calcium, and estrogen intake.

Iron

Up to 25 percent of all adolescent girls are iron deficient, resulting in a condition known as anemia. Anemia and iron deficiency are even more prevalent in adolescent female athletes because of a combination of factors, including:
- menstrual blood losses
- iron lost through sweat
- inadequate intake of iron in regular diet
- iron demands of adolescent growth spurts

These factors will be aggravated by a vegetarian diet, so if your family or your daughter is vegetarian, you'll want to pay close attention to her iron intake. Except when their condition is severe, anemic girls and women generally do not have any symptoms. Early and unexpected tiredness during exercise may be the only sign. The symptoms of severe anemia include extreme fatigue, irritability, and headaches. It is often difficult to pinpoint the exact causes of anemia in a young female athlete because there are so many factors that may be at work. Iron deficiency can be prevented or overcome by eating lean meats, like chicken, and drinking a vitamin-C beverage at mealtimes to enhance iron absorption. When dietary modifications fail and an anemic athlete's iron level remains low, she should start taking a daily iron supplement.

Calcium

Calcium builds bone strength. Young female athletes who don't get sufficient calcium are at increased risk of stress fractures and premature manifestations of the bone-thinning disease known as osteoporosis.

An adolescent female athlete who is in good health and eats a balanced diet including enough dairy products doesn't need to worry about her calcium intake. Active girls between the ages of nine and nineteen need to consume about 1300g of calcium every day. However, if your teenage daughter has stopped getting her period for any reason, she should increase her calcium intake to compensate for the lack of bone-building estrogen that is part of menstruation. Nutritionists strongly recommend that girls who stop menstruating, or who have irregular periods, increase their calcium intake (especially their intake of yogurt).

The best way to increase calcium intake is through whole foods in the diet. Here are some easy ways to help your daughter boost her calcium intake:

- At breakfast, she can pour a full cup of skim or 1 percent milk (300g) on her cereal or drink a cup of calcium-fortified juice.
- At lunch, she can sprinkle Parmesan cheese (138g) on a salad or add low-fat cheese to a sandwich.
- In the afternoon, encourage her to eat a carton of low-fat or nonfat yogurt (300-450g).

Girls who fail to eat enough calcium may also be consuming low levels of other nutrients important for good bone health (such as vitamin D), which won't be found in calcium supplements. Foods provide the other nutrients that bones need to stay healthy. Girls who don't get enough calcium often steer away from drinking milk or eating yogurt because they think it's fattening. In fact, a recent study showed that girls and women who drink three to four glasses of milk a day are slimmer than those who don't.

Estrogen

Low estrogen levels cause decreases in bone density. Having brittle bones increases an athlete's risk of fractures. One of the reasons that estrogen deficiencies occur is because of menstrual irregularities. The most common reasons that a young female athlete stops menstruating regularly are because of intense exercising, being underweight, or both. If your daughter is experiencing menstrual irregularities, she needs help returning to normal menstrual cycles. This can usually be accomplished by decreasing the intensity of her exercise regimen and/or helping her gain weight. Often, elite athletes do a lot of unnecessary training ("junk training" as it's known), and by making workout sessions more efficient and focused, this can usually be reduced or eliminated. Adding 20g of fat to an athlete's daily diet has also been shown to help a girl resume her periods.

Estrogen supplements in the form of birth-control pills were once thought to preserve or restore bone health in girls and women who are not menstruating regularly. However, "the pill" is no longer thought to be effective in doing this. Clearly, this estrogen supplementation is no substitute for good nutrition.

Stress fractures can be the end result of poor diet and menstrual irregularities. This relationship is known as the "female athlete triad." Because the end result is an orthopedic injury, we cover this issue in much greater depth in the chapter on the sports health concerns of young female athletes, chapter 12.

The Pre-game Meal—What to Eat and When

Your daughter's sports performance on the day of her competition doesn't depend on some magic pill, powder, or shake consumed right before the event—it depends on her ongoing nutritional intake as well as sensible eating practices prior to the game. "Even with the right combination of genes, training, and coaching, a poorly nourished athlete is unlikely to perform at her best," says Nancy Clark, author of *Nancy Clark's Sports Nutrition Guidebook,* and the country's best-known sports nutritionist.

The purpose of the pre-game meal is to add to the body's energy reserves and prevent hunger pangs. To supplement energy reserves, sports nutritionists recommend that meals should be high in carbohydrates and low in fat and protein. Protein is a poor source of immediate energy, and it can cause dehydration. It should be a very small part of the pre-game meal. Fatty foods take longer to digest than other foods and can even cause stomachaches during a game.

Meal timing is as important as what's on the menu. Try to schedule your daughter's pre-game meals so the food is fully digested by game time. As a general rule, your daughter shouldn't eat a large meal within three to four hours of a game. You can let her eat a small meal two to three hours before the game, and a small pick-me-up snack within an hour of the activity (good pre-game snacks include rice cakes, crackers, low-fat yogurt, fruit, or a dry bagel). Your goal should be to make sure her stomach is empty when exercise begins so she doesn't feel nauseous or get an upset stomach. The larger the meal, the longer it takes to digest.

After the game, feed your daughter plenty of high-carbohydrate foods to replace her depleted energy sources; pasta, fruits, and vegetables are good choices. Liquid carbohydrates, such as juices, are handy and tasty right after the game. They also help prevent dehydration.

The Importance of Fluids

What kids drink before, during, and after a game is as important as what they eat. The thirst drive lags behind actual needs, so stress to your children that they need to drink fluids even when they're not thirsty. Encourage your daughter to drink a glass or two of water before the game. Give your daughter her own bottle of water to take along to games. Coaches should ensure that water breaks are scheduled during long events or when it is particularly hot. Water is the perfect fluid replacement. However, it is sometimes easier to get children to consume sports drinks with their bright colors, attractive packaging, and sweet taste. There's no harm in this, but despite advertisers' claims, sports drinks are not essential and have no advantages over water.

Everyday Meal Planning for Our Young Athletes

Kids can be careless about what they eat. However, a girl who's interested in sports can be convinced to practice good nutrition if she thinks it will improve her performance. I hope to use my daughters' interest in sports as opportunities to teach them how to eat the *right way!*

It All Starts with Breakfast

The morning meal is the most important one of the day. Study after study has shown that kids who eat a good breakfast learn more in school, perform better academically, and participate more frequently in beneficial extracurricular activities—including sports.

If you're having trouble getting your daughter out of bed and fed before she goes to school, part of the problem may be that she is going to bed too late. Consider having her get her head on the pillow earlier so that all of you can get an earlier start. Of course, that means no TV in her bedroom!

It's also important to have healthy and hearty breakfast foods available every day—even if she only wants the same thing every morning. Cereal, fruit, and milk is probably the healthiest combination, and if she washes it down with a glass of juice, she's getting a great nutritional start to her day. Think about setting the table for breakfast the night before so she and the rest of your household have it in their minds that breakfast is important.

According to the American Dietetic Association, a balanced breakfast for children should include:

- Two servings from the Bread, Cereal, Rice, and Pasta group (grains)
- One serving from the Fruit group (fruit)
- One serving from the Milk, Yogurt, and Cheese group (dairy)

Here are some hints on getting the goodness into your daughter's morning meal.

Grains

Try to serve breakfast cereals with the words "whole grain" on the package, and as for breads, choose and serve products where whole-grain flour is the first flour listed.

Fruit

An eight-ounce glass of orange juice and a sliced banana, berries, or raisins on cereal give your kids a delicious and healthy fruit start to their day.

Dairy

The most efficient and convenient way to get calcium is through dairy products. To increase your daughter's consumption of dairy products—milk, yogurt, and cheese—start at breakfast.

- Have her eat cereal with a serving or more of skim or 1 percent milk.
- Make oatmeal with skim or 1 percent milk instead of water.
- Spread lowfat or nonfat ricotta cheese and honey or fruit preserves on toast.
- Add some spark to lowfat or nonfat yogurt with wheat germ, granola, or crunchy cereal.

Creating Healthy School Packed Lunches

Packing school lunches that are healthy and won't be ignored or traded away is a challenge. Here are some guidelines.

Sandwiches are a reliable choice for many kids. Start off with whole-wheat or enriched white bread. Lean varieties of ham, turkey, and roast beef are available in the deli departments of most grocery stores. Even processed lunch meats like bologna and salami now come in low-fat and fat-free varieties. Always try to slip in a couple of slices of low-fat cheese into a meat sandwich to add calcium. If your kids are into it, lettuce and tomato add texture and flavor as well as extra goodness. Sandwich-wise, let's not forget that old standby, PB & J. The healthiest choice is freshly ground or natural peanut butter.

Now what? Fresh fruit or small boxes of raisins and other forms of dried fruit are always healthy choices. If your child will eat raw vegetables, try packing some for her lunch. Baby carrots and celery sticks are popular. To round off her lunch, consider a small bag of pretzels or baked potato chips. Large quantities of these are available in snack-size bags at discount food-stores. Easy-to-pack yogurts are now available that she can drink or suck out of a tube.

Cookies are another lunchbox favorite. Fig Newtons, ginger snaps, graham crackers, and reduced-fat vanilla wafers are good lunchbox desserts.

The healthiest beverage choice for growing girls is milk. Most schools offer 2 percent or even 1 percent; chocolate milk is usually 1 percent. Second best is fruit *juice* (not a sugary fruit *drink*).

The Dinner Hour

A hearty dinner is especially important for active girls. After strenuous exercise, your daughter's meal should consist of lots of carbohydrates to replace lost energy reserves. Only carbohydrates will replace these reserves. Common carbohydrates are bread, rice, pasta, cereals, fruit, and starchy vegetables.

For your daughter's body to most effectively replenish its depleted energy reserves, it's important that she eat soon after vigorous exercise—preferably within one to two hours. Even if she doesn't eat a full meal in this time frame, she should consume at least two hundred to four hundred calories of carbohydrates within two hours of a strenuous workout. She can get this amount of carbohydrates in sixteen ounces of 100 percent fruit juice, 1½ cups of pasta with tomato sauce, a banana with four graham crackers, or a cup of yogurt with fruit and cereal.

High-carbohydrate meals that are popular dinners with kids are pasta dishes (including lasagna), baked potatoes, and pizza (especially thick crust).

Also make sure your daughter drinks plenty of fluids at dinner—at least two cups of water or juice. Fruit juices are an excellent fluid source after exercise as they are rich sources of carbohydrates and other important nutrients, but be sure you select products that say 100 percent juice on the label.

No matter how busy you and your kids are with work and sports, try to make it a priority to sit down together for dinner at home most nights as a family. Eating together at home helps create a stable, nurturing family life. Dinnertime is an opportunity to talk one-on-one with our children, finding out how they feel about what's happened in their day, including their sports experiences. This is a good time to ask about the game or practice and discuss your child's accomplishments and efforts.

chapter 9

Physical Fitness for Girls Six to Seventeen Years Old

● ● ●

Despite the explosion in organized sports for children, the fact is that, as a nation, our kids' physical-fitness levels have never been lower. How can this be true? The reasons are easy to comprehend once one understands the difference between sports and physical fitness. Sports are games of physical exertion with set rules, while physical fitness refers to various aspects of health.

Although there is overlap—some sports do improve certain areas of physical fitness—it's important to realize that just because a girl plays sports doesn't necessarily mean she is physically fit. Not all sports significantly enhance physical fitness—in softball and volleyball, for example, players never have to be moving for more than a few seconds at a time. Plus, there may be too much standing around in a sports program to make even those such as soccer and basketball, which are considered good physical-fitness builders, effective. And let's not forget that a couple of hours a week on the sports field doesn't make up for extended periods of inactivity. In addition, we can't count on our child's school making sure that our kids are getting enough exercise throughout the week.

All this explains how, even though more kids than ever before are playing organized sports, physical fitness levels are much lower than they should be.

The most effective and safest way for kids to get physically fit is free play. In an ideal world, kids should run, bike, and in-line skate around the neighborhood, climb trees, and play pick-up games of basketball with their friends from down the street. Unfortunately, this is not the world most of us live in. Kids today simply don't have the same opportunities for free play. Sports are supposed to have replaced free play, but in many cases, they don't do as good a job at building physical fitness. Therefore, girls who are not getting enough exercise through sports or free-play activities may need to participate in a directed exercise program to build physical fitness. We'll describe such a program later in this chapter.

What Is Physical Fitness?

We often throw the term "physical fitness" around, but not many of us know exactly what physical fitness is. In a general sense, being physically fit is the ability to perform daily tasks without getting tired and also being able to respond to demanding situations that arise—having to run to catch a bus, for example, or carry a heavy backpack home after clearing out a locker. Tasks such as these are not a challenge for our kids if they use their bodies regularly, as nature designed them to be used. But as society has become more technologically advanced, our children use their bodies less often to move, lift, and stretch.

It's impossible to reverse the advances in our culture, so we need to look for ways to help our kids maintain physical fitness in their lives.

There are four components to physical fitness: heart/lung endurance, strength, flexibility, and appropriate body composition. Each is important for our children's health.

Heart/Lung Endurance

Sometimes known as "cardiovascular endurance," heart/lung endurance refers to the ability of our heart and lungs to efficiently pump blood and deliver oxygen throughout our bodies. The heart is a muscle and, like our other muscles, responds to exercise by getting stronger. The lungs also get better at exchanging the carbon dioxide that we produce for the oxygen that we need. People with low levels of heart/lung endurance tend to find that their hearts start pounding quicker and they get out of breath more easily than those who have better heart/lung endurance.

Poor heart/lung endurance is responsible for a host of chronic medical conditions thought to begin in childhood, including heart attack, stroke, and high blood pressure. People who do not participate in the kinds of weight-bearing exercise that improve heart/lung endurance are also at greater risk of the bone-thinning disease osteoporosis.

To improve her heart/lung endurance, your child needs to do exercises that involve repetitive movements of large muscle groups (especially the legs) and get the heart and lungs working. This kind of exercise is known as "aerobic" exercise. Aerobic exercise can be biking, dance classes, jogging, walking, swimming, cross-country skiing, as well as running and jumping around the backyard, playground, or living room.

Experts say that everyone should do aerobic exercise at least three times per week and for a minimum of twenty minutes each workout session. Your daughter is exercising hard enough if her heart and lungs are working harder than when she is inactive—her heart is beating faster and she is breathing harder and faster. You can teach your daughter to measure her heart rate so that, when it's beating faster than usual, she knows she's exercising aerobically.

Strength

Strength refers to our ability to use our muscles to lift and move objects. We need strength and muscle endurance to perform individual tasks as well as continue to use our bodies throughout the day.

People with weak muscles—even kids—are more likely to develop lower back pain. Also, girls who don't use their bodies in such a way that they get strong are more likely to develop osteoporosis later in life. Poor muscle strength is also responsible for sports injuries.

Kids can build strength by doing normal activities such as climbing and roughhousing. Other ways to build strength include lifting weights or performing callisthenic exercises such as push-ups, pull-ups, and sit-ups, modified appropriately for their age. To see a definite improvement in strength, kids need to work a muscle group three times a week.

Flexibility

Flexibility is our ability to move our joints freely and without pain through a wide range of motion. Flexibility depends on the structure of the joint itself, the muscles, and the connective tissue that span the joint (ligaments and tendons). Although most of us think that kids are naturally flexible, the fact is that kids who are not very active can be quite "tight." Poor flexibility is a main cause of lower back pain as well as injury.

Your daughter can improve her flexibility by doing stretching exercises. "Static stretches" are most common. These involve putting the muscle she wants to stretch into a lengthened position and holding that stretch for a certain amount of time, preferably between thirty and sixty seconds.

Body Composition

Body composition refers to the proportion of fat in our bodies compared to lean tissue—muscle, bones, organs, and so on. Body composition is normally expressed as a percentage of body weight. Children should have fat levels no greater than 20 percent of their total body weight. Children who have too much fat on their bodies have a higher risk of a host of life-threatening diseases. The skyrocketing incidence of heart disease, diabetes, and hypertension in children is directly associated with the increase in obesity in this age group. Adults who are overweight were often overweight as kids. Adults and kids alike can keep their body fat at appropriate levels through good nutritional habits and exercise.

Monitoring your daughter's Body Mass Index (BMI) is the best way to keep track of whether her body composition is within the acceptable range. To find out how to calculate your daughter's BMI, refer to page 140.

It's also important for parents to remember that being active is essential for normal growth. Your daughter's heart, lungs, muscles, and bones cannot develop properly unless they are used. Exercise is the most effective way to make sure they are used optimally. Compared to girls who are inactive, active girls have bigger and stronger hearts, stronger bones, and leaner bodies.

How Do I Know If My Child Is Physically Fit?

Many parents assume that their kids are fit just because they are kids. Children are supposed to be fit, after all. Yet for various reasons, this isn't necessarily true. Even if your daughter isn't overweight, she may not be fit. Here are a few ways to tell if your child is in shape.

Heart/lung endurance: she should be able to walk long distances at a moderate pace and climb short flights of stairs without getting out of breath.

Strength: she should be able to do twenty curl-ups within one minute, twenty modified pull-ups within one minute, and twenty modified push-ups within one minute.

A curl-up resembles the old-fashioned sit-up except that it is a little easier on the back. Your daughter should lie with her knees bent at 90 degrees, feet flat on the floor. She crosses her arms over her chest so her hands are on opposite shoulders. She should slowly lift her head, shoulders, and upper back off the floor and touch her thighs with her elbows. Remind her to breathe out as she curls up and then breathe in as she returns to the starting position.

To help your daughter do a modified pull-up, place a strong pole on the seats of two sturdy chairs set four feet apart. She should lie on her back, slide under the bar, then grasp it palms upward with two hands, hands shoulder-width apart. She should then pull herself upward until her chest almost touches the bar (if she find this easy, raise the bar).

A modified push-up is the same as a regular push-up, except the knees stay on the ground. Your daughter should get down on her hands and knees, keeping her back straight and her head in line with her spine. Her hands should be slightly wider than her shoulders and her fingers should point forward. Her knees and feet should stay on the ground. She should then lower herself until her chest touches the floor, then after a pause, push herself back to the starting position.

Flexibility: she should be able to bend over and touch her toes without bending her knees.

Body composition: her Body Mass Index should be below the 85th percentile for her age (see page 140).

General Decline in Physical Fitness

The reasons for the overall fitness decline in American kids are complex, and include the advent of the automobile, television, and video games; the decrease in the amount of open space in neighborhoods available for free

Health Benefits of Physical Fitness for Children

- stronger heart and lungs
- harder, thicker bones
- lower cholesterol levels
- bigger, stronger muscles
- healthier blood pressure
- lowered risk of diseases such as diabetes and heart disease
- more desirable ratio of body fat to lean muscle

play; and the increase in concerns about child safety, which has made "going out to play" more difficult.

However you look at it, the statistics are frightening:

- 50 percent of American children do not get enough exercise to develop healthy hearts.
- 98 percent of American children have at least one heart disease risk factor.
- 13 percent of American children have five or more risk factors.
- 20–30 percent of American children are obese.
- 75 percent of American children consume excess fat.
- 70 percent of girls can't do a single chin-up.
- 70 percent of girls can only do one push-up.
- 40 percent of girls can't touch their toes.
- 25 percent of all kids can't do a single sit-up.

Improving Your Daughter's Physical Fitness

Younger children who need to improve their physical-fitness levels should be encouraged to get out and play more often. You will need to help make this possible. Family bike rides, afternoons playing at the park, and backyard games of tag or soccer are all excellent ways to build physical fitness. It may be appropriate for older girls to participate in a directed exercise program, such as a jogging or weight-lifting program whose specific purpose is to improve fitness, or an aerobics or martial arts class.

Any effective physical-fitness program is based on the principles of increasing the intensity of the exercise, working out regularly, working slightly above what the body can do easily, and choosing the right exercises. This is known as: Progression, Regularity, Overload, and Specificity.

Progression. Steadily increase the intensity, frequency, and/or duration of activity.

Regularity. At least three balanced workouts a week are necessary to maintain a desirable level of physical fitness.

Overload. Work at levels above what the body is used to in order to bring about improvement.

Specificity. Pick the right kind of activities to improve each component of physical fitness.

For example, soccer is good for heart-lung endurance, while training with weights can build strength and help prevent injury. Many activities improve more than one of the components of physical fitness. For example, running increases heart/lung endurance as well as muscular endurance in the legs. Swimming develops the muscles of the arms, shoulders, and chest. By choosing the right physical-fitness activities, your daughter could fit aspects of a muscle workout into her heart/lung workout and save time.

A Physical-Fitness Program for Girls

The best way for kids to get physically fit is to engage in the normal kinds of activities for which young bodies are designed: running, jumping, climbing, lifting, those sorts of things. Unfortunately, many children don't participate in these kinds of activities these days. For those who don't—and for any girl who may be interested in taking a more organized approach to getting in shape—here are ways to develop all areas of physical fitness.

Heart/Lung Endurance

To improve her heart/lung endurance, your daughter has to participate in aerobic activities—those that get her heart and lungs working hard. Walking, swimming, in-line skating, and running are examples of aerobic exercise. No one form of aerobic exercise is better than another—each has its pros and cons. For instance, running can be done anywhere, and all that

Teaching Kids How to Take Their Pulse and Why It's Important for Physical Fitness!

"Taking your pulse" means counting the number of times that your heart beats in a minute. Teaching your child to take her pulse and understand how it speeds up when she's being active is a good way to teach her something very important about physical fitness and health. She can do this as young as fourth grade.

There are three ways your daughter can take her pulse.

On the Wrist

Your daughter holds one arm in front of her. She places the tips of the first two fingers of her other hand on the wrist of her outstretched arm, applying slight pressure. The thumb can be placed lightly on the back of her wrist to create more pressure from behind. She may have to move her fingertips around a little until she can find her pulse.

On the Neck

Your daughter places two fingertips at the side of her neck right beside her windpipe. She applies slight pressure. She may have to move her fingertips around until she finds her pulse.

On the Temple

Your daughter places two fingertips of one hand on one of her temples. She applies light pressure. She should be able to feel her pulse.

For your daughter to find out her resting heart rate, she should sit quietly for a few minutes, then do the following:

- Look at a watch and wait for the second hand to reach the next quarter-minute mark.
- Count her pulse beats for the next fifteen seconds.
- Take that number and multiply it by four.

That total is her resting heart rate.

Most children have resting heart rates of between seventy and one hundred beats. Kids who are especially physically fit have heart rates lower than that.

Once your daughter knows what her resting heart rate is, she can find out what it is when she's active. She'll be interested in finding out that it beats much faster when she's exercising.

Explain to her that anytime she raises her heart rate for a significant time, that means her heart is being strengthened. Significant improvements in heart health can be achieved if your daughter achieves her "target heart rate" for twenty minutes at a time three times a week (see page 118 to calculate what your daughter's target heart rate is).

the participant requires for equipment is a good pair of running shoes. In-line skating is an immensely popular activity, but requires skates and protective equipment and a long, flat surface to skate on. As for swimming, your family needs to live near an ocean or an affordable pool for your daughter to be able to. Injuries are also a consideration—some girls' bodies don't cope well with the stresses of certain physical-fitness activities. Allow your daughter to try different things and find the activity that she enjoys the most. If she doesn't enjoy a particular activity, there is no need to force her—there are plenty of choices.

For exercise to improve your daughter's heart/lung endurance—and to have a beneficial effect on her health—she has to significantly accelerate her heart rate for twenty minutes at a time three times per week. Teach your daughter to figure out her "resting heart rate" so she can compare it to her heart rate when she's exercising. A young child really only needs to know that it's good for her if she keeps her heart beating fast while she's playing or exercising.

One of the most important things you can teach your daughter about her health is that when she's exercising and her heart is beating fast, that's really good for her because it means her heart is getting stronger. What a fundamental but easy-to-describe principle! Later you'll be surprised how, when the two of you are doing something active, she'll stop to check her heart rate and make the point of telling you her heart is beating fast.

Older children and adolescents who participate in physical-fitness activities specifically to improve heart/lung endurance should know how to calculate their target heart rate and how to measure it while they are exercising. They should know that to build heart/lung endurance, it is necessary to maintain the target heart rate for twenty minutes at a time three times a week.

The target heart rate is the number of beats per minute that the heart should be beating during an efficient aerobic workout. Your daughter can monitor her heart rate while she is exercising by counting her pulse—the number of times her heart beats per minute. The easiest way for her to do this is to count the number of times her heart beats in fifteen seconds and multiply it by four. You may have to help younger kids with the math.

To get the most out of her workout, your daughter needs to keep her heart rate within the 65 percent to 85 percent range of her estimated maximum heart rate. If she's below 65 percent intensity, she should probably be working harder. If she's above 85 percent intensity, she's working too hard and her body isn't able to take in the oxygen it needs to strengthen her heart and burn calories. Refer to the table below to see what target heart rate is for children depending on age.

Target Heart Rate for Children 6–17

Age	65 percent	75 percent	85 percent
6	139	160	182
7	138	160	181
8	138	160	180
9	137	158	179
10	136	157	178
11	136	157	178
12	135	156	177
13	135	155	176
14	134	154	175
15	133	154	174
16	133	153	173
17	132	152	173

Participating in strenuous exercise is vital for heart and lung health. It's also important to encourage your daughter to make choices throughout the day that benefit her health. Offer her some outdoor play time every day that weather permits, and encourage her to look for other ways to be active. When you go places together, make it a practice to take the stairs instead of the elevator or escalator, park at a distance so you and she can walk farther, see if chores can be an opportunity to stretch, bend, and otherwise be active. Remember, you are her best example.

Strength Training

When taught by an instructor experienced in training children and adolescents, strength training with weights can be a fun and rewarding activity for kids. Raise the possibility with your daughter, and if she's interested, encourage her to get involved in a strength-training program.

So long as she's supervised, working out with weights is perfectly acceptable for kids as young as seven or eight. If your daughter doesn't play sports, a strength-training program may be one way of introducing her to exercise. Children who are elite athletes should definitely participate in strength training to prevent injuries and enhance performance.

Strength training for girls is extremely beneficial. Two pioneers in strength-training research and instruction for kids, Dr. Wayne Westcott and Dr. Avery Faigenbaum, found that when girls train properly with weights, their strength can improve by 50–75 percent in just two months!

Still, there are a lot of old wives' tales concerning kids and strength training. Many people believe that when kids lift weights, their growth gets stunted, or that girls who train with weights will turn into musclebound behemoths. None of this is true. "So long as certain guidelines are followed," says Dr. Angela Smith, president of the American College of Sports Medicine, "strength training is beneficial for all children—and girls in particular."

Strength training has special benefits for girls because it builds bone density and helps them combat osteoporosis in later life. Because females don't have the hormone testosterone that enables adolescent boys and men to "bulk up," there is no danger of developing the rippled body types of the professional bodybuilder . For girls, the likely outcome of a strength-training program is a body that is healthier and more resistant to sports injury.

Helping Your Daughter Start a Running Program

Running is one of the easiest physical-fitness activities to take up. If your daughter is not involved in any particular sport or physical-fitness activity, and you have concerns about her physical fitness, why not help her start a running program? The following running program is adapted from the one suggested by the President's Council on Physical Fitness and Sports.

First, look for an area where a one-mile distance can be marked off. Four times around a school track is usually one mile. If your daughter has never run a mile before, have her follow the Beginner program shown below. If she's a pretty good runner, but hasn't been following a regular running routine, she should follow the Intermediate program. If she's done a lot of running, encourage her to follow the Advanced program. Remind her to always warm up and stretch before going for a run.

Beginner

Jog two minutes/walk one minute for a total of fifteen minutes. Repeat. Do this at least three times a week for two weeks. Don't worry about the distance yet.

Intermediate

Jog four minutes/walk one minute. Do this for about fifteen to twenty minutes at least three times a week. After about two weeks, reduce the amount of walking time to thirty seconds. Gradually build up to about thirty minutes using this pattern.

Advanced

Continuously jog for twenty minutes. Of course, there is no limit here. If she decides she likes jogging, she can run longer distances.

Be sure your daughter has running shoes that have plenty of cushion and support, and replace them regularly, at least every six months, and more often if she runs more than three or four times per week. You'll also want to teach her proper running technique—a smooth gait is desirable, one in which her heel touches down first, followed by the arch and then the ball of her foot. Both a springy gait or one where the heel hits the ground too hard can cause foot and lower-leg pain. Remind her to keep her upper body relaxed. Her elbows should be slightly bent, her shoulders relaxed, and she should look straight ahead. She should let her arms swing naturally and in opposition to her leg strides. Teach her to set a rhythm with her breathing, to take deep breaths, and to cool down at the end of her run with brisk walking and more stretching.

The most important thing is to make sure that your daughter is being taught and supervised by a qualified instructor. The YWCA or YMCA is an excellent place to receive such instruction and supervision. The person who teaches your daughter to build strength with weights should be certified by an organization such as the American College of Sports Medicine, National Athletic Trainers Association, or the National Strength and Conditioning Association. If you are willing to learn the basics of strength training for children through a book (such as *Strength & Power for Young Athletes* by Drs. Faigenbaum and Westcott), then you can supervise your daughter at home or at a health club.

The world's top health and sports-medicine organizations—the American Academy of Pediatrics, the American Orthopaedic Society for Sports Medicine, the Society of Pediatric Orthopaedics, and the American College of Sports Medicine—have issued position statements in support of strength training for children and adolescents. The American College of Sports Medicine recently published a concise but comprehensive series of guidelines for people interested in strength training for children, including the parents of daughters.

Developing a Strength-Training Program

If you would like to develop a strength-training program for your child, you can refer to appendix 2 for a program of exercises done with "free weights" (either dumbbells or barbells). Both dumbbells and barbells are featured, though dumbbells are preferable because they are easier for young kids to control. There are other ways for kids to build strength, but free weights are inexpensive and can be stored easily in a cupboard or under a bed. Also, most strength-training machines are too big for anyone under five feet tall, but free weights are right-sized for any child (there are companies that make strength-training machines specially for kids, but they are not widespread).

Consider designing a program that is divided into upper- and lower-body exercises because it is convenient to focus on the upper body one day and the lower body the next. Remember, strength training for children is intended to increase the child's abilities—it has nothing to do with lifting a maximum weight.

Flexibility Training

According to Drs. Faigenbaum and Westcott, "Children who don't play sports or aren't physically active in other ways should participate in flexibility training, better known as 'stretching.'" Knowing how to lead your kids in a stretching program will benefit you, too! Regular stretching relaxes the body, makes muscles less stiff, increases the range of motion in the joints, and increases circulation.

You can work stretching in with other family physical-fitness activities. For example, you can take a brisk walk or slow jog to the park with your daughter and her friends, do some stretching, then play a game of Frisbee or soccer together. Don't underestimate your kids' interest in doing something good for themselves: if you explain the benefits of flexibility, you may well find that they become enthusiastic participants.

It's always a good idea to warm up before stretching. Muscles that are warmed up before a stretching session are more flexible and less likely to feel sore after the stretch. Good ways to warm up include a brisk walk around the block, running in place for a few minutes, or jumping rope. If your daughter has access to a stair-climbing machine or a treadmill, even better.

For flexibility to improve, kids should stretch every day. Some children who are especially "tight" should try to stretch twice a day, according to Dr. Lyle Micheli, director of the Boston Children's Hospital Division of Sports Medicine.

American College of Sports Medicine Guidelines on Youth Strength Training

Physical-fitness training has traditionally emphasized aerobic exercise such as running and cycling. More recently, the importance of strength training for both younger and older populations has received increased attention, and a growing number of children and adolescents are experiencing the benefits of strength training. Contrary to the traditional belief that strength training is dangerous for children or that it could lead to bone-plate disturbances, the American College of Sports Medicine (ACSM) contends that strength training can be a safe and effective activity for this age group, provided that the program is properly designed and competently supervised. It must be emphasized, however, that strength training is a specialized form of physical conditioning distinct from the competitive sports of weight lifting and powerlifting, in which individuals attempt to lift maximal amounts of weight in competition. Strength training refers to a systematic program of exercises designed to increase an individual's ability to exert or resist force.

Children and adolescents can participate in strength-training programs provided that they have the emotional maturity to accept and follow directions. Many seven- and eight-year-old boys and girls have benefited from strength training, and there is no reason why younger children could not participate in strength-related activities, such as push-ups and sit-ups, if they can safely perform the exercises and follow instructions. Generally speaking, if children are ready for participation in organized sports or activities such as Little League baseball, soccer, or gymnastics, then they are ready for some type of strength training.

The following guidelines for youth strength training were issued by the American College of Sports Medicine and written by Avery D. Faigenbaum, Ed.D., and Lyle J. Micheli, M.D., FACSM.

How much should the muscle be stretched? Instead of stretching to the point where a muscle hurts, children should stretch until they feel the "action point"—that is, where they feel that slight point of tension in the muscle. Your daughter should not feel as though she is overstretching, she should be able to relax while she is stretching and therefore hold the stretch for longer.

How long should a stretch be held for? According to Dr. Micheli, it takes children's muscles between twenty and forty seconds to relax when they're being stretched. Therefore, he recommends that children hold each stretch for sixty seconds, and for a minimum of thirty seconds. By encouraging your daughter to hold her stretches for sixty seconds, she will be slowly stretching her muscles, tendons, and ligaments, which lessens the chance they will be sore afterwards. The best way to get your daughter to hold the stretches for long enough is to do them with her and set an example. See appendix 2 for a program of flexibility exercises.

Body Composition

Kids need to have an appropriate ratio of body fat to lean tissue. How to find this out in your daughter is by calculating her Body Mass Index (BMI). A BMI in the 85th percentile (i.e., in the top 15 percent of the age group) indicates that she is overweight. A BMI in the 95th percentile (i.e., the top 5 percent of the age group) signifies obesity. For information on how to calculate BMI and to find out in what percentile your daughter's BMI is, refer to page 140.

If you have any concern whatsoever about your daughter's weight, take her to see your family doctor or pediatrician.

How to Lose Body Fat

If your daughter is overweight, encourage her to start a program to lose the fat. The same activities that help a child build heart/lung endurance are the ones that can help her lose body fat—aerobic activities such as walking, hiking, running, jogging, biking, cross-country skiing, dance, rope skipping, in-line skating, swimming, and skating. To lose body fat, a child needs to exercise more often and for longer periods than if she's trying to build heart/lung endurance, but she doesn't need to work out quite as hard. As a guideline, if your daughter needs to lose weight, she should exercise moderately four or five times a week for thirty minutes at a time. Moderate exercise might include brisk walking or bike riding.

Keep in mind that without changes in diet, exercise usually does little to help a person lose body fat. Exercise combined with an improved diet is the most effective way to lose weight. Diets that promote rapid weight loss without exercise usually result in an undesirable loss of muscle as well as fat.

Because the problems of being overweight and obesity are such serious ones for girls in the United States—and increasingly throughout the western world—we devote an entire chapter to the issue later in this book.

Make Physical Fitness a Family Affair

If we live a couch-potato lifestyle, we shouldn't be too surprised if our kids turn out to be little spuds as well! Parents who are active have an easier time motivating their children to exercise. Try to make exercise a part of your family's daily life by finding fun physical-fitness activities that the whole family can do together. There are so many of these, such as swimming, cycling, canoeing, tennis, nature hikes, or even walks with the family dog.

Your daughter is much more likely to get into a fitness activity if she helped come up with the idea, so work with her on developing ideas for family fitness activities. Keep in mind that you are the biggest influence on your daughter, so if you exercise regularly she is likely to emulate your behaviors. Remember to always be affirmative about exercise. Never make exercise seem like a chore—always frame it in a positive light, and let your daughter see that you're enjoying yourself.

chapter 10

Good Sports Grooming

● ● ●

Particular areas of concern for girls involved in sports include keeping skin clean, keeping hair out of the way, removal of body hair, using sunscreen and deodorant, chapped lips, and makeup, particularly around the eyes. Eye glasses or other eye protection are also an issue, as is the proper fit of a sports bra. These issues are all important because they affect how your daughter performs on the sports fields. In order for your daughter to truly enjoy her sports experience, she must be comfortable and free to concentrate on the game. With the help of makeup artist and skin-care expert Rhonda Barrymore (www.helpmerhonda.com), this chapter covers all these areas so you can steer your daughter in the right direction.

Getting Started

Your active daughter will enjoy the benefits of good grooming if you help her to choose the right products and procedures for her individual needs. Equipped with correct information and the right tools, your daughter will be less likely to become obsessed with how she "looks" to others and more likely to have a healthy self-confidence about her appearance.

Clean, Healthy Skin

For girls in their tween (eight to nine) and preteen (ten to twelve) years, there seems to be little information to help with ever-changing skin-care needs. Teens have dozens of magazines and books to guide them with their own skin-care and makeup needs. For this age group, you'll want to observe your daughter's skin and make sure she is keeping it clean on a daily basis. It is always a good idea for her to cleanse her face before and after practice or a game, especially if she perspires a lot or the field is dusty or muddy. Your daughter is likely to have a different skin type than yours, so it won't be enough to simply share your own skin-care products with her.

It may take some experimentation to find the correct solution and products for her. Many products oriented toward teenagers have acne as their focus and may contain harsh ingredients. Look for hypoallergenic products, or visit www.helpmerhonda.com for a full line of all-natural skin-care products.

The following is a list of recommended solutions and products for common skin care needs of tween, preteen, and teenage girls. Much of this is common sense, but as your daughter becomes active in sports, she'll be talking to other girls her age and becoming more aware of her appearance. Help her start good habits at an early age.

General Skin Care

Skin Hydration. Be sure that your daughter is drinking plenty of clear water daily to hydrate the largest organ of her body, the skin. She should drink water both before and after practice or a game, and should drink more than she is thirsty for, as thirst doesn't reflect the body's actual fluid needs.

Skin Detoxification. Encourage your daughter to detoxify her skin by sweating, but to remove the sweat from her face and body as soon as possible with clear water to avoid skin irritations. For situations where no water is available, pack some sports wipes or skin wipes in her gym bag so she can wipe away the released toxins and clean and balance her skin after sports.

Sleep. A physically active child needs plenty of rest, so make sure that your daughter is getting at least eight hours of restful sleep a night. Younger children may need as much as 9 to 9.5 hours of sleep. Adequate sleep will help her appearance, performance, and attitude.

Rest and Relaxation. Encourage your daughter to take breaks during the day to relax her mind and body. This promotes a greater sense of well-being and helps her stay energized and have fun in her sports activities.

Blemish/Sensitivity Prevention

Have your daughter brush and floss her teeth before she washes her face in the morning and in the evening. This will help to prevent blemishes and skin irritations, since brushing and flossing can splash unwanted bacteria onto the face.

Clean the telephone receiver often to ward off skin irritations and blemishes. Encourage your daughter to shower instead of bathing, since taking a tub bath can leave a film of dirt, soap, and oil on the skin as she exits the tub. This film can cause irritation and blemishes on the skin and scalp.

Bathing and Shampooing. If your daughter's sports activities are strenuous and make her sweat, or if she's swimming, she may end up bathing and shampooing more often than she would otherwise. In order to make sure that her hair and skin don't dry out, help your daughter choose shampoo, conditioner, and hairstyling products that are appropriate to the condition of her scalp, hair, body skin, and facial skin. Have your daughter shampoo and condition her hair before she cleanses her face so that any residue from the shampoo and conditioner is washed away from her skin. She should stay away from antibacterial body wash that can strip away the good bacteria from her body, making her more prone to developing body odor. She should also avoid using bar soaps to bathe with, as they can strip away the natural body oils that keep her body skin in healthy condition. Botanically based skin-care and bath products that contain very few preservatives and only naturally occurring fragrances are best used by everyone in the family, including babies and young children. Her facial cleanser should be within easy reach of the shower. Cleansing the face with an appropriate cleanser should be the last thing she does before toweling off and exiting the shower.

Once your daughter is out of the shower, she should apply any additional facial products before applying body lotions, hairstyling products, and deodorant. This cuts down on bacteria transference that can lead to skin irritations and blemishes.

Keep grooming and hygiene product containers clean and dust free so that irritants from them do not transfer to the skin as they are used.

Skin-Care Regimen

To prevent or correct skin problems or to maintain a healthy complexion, encourage your daughter to cleanse, tone, and moisturize her face daily. For best results, this should be done once in the morning and once in the evening. She may also need to cleanse her face after a game or practice.

Tweens, preteens, and teenagers can experience all the same skin symptoms and conditions as adults do, such as dry skin, oily skin, sensitive skin, blemished skin, and the most common skin condition: combination skin (oily and dry areas). Normal skin (no problems) is the skin condition most desired. You can help your daughter determine her skin type on the www.helpmerhonda.com website.

Dry or Chapped Lips

Let your daughter know that licking her lips will only worsen the problem. To heal and prevent dry or chapped lips, choose lip-care products that will hydrate and treat her lips with botanical ingredients such as fruit, flower, and seed oils, aloe extract, and vitamins C & E. A product with sunscreen will protect lips while in the sun. Apply as often as needed and when exposed to the sun.

Sensible Sun Exposure

You've probably heard the saying "No tan is a safe tan." If your daughter spends a great deal of time outdoors, she may not think about the effects that the sun has until she gets a sunburn. Following are guidelines that may help you decide what is best for your daughter's sun protection.

Limit your daughter's midday (between 10 A.M. and 2 P.M.) sun exposure when the sun's ultraviolet (UV) rays are the strongest. If your daughter has to be exposed to the sun during this time of day, take extra precautions to prevent overexposure to the sun.

Sunscreens are useful, but don't rely on them to give your daughter full protection from the sun. When possible, use physical sun blocks (something between her skin and the sun) such as clothing that is made from tightly woven fabric or that has been treated with UVP (ultraviolet protection factor). She should wear a hat and sunglasses, or get under an umbrella or tree to shield her from the damaging effects of the sun, when she's not on the field or court.

Sunscreens have a shelf life of about a year. After that they lose their effectiveness. They also lose their effectiveness when exposed to heat, so keep them out of the car and in a cool place.

When choosing a sunscreen, nothing higher than SPF (sun protection factor) 15 is needed, provided it is used properly and it contains full-spectrum protection from UVA (longer-wave rays) and UVB (shorter-length rays) radiation. The higher the SPF, the more the likelihood of irritation on young and/or sensitive skin will be. Choose a product especially designed for use on babies and children with any SPF from four to thirty-five, and realize that the safe time in the sun will vary with each SPF. It's best to also do a patch test when in doubt about sensitivity. Proper use of sunscreen means using it thirty minutes before exposure; using it often, all over the exposed body; and reapplying it every time the skin gets wet (even sweat).

Sunscreens with an SPF higher than 15 are more likely to cause allergic reactions. Whatever the SPF, children's sunscreens are the least likely to cause adverse reactions on the body, including blemishes. For best results, choose a formulation that is unscented and oil free, such as Waterbabies by Coppertone.

The skin in the undereye area is much thinner than the rest of the face. Therefore, it tans faster, resulting in dark circles. It is usually the first area to show signs of premature aging and wrinkles due to sun damage. Be sure to use a specially formulated sunscreen intended for use around the eyes.

Your daughter's lips, hair, scalp, ears, and nails need protection from the sun, too. Choose lip gloss with an SPF of 15, and hair-care products that contain sunscreens, such as Redken's Sun Shape line, that will protect her hair from the effects of UV rays, saltwater, and chlorine. Colored nail polish or a clear topcoat with sunscreen will protect her nails from exposure to the sun.

Mechanical blocking agents (sun blocks) containing zinc oxide and titanium dioxide reflect the sun's rays and protect against the entire UVA and UVB spectrum. If your daughter is fair-skinned and burns easily, you'll want to go with a sun block.

Deodorant and Antiperspirant

Your athletic daughter may come to you and propose using deodorant, or you may be the one to recommend it to her. In either case, you should know that there is a big difference between deodorant and antiperspirant. Deodorants don't inhibit perspiration, which is the salty, watery fluid that is secreted by the sweat glands through the pores of the body. They do, however, destroy, inhibit, or mask the odors of the body. Antiperspirants are known for very successfully retarding and reducing perspiration; however, it is not recommended that young people use them until the research is complete concerning the potential health risks that are associated with aluminum chlorohydrate, the most commonly used substance in antiperspirant. This substance contains heavy metals that are reported to be extremely toxic.

You may want to start your daughter off with a mild deodorant product in a spray bottle, as roll-ons and stick deodorants can harbor bacteria. Encourage your daughter to use her deodorant after bathing, and before and after practice or a game.

Hairstyles for Female Athletes

Unless your daughter's hair is super short, it has probably been an issue when deciding what to do with her hair when she's competing in sports. For long hair, a ponytail is ideal. (It is even possible to get a batting helmet with a ponytail hole in the back.) The only problem that can arise is that shorter pieces of hair can become loose, causing a very distracting tickling of her nose, arms, or back. These distractions could grab your daughter's concentration away from the game. Long bangs (fringe) can be the hardest to get out of the way. They are too long to leave hanging and they're too short to include in a ponytail.

The best and most stylish ways to secure fringe or long bangs are to include the fringe into braiding or secure the loose hairs with hair clips. These metal, plastic-coated, or rubberized clips (also known as swimmer's clips) are better at holding even baby-fine hair securely and they are flat, making them a safer choice for sports activities. They also come in a very wide assortment of sizes and colors and are widely available at drugstores and department stores. This kind of clip won't hurt the hair and they can be used to secure braids as well.

Another option for securing the hair or bangs is with a terrycloth headband, which won't cause injuries and could help to absorb sweat. Avoid using claw clips of any size during sports activities as they have "teeth" that could dig into the scalp if your daughter gets bumped. If the hair is long, avoid using beads as a styling option as they can cause excessive tension on the scalp and roots and they could "slap" your daughter and others.

The best ponytail holders are Poly Bands that are made by Scunci. They will not pull out, tangle, snag, or damage any type of hair. A clever way to make stylish variations of the ponytail is with a Topsy Tail hairstyling tool, also widely available at drug and department stores. It can be used to create many ponytail variations on any type of hair. Braiding is another neat and tidy, yet stylish, way for your daughter to wear her hair during sports. Experiment with current hairstyles that allow your daughter a full range of head and body motion without compromising her safety or vision.

Hair Removal

Hair removal is a very personal issue and you may have strong feelings about the appropriate age for your daughter to remove leg and underarm hair. When you feel she is ready, the safest and least painful way to remove hair from the body is by shaving it off with a razor such as Schick's Silk Effects. This razor is designed especially for women and the blades have a protective band of wire that prevents nicks and cuts. It also has a strip that glides on a soothing layer of aloe as it removes the hair. This razor and the blades that fit it are available at most drugstores.

When your daughter is ready, you will want to supervise her experience with shaving. Perhaps she can watch you do it the right way so that it eases her mind and yours when the time comes for her to shave on her own without your assistance. You don't need special shaving foam to successfully remove hair with a razor from your legs and underarms. Simply use your favorite body wash. Shaving your legs and underarms in the shower prevents a need for cleanup in the tub.

Always begin by giving the skin and hair a chance to soften up and become thoroughly wet. Then apply body wash and begin to shave. The hair under the arms grows in many directions, so your daughter will want to shave first from the top down direction, then from the bottom to the top. If this is the first time that your daughter is shaving the hair from her underarm area, the hair may be long. You'll want to check the razor and remove any buildup of hair from the blades by dragging it in a backwards motion onto a thick, wet washcloth or heavyweight, wet paper towel that has been folded into quarters. This will free up the blade to shave the next section of underarm hair.

For shaving the legs, you will want to use a new blade so that any body odor left on the blade will not transfer to the legs. If this is the first time that your daughter is shaving the hair off her legs, it may be long. Check the razor and remove any buildup of hair from the blades by stroking it in an upward motion and in the opposite direction that you would shave in, onto a thick, wet washcloth or heavyweight, wet paper towel that has been folded into quarters. You may want to encourage your daughter to shave from the ankle, stopping at the base of the knee. To shave the knee area, have her remain standing and apply body wash to the area, front and back. She should not bend the knee, as it is more likely that she could get a nick if the knee isn't straight as she shaves it. If the upper leg and thigh are to be shaved, start at the area just above the front of the knee and drag the razor up the front of the upper leg to the thigh, then continue around the leg. Your daughter may want to apply a light moisturizer or body lotion to newly shaved legs.

Sporty Makeup

Even though wearing makeup isn't a good idea while working out or playing sports, many girls are determined to do it anyway. So if that's the way it's going to be, here are some tips that might make it safer and more fun for your daughter.

Before she applies makeup, she should always start with a clean and properly moisturized face. Waterproof foundation and concealer is ideal for athletes, because it lasts longer through sweating and wet sports. Just remember that waterproof makeup requires special makeup dissolvers that your daughter's normal facial cleanser may not have.

If your daughter must wear eyeliner, help her choose an automatic pencil, for three reasons: 1) it is less harsh looking than waterproof liquid eyeliner, 2) it stays on about as long, and 3) it does not require sharpening, so it is safer to use around your daughters eyes.

If she wants to curl her lashes, your daughter should use an eyelash curler that has a silicone pad in it. It is less likely to pull out lashes that stick to it. She should never curl her lashes after she has applied mascara. The mascara will grab onto the curler and she could pull out her lashes with the slightest jerk of the wrist.

Clear mascara products work terrifically at separating and glossing the lashes and brows. It may be the only mascara your daughter needs, but it is not waterproof! Color waterproof mascara works well, but it does take much longer to dry than normal mascara does because it is oil based.

Blush in a crème or gel formulation is best used on skin without foundation. It is the best at withstanding moisture and sweating of all blushers. For blush used over foundation, encourage your daughter to stick with a powder bronzer.

If your daughter must wear color eye shadow, she should choose powder shadows.

Sheer lip gloss looks more appropriate than opaque color on girls and young women playing sports. Be sure that it includes sunscreen if you will be outdoors. Choose lip gloss with an SPF of 15.

Watch out for sweat that could run down your daughter's face. It could carry her makeup right into her eyes causing them to itch and burn. No makeup or sunscreen is intended for use inside the eyes. Have her wear a terrycloth headband if she tends to sweat during sporting activities.

Just remember that there are no guarantees that what your daughter wears on her face before a sports activity will stay put. Encourage her to experiment until she gets it right, and remind her that no makeup at all is the best choice. She can cleanse, tone, and moisturize, and then apply her makeup right after the game!

Sports Eyewear

As you prepare to outfit your daughter in the gear needed for her chosen sporting activities, consider her eye care and eyewear as well. Dust, dirt, mud, wind, chlorinated water, and overexposure to the sun are just a few of the potentially hazardous elements that can cause eye irritation, injury, and even disease. About 90 percent of all sports-related eye injuries can be prevented with eyewear created from shatter-resistant propionate, a high-impact polycarbonate-like material. Do not choose plastic or glass lenses or frames, as they can be extremely hazardous. An eye-care professional, such as an optician or ophthalmologist, can help you and your athletic daughter choose the correct eyewear depending on her sport, even if she does not need corrective (prescription) eyewear. If she participates in several different sports, chances are she will need to have separate pairs of protective eyewear for each sport just as she would wear appropriate shoes for these various sports. For instance, if your daughter will be playing racquetball, soccer, basketball, or baseball, no tint in the lens is necessary; however, a nose and temple guard is appropriate since the main objective of this eyewear is to protect the eyes and face from impact. In some sports, seeing better is key, so tinted lenses are in order. A gray cast to the lens will only give a two-dimensional field of vision, whereas a brown or rosy tint will give a three-dimensional field of vision for greater contrast, making it perfect for seeing those moguls when skiing and the golf ball if it goes into the tree line. Special eyewear created for sports may not be appropriate for other activities. For instance, professional tennis players are now using eyewear with a blue tint to give greater contrast and reduce glare, but they are not appropriate for driving. Contact lenses may be worn during sports if appropriate protective eyewear is in place, but think twice about it. Swim goggle lenses can be made with correction and ski goggles and diving masks can have a corrective insert, making them a safer alternative to wearing contacts during sports. Wrap-around eyewear with UVA and UVB protection will keep the eyes better protected from refracted sun rays. With proper protective and corrective eyewear in place, your daughter can focus more clearly on her game while reducing her risk of injury.

American Council on Exercise Guidelines for Selecting a Sports Bra

Some girls and women experience breast discomfort while exercising. Often they either suffer in silence or avoid exercise altogether because they don't know where to go for advice on this sensitive subject. The American Council on Exercise (ACE) offers the following pointers to pass onto your daughter:

- There are two types of sports bras to consider: compression bras and encapsulation, harness-type bras. The compression bra works best for smaller-busted girls and women, because it compresses the breasts against the chest. The harness-type encapsulates each breast and is typically better suited for larger-busted girls and women due to its heavy-duty construction.
- Don't go by the size of the bra, go by the fit. Breast size changes with weight loss or gain, menstrual cycle, or medication.
- Choose a bra that has good ventilation so sweat won't be trapped, which increases friction and chafing. New fabrics such as CoolMax and Nike's DriFit help keep skin cool and dry.
- Make sure the clasps or straps don't dig into the skin. A good sports bra should fit comfortably from the very first wearing.
- When trying on a bra, the athlete should jump around to mimic the activity she'll be doing while wearing the bra.
- Over time, elasticity is lost. Sports bras should be replaced every six to twelve months.

The most important thing to remember in grooming for your daughter is that your ultimate goal is that she be comfortable and free of distraction on the playing fields. This means that she should be happy with how she looks, comfortable with how her hairstyle feels and how her clothing fits, and free to concentrate on playing sports and having fun. Don't hesitate to experiment until you find the right products, styles, and clothing for your daughter, or to seek help from a dermatologist or other resource, if you need to. Good grooming and good health go hand in hand and will both make a difference in your daughter's sports experience.

chapter 11

Weight Issues

● ● ●

As parents it's natural to worry about whether or not our children are "normal." Usually our concerns are unfounded. Most kids are as normal as can be. That said, there *are* sometimes justifiable reasons for serious concern where it comes to our daughters' growing bodies. It's ironic that the most common of these concerns are at opposite ends of the spectrum—obesity caused by overeating and malnourishment as a result of restrictive eating disorders.

Team sports and physical activity are fundamental components of a program to treat obesity, and are effective *preventive* medicine for both obesity and eating disorders.

From the time your daughter was an infant, your pediatrician has been marking her height and weight on a growth chart and telling you where she falls in a percentile of her age group. This growth chart was created by the Centers for Disease Control, and you can find it on the web at http://www.cdc.gov/nchs/about/major/nhanes/growthcharts/set1clinical/CJ41L022.pdf. You can use this chart to see for yourself between doctor visits where your daughter's height and weight fall.

The percentile curves on these charts tell us what percentage of children are of the same height or weight. The fiftieth percentile represents the median height or weight for each age group. In other words, 50 percent of children will be above this point and 50 percent will be below it. If a two-year-old girl weighed twenty-four and a half pounds, then she would be at the tenth percentile for her weight at this age. This means that 90 percent of two-year-old girls weigh more than she does, but it also means that she weighs more than 10 percent of children of this same age.

It is normal for children to change percentiles between birth and eighteen months of age, but after this stage, they tend to follow their growth curves fairly closely.

Obesity and Being Overweight

Obesity and being overweight are an epidemic in the United States. It's not just adults who are tipping the scales—our kids are getting heavier, too. Although most of us have heard the numbers, they bear repeating. During the past forty years, obesity increased 54 percent among children ages six to eleven and 40 percent among adolescents. In 1995, the average ten-year-old weighed eleven pounds more than the average ten-year-old in 1973. Results from the most recent National Health and Nutrition Examination Study show the prevalence of obesity among children ages six to eleven ranges from 9.2 to 17.4 percent. The statistics are no more encouraging for older children. Among adolescents ages twelve to seventeen, findings from that same study showed the prevalence of obesity at 8.5 to 15.7 percent.

I'm determined that my daughters *not* join the ranks of the millions of obese and overweight American children. That's one of the reasons that I encourage them to be active and would love it if they developed sports skills they can use for life. It's not just for their comfort and confidence that I want them to have an appropriate body composition—there are serious health risks associated with being obese.

Is Your Daughter Either Overweight or Obese?

You can figure out whether your daughter's weight puts her in the category of being overweight or obese by calculating her "Body Mass Index." The Body Mass Index, or BMI, is simply a number you arrive at after performing a calculation involving her height, weight, and age. You use that number to see where your daughter is in relation to her peers on a percentile chart.

The formula for measuring BMI is as follows: multiply your daughter's weight in pounds by 705, divide by her height in inches, then divide again by her height in inches.

Example: A 9-year-old, 4' 6" girl weighs 100 pounds.

100 x 705 = 70,500

70,500 ÷ 54 = 1305.5

1305.5 ÷ 54 = 24.17

The 9-year-old, 4' 6", 100-pound girl's BMI is 24.17.

Once you have calculated your daughter's BMI, look it up on the BMI-for-age percentile chart on the Internet at www.cdc.gov/nchs/about/major/nhanes/growthcharts/set1/chart16.pdf.

A child is defined as *obese* if she has a Body Mass Index above the 95th percentile for her age. Having a Body Mass Index that is above the 85th percentile for her age means that a girl is *overweight*. Being overweight is not just a matter of carrying around a few pounds. A girl who is overweight has a very strong chance of becoming obese. If your child is defined as "overweight," take this as a warning sign to act now!

A word of caution: if your daughter has the stocky, very muscular physique of a gymnast, her BMI may incorrectly suggest that she is overweight or even obese, even though she may be in great shape. That's because muscle is heavier than fat and it throws off the calculation. Situations like this, however, are extremely rare, and otherwise BMI readings are extremely accurate. If what you find when you do these calculations concerns you, discuss your concerns with your pediatrician or family doctor.

Causes and Consequences

The consequences of childhood obesity are scary for parents. Most importantly, obese children are more likely to grow up to be obese adults and suffer the range of associated health problems. Studies have shown that a child who is obese between the ages of ten and thirteen has an 80 percent chance of becoming an obese adult. But obese children don't have to wait until adulthood for the onset of health problems. Childhood obesity is a primary cause of pediatric hypertension/high blood pressure, Type II diabetes mellitus, heart disease, and skin disorders.

Some experts believe that the most significant consequences of obesity in children aren't even physical—they're the psychological problems that being overweight can cause. Our society glorifies leanness, and kids who are fat may grow up with low self-esteem.

You may be thinking to yourself, whether or not a kid is overweight or obese can't be as straightforward as calories in/calories out. In fact, *it is!* Less than 1 percent of all obesity is caused by medical problems. The reason American kids—and adults, too—are heavier today than ever in our history is that they're consuming more calories than they expend. The multi-billion-dollar diet industry would have you believe that our fatness has more to do with complex concepts such as metabolism and insulin levels. It's not. It's simple mathematics—if you consume more calories than you expend, you are going to put on weight; if you expend more calories than you consume, you are going to lose weight. I think one of the reasons we don't want to believe weight loss is so simple is because it means accepting that the solution is simple, too. When we know the solution is simple, we have no excuse not to act!

Treating Obesity in Girls

Parents need to follow a multifaceted approach to getting their children's body composition to an appropriate level. Unless her obesity is immediately life-threatening, a treatment program for an obese child or early adolescent rarely has weight *loss* as its objective. Instead, what we want to do is slow or stop weight gain so that a girl will grow into her body weight over a period of months or years. Actual weight loss may be a goal for girls in later adolescence who are most likely not going to grow much more.

The earlier you address the problem of an overweight or obese child, the better. It's easier for young children to learn good eating and exercise habits than adolescents or adults.

The three pillars of a multifaceted treatment program for overweight and obese children are *exercise*, *diet*, and *behavior modification*. Let's look at each one.

Exercise

Encouraging your daughter to begin an exercise program or simply be more active is an important way for her to slow or stop weight gain. However, most studies show that exercise doesn't work well unless it's done in conjunction with at least one of the other two components—diet and behavior modification. Even when a child exercises and still doesn't lose body fat, her health still benefits as physical activity lowers cholesterol and blood pressure, two factors that reduce the risk of heart disease.

The kind of exercise that is most effective at helping a person lose weight is aerobic exercise—that which makes the heart and lungs work hard. Getting your daughter to participate more often in normal children's play is the best way to increase her physical activity. Playing in the backyard, biking around the neighborhood, in-line skating—these are all good ways to burn fat. However, it's important to remember that there are many kids who've gotten in the habit of coming home from school and plopping themselves in front of the TV with a bowl of chips for the rest of the afternoon. Video games and personal computers are equally seductive. It's important that we restrict the time they have for TV, video games, and personal computers so they have time to participate in strenuous play activity.

Certain forms of aerobic exercise may be too strenuous for children who are obese, as they are predisposed to injuries of the knee and hip joints, as well as to heat exhaustion. For these kids, a walking program is an excellent way to get started with an exercise program. If you're trying to motivate your daughter to participate in a walking program, one of the best ways to do this is to lead by example and get involved yourself in a walking program.

The accompanying table features a walking program of three different intensities. If your daughter has been extremely inactive for some time, she should start with the beginner's program. If she starts with the quarter mile and it's not a strain, she should advance to the half-mile the next time she walks. But if a quarter mile makes her tired, she should stick with that distance for two or three more sessions until her lungs and legs get stronger.

Beginner's Walking Program
(If your daughter has not exercised for some time)

WEEK	DISTANCE (Miles)	DURATION (Minutes)	FREQUENCY (p/week)
1	n/a	10–15	2–3
2	n/a	12–15	2–3
3–4	0–1	20–25	3
5–6	1–1.5	20–30	3–4
7–8	1.5–2	27–36	3–4
9–10	2–2.5	35–44	4
11–12	2.5–3	43–51	4
13–14	2.5–3	40–48	4
15+	3–3.5	48–56	4-5

Moderate-Intensity Walking Program
(If your daughter is occasionally active)

WEEK	DISTANCE (Miles)	DURATION (Minutes)	FREQUENCY (p/week)
1	.5–1	8–15	2–3
2	1.5	23	2–3
3–4	1.5–2	21–26	3
5–6	2–2.5	29–39	3–4
7–8	2.5–3	35–42	3–4
9–10	2.5–3	34–41	3–4
11–12	2.5–3	33–39	4
13–14	3–3.5	39–46	4–5
15+	3.5–4	46–52	4–5

Advanced Walking Program
(If your daughter is somewhat active.)

WEEK	DISTANCE (Miles)	DURATION (Minutes)	FREQUENCY (p/week)
1	.5–1	6–12	2–3
2	1.5	18	2–3
3–4	1.5–2	18–24	3
5–6	2–2.5	23–29	3–4
7–8	2.5–3	28–33	3–4
9–10	3–3.5	33–39	3–4
11–12	3–3.5	32–37	4
13–14	3.5–4	37–42	4–5
15+	3.5–4	35–40	4–5

Biking is another excellent fitness activity that can be done as a family. Like any other experience, if you make it enjoyable and build up your daughter's confidence by keeping the initial rides fairly short, she'll want to do it again. If you enjoy biking together and plan to do it often, look into joining a local bike club. These clubs plan outings with pre-established routes. Among the advantages of family-oriented bike clubs are that parents have other adults to talk to, and your daughter can make new friends.

Diet

Fasting or crash dieting is definitely not a good idea for children. Not only is it stressful, but it can distort a girl's perception of what constitutes "normal" eating. The most effective dietary plans to address obesity are balanced diets with an emphasis on reducing calorie consumption, and in particular, reducing the consumption of dietary fat. Teaching kids what good nutrition is and what it isn't is also beneficial; these early lessons can stay with them forever. The most effective treatment for childhood obesity is diet management combined with exercise.

Break the TV Habit

Too much television is bad for our children's health. According to a recent study done at Johns Hopkins School of Medicine, the more TV that children watch, the more likely they will be overweight. Children who are the least active and who watch the most TV tend to be the heaviest.

Addressing this serious problem requires a change in the way our families think about electronic entertainment. Here are some suggestions:

- Set a good example. Your daughter's biggest influence is *you*. Setting a good example means spending *your* free time in ways other than watching TV.
- Watching TV is not a right, it's a privilege. Make TV viewing contingent on good behavior and following through on specific positive activities, especially those involving physical activity. For instance, for every hour she spends engaged in physical activity, she can spend thirty minutes watching TV.
- It is difficult to have any control over TV viewing if there is a TV in your daughter's room. If she has a TV in her room, remove it. This move is likely to spark protest if it's a major change from what she's used to. Admit to your daughter that you made a mistake by letting her have a TV in her room. Schedule a family meeting and emphasize that the changes are not a punishment. Instead, stress that you are trying to make a positive change within the family by making TV watching a family activity. Follow through on what you say. Schedule time to watch your daughter's favorite TV shows with her. When necessary, discuss the show's content with her and answer her questions.

A Weight Management Program

Weight loss occurs when a person consumes fewer calories than they burn. Eating two- to three-hundred fewer calories per day will slow or stop a child's weight gain so she can grow into her body weight. In an adolescent—for whom actual weight loss may be a goal—eating five hundred fewer calories per day will result in a loss of one pound of body fat per week. This is a good, safe rate of weight loss for an overweight or obese adolescent. She will have plenty of energy and will not feel totally deprived of food.

One of the most effective ways to cut calories out of a child's diet without eliciting howls of protest is to substitute low-fat foods for foods that are high in fat. Don't keep this a secret from your child. In fact, it's a good idea to get her input about what substitutions she wants to make. Before long she will find herself choosing healthier foods out of habit.

From *The DASH Diet for Hypertension—Lower Your Blood Pressure in 14 Days—Without Drugs* by Thomas Moore, M.D., here are some ideas for substituting healthier foods for ones that are less healthy:

Instead of...	Try...
Ice cream	Low- or non-fat frozen yogurt
Whole milk	nonfat dry milk, skim or 1 percent milk
Regular cheese	Reduced-fat cheese
Rich desserts	Angel food cake or sorbet
Pudding	Sugar-free pudding or gelatin
Potato chips	Pretzels
Butter	Reduced-fat margarine
Doughnuts	Bagels
Fried foods	Baked, broiled, steamed, microwaved, or roasted meat, fish, poultry, and vegetables
Oils, salad dressings, sour cream	Reduced-calorie salad dressings and sour cream, low-fat or nonfat plain yogurt
Mayonnaise	Mustard
Butter, margarine	Jam jelly, preserves, low-calorie apple butter as a spread
Cake, pie, cookies, pastries	Angel food cake, baked apple, fruit crisp, oatmeal cookies, ginger snaps, fresh fruit or juice-pack
Snack crackers, chips	Crisp breads, matzo, pretzels, rice cakes, melba toast, air-popped or microwaved popcorn

It is particularly important if your daughter is overweight or obese that you try to cut some fats out of her diet, especially saturated fats (those from animal products).

In fact, this should be your goal for your entire family's diet. Foods that are high in saturated fats don't just cause us to put on weight—they cause cholesterol and other fatty substances to collect on the walls of our blood vessels, which in turn leads to heart disease. Most Americans eat a diet that is 34 percent fat. Your goal should be to make sure your family's diet is less than 30 percent fat, according to the American Heart Association. You can achieve this by following the Food Guide Pyramid described in chapter 8, "Nutritional Needs."

Here are tips on how to trim fat from your family's diet:

- Use a non-stick pan when sautéing vegetables or browning meats.
- Use vegetable spray when sautéing foods and preparing baking pans.
- Add flavor to sauces using herbs and spices instead of high-fat flavorings.
- Use vinegar, lemon juice, red or white wine, broth, stocks, tamari, soy sauce, low-fat cream soups, or yogurt to make foods richer in flavor, but not in fat.
- Choose lean cuts of meat (loin and round cuts, for example), and trim away all visible fat when preparing them to be cooked.
- Purchase low-fat, reduced-fat, or non-fat varieties of products such as salad dressings, mayonnaise, yogurt, and sour cream.

Behavior Modification

Many of the strategies adults have successfully used to treat obesity can be taught to children and adolescents. These strategies include setting and shaping goals, self-monitoring, paying attention to food cues, and slowing down how fast you eat.

Setting goals is an important first step to losing weight. Instead of having your child focus on those numbers on the bathroom scale, encourage her to focus on the dietary and exercise changes that will *lead to* that long-term goal of an appropriate weight.

The key to successful weight management lies in selecting two or three goals at a time to take on, which are 1) measurable; 2) achievable; and 3) forgiving (less than perfect). For example, "exercise more" is a commendable ideal, but it's not specific. "Walk five miles everyday" is specific and measurable, but is it attainable if you're just starting out? "Walk thirty minutes every day" is more attainable, but what happens if she gets stuck at school one day and there's a thunderstorm during her walking time another day? "Walk thirty minutes, five days each week" is exact, achievable, and forgiving. In short, a great goal!

Self-monitoring means keeping track of what you're doing to change your behavior, such as reducing calorie intake, increasing servings of fruits and vegetables, and exercising more often, or an outcome of these behaviors, such as stable or lower weight. Adolescents and more mature children can use self-monitoring, but if your daughter is younger, you will need to keep track with her (you are the best judge of whether your daughter is mature enough to keep track of her progress). Encourage your daughter to use self-monitoring at times when she's not sure how she's doing, and at times when she wants her behavior to improve.

Self-monitoring a behavior usually improves that behavior and produces handy records for you and your daughter to review. For example, by keeping a record of how much your daughter is exercising, both of you can know right away how she's doing, and when the record shows that her exercise frequency is increasing, she'll be encouraged to keep it up. Some children find that specific self-monitoring forms make it easier, while others prefer to use their own recording system. You may wish to use a form such as that created by the National Institute for Health, available on the web at http://whi.nih.gov/health/public/heart/obesity/lose_wt/diary.pdf.

Your daughter may or may not wish to weigh herself frequently while trying to manage her weight, but regular monitoring is essential to tracking desired weight. Sometimes kids prefer a graph to a list of numbers, because it is more visual and easy to read, so you might consider representing her weight changes that way. Remember that day-to-day fluctuations do occur due to changes in water weight, so it's a better idea to monitor your daughter's weight on a weekly basis.

Rewards can be used to encourage meeting goals, especially those that have been difficult to reach. You and your daughter should discuss which rewards she thinks are appropriate for particular achievements. For children and adolescents, the most effective rewards are tangible (such as a movie or music CD). Numerous small rewards, delivered for more modest goals, are more effective than bigger rewards, requiring a long, difficult effort. Small rewards might include payments into a bank account that are to go toward buying a more costly item.

Cue control is learning which social or environmental cues encourage undesired eating, and then changing or avoiding those cues. For example, you and your daughter may learn from her self-monitoring records that she's more likely to overeat while watching television, whenever treats are on display at a friend's house, or when around a certain group of friends. She might then try to sever the association of eating with the cue (don't eat while watching television), avoid or eliminate the cue (immediately leave the area in her friend's house where the treats are laid out), or change the circumstances surrounding the cue (plan to meet with friends in non-food settings). Explain to your daughter—and discuss the issue with her—that situations when you can see and help yourself to food items are often cues for unplanned eating.

Helping your daughter change *how* she eats can make it easier for her to eat less without feeling deprived. It takes fifteen or more minutes for the brain to get the message that the body has been fed. Explain to your daughter that if she slows down how fast she eats, this will allow fullness signals to begin to develop by the end of the meal. Specific ways she can do this include putting less in her mouth with each forkful, and chewing each mouthful ten times. Eating lots of vegetables can also make one feel more full. Another tactic you can use is to serve food on smaller plates so that moderate portions do not appear meager. Changing your daughter's eating schedule, or setting one for her, can be helpful, especially if she tends to skip or delay meals and compensates later by overeating and/or eating too fast.

We know that 80 to 90 percent of children who lose weight eventually gain it back again, so nowhere is the adage "prevention is better than cure" more applicable than in the case of childhood obesity. The onus is on us as parents to prevent our kids from becoming overweight in the first place. Our efforts should begin when our kids are in infancy, where breastfeeding has been shown to prevent obesity, and it is important not to start them on solids too early or continue to feed them even when they're full. In early childhood, we need to teach our daughters about proper nutrition using the Food Guide Pyramid as a guide. We need to explain how to select healthy, low-fat snacks. It's crucial that we also teach them about the importance of exercise and being active, and why watching television and participating in other forms of electronic media need to be limited.

As our children grow older, we need to remind our daughters that a healthy body does not necessarily look like the ones we see on the covers of women's magazines. Few of us are naturally as slim as those wafer-thin models. However, almost anyone can have an appropriate proportion of body fat compared to lean tissue, and live a happier, more fulfilling life, maintaining or achieving this goal through sports and exercise.

Eating Disorders

It is seemingly a contradiction. In this land of plenty, overeating is a growing problem, but so are eating disorders characterized by self-starvation. Maybe this isn't a contradiction at all. When being overweight is so prevalent, what becomes desirable is the opposite—hence those bony, hollow-cheeked models staring out at us from the fashion-magazine covers. Adolescent girls who are trying to fit in often latch onto thinness as their entrée to acceptance by their peers and society as a whole.

Among adolescent girls there has been an increase in the incidence of two psychiatric illnesses: *anorexia nervosa* and *bulimia*. These two illnesses are characterized by a preoccupation with food and a distorted body image. Anorexics drastically restrict their food consumption, while bulimics engage in eating binges followed by self-induced vomiting. Often, teens with anorexia may also have bulimia—after a period of restricted eating they will lose control and binge on food, which is followed by "purging."

As many as 10 percent of adolescent girls in the United States suffer from anorexia, bulimia, or both. These illnesses usually begin at either the age of fourteen or fifteen, or around eighteen years of age. Although boys do develop eating disorders, they are much more common in girls.

A girl with anorexia nervosa is typically a perfectionist and a high achiever in school. At the same time, she suffers from low self-esteem, irrationally believing that she is fat regardless of how thin she becomes. The girl with anorexia nervosa experiences a sense of control only when she says "no" to the normal food demands of her body. In a relentless pursuit to be thin, the girl starves herself, with serious health consequences. The semi-starvation characteristic of anorexia can damage organ systems and cause anemia, kidney dysfunction, heart problems, changes in brain structure, hormonal disturbances, menstrual changes, and osteoporosis.

The symptoms of bulimia are usually different from those of anorexia nervosa. The girl binges on huge quantities of high-caloric food and/or purges her body of dreaded calories by self-induced vomiting, and often by using laxatives. These binges may alternate with severe diets, resulting in dramatic weight fluctuations. Teenagers may try to hide the signs of throwing up by running water while spending long periods of time in the bathroom. The purging of bulimia presents a serious threat to the patient's physical health, including dehydration, hormonal imbalance, the depletion of important minerals, and damage to vital organs.

Eating disorders are life-threatening, so if you suspect your daughter suffers from one, do not delay in getting help for her.

What Causes Eating Disorders?

Doctors don't know exactly what causes eating disorders. However, a girl is more likely to become anorexic or bulimic if she has a close relative with an eating disorder, which may point to a genetic origin for these diseases.

There is also an apparent relationship between eating disorders and participation in athletic activities where appearance is important—ballet, diving, figure skating, and gymnastics. Girls who participate in these sports are more linked to eating disorders than those who play team sports such as basketball, soccer, or field hockey. This issue is covered in depth in chapter 12, "Sports Health Concerns."

A perfectionist or obsessive personality is another red flag, as is a past history of physical or sexual abuse.

Signs and Symptoms That Your Daughter May Have an Eating Disorder

Eating disorders are extremely harmful—and can be deadly—so it is extremely important if you are the parent of an adolescent girl to know how to identify symptoms of anorexia and bulimia. The mortality rate in people with eating disorders is between 10 and 15 percent. Unfortunately, many teens successfully hide these serious and sometimes fatal disorders from their families for many months or even years. This reinforces the importance of being on the lookout for various signs or symptoms of anorexia and bulimia:

- recent weight loss (growing children should be gaining weight)
- a Body Mass Index in an "underweight" category
- outward physical changes such as thinning hair or dry and sallow skin
- an apparent fear of putting on weight or being overweight
- "purging" (deliberate vomiting or using laxatives to lose weight)
- an apparently distorted body image, and especially, a repeated insistence that she is "fat" when this is obviously not true
- an obsession with issues pertaining to food such as calorie content of individual foods
- going on fad diets that involve fasting, or eliminating entire food groups
- menstrual abnormalities (she hasn't yet started menstruating by her mid teens or her periods stop or become irregular)
- exercising compulsively
- strenuously denying that she has an eating disorder
- withdrawing from friends and family activities
- wearing bulky clothing to hide weight loss

What Should You Do If You Think Your Daughter Might Have an Eating Disorder?

If you think your daughter has an eating disorder, confronting her will be difficult because she almost certainly won't acknowledge that she is ill. It must be done, however, and the sooner the better.

Find a time to talk to your daughter. As sympathetically as you can, tell her that you are concerned about her health and want her to get help. Cite examples of specific behavior that make your point. You might say, "I've noticed that you are preoccupied with dieting and are looking quite thin."

A girl in this position will often react angrily and deny she has a problem. That's not surprising: she will be embarrassed and humiliated at realizing that someone has found her out. Keep that in mind and avoid getting into an argument with her. Don't think you can cure your daughter yourself—if you are concerned that she has an eating disorder such as anorexia or bulimia, have her seen by a physician as soon as possible. Technically, a person must be 15 percent below her normal weight and must have menstrual abnormalities to be diagnosed as anorexic. However, a doctor can begin to treat your daughter even if these criteria are not met, and a complete physical exam is important to check for any damage the illness may have caused.

How Are Eating Disorders Treated?

Eating disorders are treated in two steps. At first, the doctor will focus on addressing any immediate and pressing health concerns. Sometimes hospitalization is necessary, especially if the person's weight has fallen below 75 percent of what's normal, if there is damage to a major organ such as the heart or kidneys, or if there is a risk of suicide.

Restoring body weight is a complicated undertaking, since gaining weight is what someone who's anorexic or bulimic fears most. It usually calls for the help of a psychologist and a nutritional counselor as well as a physician, and can be done on an outpatient basis.

The second phase is more long-term and is aimed at treating the psychological component of the illness. There may be medical monitoring by a physician, treatment by a psychiatrist or psychologist (preferably a specialist in eating disorders), and often family therapy when the patient is living at home. Antidepressants may be prescribed as they have frequently proven to be effective in helping people with eating disorders get a handle on their disease.

Where Do I Get More Information?

More information on eating disorders is available from The National Association of Anorexia Nervosa and Associated Disorders, P.O. Box 7, Highland Park, IL 60035, (847) 831-3438. Contact this organization and it will send you information and provide referrals to experts and support groups near you. The same information is available on its website at http://www.anad.org.

Remember also to take care of yourself. Anorexia is hard on family members and other loved ones. Look into joining a support group where you can air your feelings and get additional information.

Sports Are Preventive Medicine for Eating Disorders

It's true that eating disorders are sometimes seen in girls who participate in activities in which appearance is a factor—diving, gymnastics, and figure skating, for example. If your daughter participates in one of those sports—or in ballet or modeling for that matter—you need to be extra vigilant about eating disorders. You also need to be concerned if your daughter exercises obsessively, which can be a sign of having an eating disorder.

There's good news, too! For most girls, participating in wholesome sports programs is important preventive medicine against anorexia and bulimia. That's because sports improve our daughters' psychological health in areas such as self-esteem, self-confidence, and their perceptions of their own abilities. Sports also reduce the risk of mental illnesses such as anxiety and depression.

The positive influence that a healthy sports experience can have on our daughters' psychological and mental health—important factors in preventing eating disorders—reinforces the need to get girls involved in sports and keep them involved throughout their adolescence.

chapter 12

Sports Health Concerns

● ● ●

I spent the first part of my career at NBC Sports "in the trenches"—working as a sideline reporter. I was the person you see on TV who stands behind the bench at a basketball or football game and reports on what's happening there. Since coaches tend to be secretive about strategy, oftentimes the only thing to report on was injuries! Sometimes I felt like my entire day was spent talking about how this person was being taped or that person was bleeding, whether an injury was a "sprain" or a "strain," or waiting for trainers or doctors to give me their reports. I feel as though I've seen it all, from freak accidents to career-threatening injuries, during competition.

The common denominator in the hundreds of hurt athletes I've seen over the years is intense frustration, which is sometimes more painful than the injury itself. In some cases, that frustration is heightened by the fact that the injury could have been prevented, or its severity reduced so the athlete could have been back in action sooner. There is much we parents can do to prevent and treat injuries in our kids so that their sports participation isn't disrupted. And, of course, no parent wants to see his or her child injured in any way.

Sports Injuries in Children's Sports

Sports and physical activity are good for children, and have special benefits for girls. However, it's impossible to ignore the fact that injuries *do* occur in sports. Every year, millions of children are treated for sports injuries by their doctors and in emergency rooms. Certain sports injuries and sports-related medical conditions are seen more often in girls—and some are unique to young female athletes.

Acute versus Overuse Injuries

There are two main types of sports injuries—acute and overuse. An acute injury occurs instantaneously as a result of a dramatic twist or stretch, for example, a sprained ankle, broken leg, or pulled hamstring. An overuse injury occurs as a result of repetitive, low-intensity stress, for example, tennis elbow, gymnast's back, swimmer's shoulder, shin splints, or heel-bone stress fracture.

Until the rise of organized youth sports, overuse athletic injuries were almost never seen in children. Now they are commonplace in the millions of youngsters who participate in organized sports programs. Overuse injuries are *especially* common in young female athletes. This will be explained in more detail later in the chapter.

Acute Sports Injuries

Most of us know what an acute injury is. This kind of injury is one that happens suddenly. You don't just see acute injuries in sports—they also occur in daily life. A sprained ankle, a broken arm, or a black eye are unfortunate but not uncommon parts of growing up. There is sometimes a tendency to not take acute sports injuries seriously. As Dr. Angela Smith puts it, children are too often expected to "tough it out." But as any sports-medicine expert will tell you, a sports injury to a child that isn't treated appropriately has the potential to cause serious problems later on.

These problems can be especially severe if there has been damage to a "growth plate." Growth plates are the softer ends of the bones where growth is taking place. Sometimes called "pre-bone," the more vulnerable growth plate is often where fractures take place as a result of a fall or impact. If a child is growing and she fractures a growth plate, the bone will stop growing while the body repairs the growth plate. Let's say the fracture is to one of the long arm bones. What happens is that the bone on the unaffected side will keep growing, which can result in discrepancies in the length of bones on one side compared to the other. If a growth plate fracture occurs near a joint—such as the wrist, elbow, knee, or ankle—that joint may not work properly unless the fracture heals properly.

Anytime a child sustains a fracture—especially to the growth plate—it is important that she be taken to an orthopedist who *specializes* in treating children.

Overuse Injuries

What about overuse injuries? These were almost never seen in kids before the rise of organized sports. Nowadays, the young female athlete is at risk of a host of overuse injuries, including stress fractures, tendonitis, bursitis, and joint disorders. "Kneecap pain syndrome was once rare in children," says Dr. Lyle Micheli, director of the sports medicine division at Boston Children's Hospital and the author of *The Sports Medicine Bible for Young Athletes*. "However, it is now the number one diagnosis in my clinic." It doesn't matter what time you call the Sports Medicine Clinic at Boston Children's Hospital, they're always busy!

Overuse injuries are caused by repetitive, low-level impact or stress to a part of the body. Running to catch the school bus a couple of times a week won't damage the bones in your daughter's feet and shins, but if she runs dozens of miles a week on hard surfaces, the bones may sustain tiny cracks known as stress fractures. Sports-medicine experts believe that more intensive sports-training regimens are partly to blame for the rise of overuse injuries. They also point to the fact that more kids than ever before are specializing in one or two sports over the course of the year, instead of playing whatever sport is in season. Specializing in one sport can put too much stress on certain parts of the body—the feet and legs of runners, the wrists and backs of gymnasts, and the shoulders of swimmers.

How Much Training Is Too Much?

Fitness and skill development must be balanced with the need to avoid overtraining, which can cause overuse injuries. This raises the question: *How much is too much?* These are some recommendations from Dr. Lyle Micheli adapted from *The Sports Medicine Bible for Young Athletes.*

How Many Hours Per Week Can Children Train?

As a general rule, children shouldn't train for more than eighteen to twenty hours a week. Elite athletes may be pressured to train for longer. Anytime a child trains for longer than this recommended length of time, she must be monitored closely by a qualified sports doctor with expertise in young athletes. This is to make sure abnormalities in growth or maturation do not occur. Any joint pain lasting more than two weeks is reason to see a sports doctor.

How Much of an Increase in Training Is Safe?

Increasing the frequency, duration, or intensity of training too quickly is one of the main causes of injury. To prevent injuries caused by too-rapid increases in training, athletes should follow the "10 percent rule." This refers to the amount a young athlete's training can be increased every week without risking injury. For example, a child running twenty minutes at a time four times a week can probably safely run twenty-two minutes four times a week the week after, an increase of 10 percent.

Most injuries are the product of violations of the 10 percent rule, when young athletes have their training regimen increased too much, too soon.

How Hard Should Young Athletes Train?

Remember, when young athletes are growing the emphasis should be on developing athletic technique and building fitness. Although power and speed are important qualities in sports, stressing them to children at the expense of technique can lead to injuries. Once good technique is mastered, power and speed can be introduced.

Children don't cope well with heat. They are more susceptible than adults to the two main types of heat-related disorders: heat exhaustion and the much more serious heat stroke.

Heat exhaustion is caused by dehydration and salt loss. Children with heat exhaustion become cool and damp while running a normal temperature, and often feel dizzy and tired. They should be given plenty of fluids and should rest in a cool, shady place.

Heat stroke is caused by a disruption of the body's heat-regulation system. The athlete becomes hot and dry, turns bright red, and runs a high fever. She may also act irrationally, often aggressively. Heat stroke must be treated by rapidly cooling the athlete with ice water, towels soaked in ice-cold water, and fanning. Any child who suffers heat stroke should be taken to a hospital immediately for observation.

These are some suggestions to lower the risk of heat-induced injuries:

- *Exercise Intensity.* Coaches should reduce exercise intensity when the temperature is hotter than 70° F. You may have to discuss this with your child's coach, and stay around through practice to make sure your child's exercise intensity is appropriate for the weather.
- *Fluid Replacement.* Coaches should provide unlimited supplies of drinking water and players should be encouraged by parents to drink a cup of water fifteen minutes before training and one and a half cups at twenty- to thirty-minute intervals throughout practice. Younger, smaller athletes will need slightly less than this amount. After a workout, it's not enough that kids drink to quench their thirst, because this only replenishes one-third to one-half of fluid losses; they should be encouraged to drink more than they think they need.
- *Clothing.* Appropriate clothing for training in the hot weather is lightweight, single-layer, and absorbent. As much skin as possible should be exposed to air and sweat-saturated articles should be changed. Sauna suits for weight reduction should *never* be allowed.
- *Fitness Levels.* Athletes should start the season as physically fit as possible. A preseason conditioning program will give the child a good baseline fitness level. This not only decreases the risk of heat illness, but will help prevent other problems such as overuse injuries. An attempt also should be made to acclimate the child before beginning a strenuous program or traveling to a warm climate. Talk to your daughter's coach about what a preseason program might look like for your daughter. If the coach isn't available or isn't able to tell you, you may wish to simply encourage your daughter to be active in the weeks leading up to the season.

Dr. Micheli's Sports Injury Terminology

Acute Injuries

Fractures. A fracture is a crack, break, or complete shattering of a bone. *A fracture is the same as a break.* Fractures are either "open" or "closed." An open fracture is when the bone breaks the skin's surface. In closed fractures, the bone doesn't break through the skin.

Strains. A strain is a stretch, tear, or complete rupture of a muscle or tendon. Strains are classified according to severity: first, second, or third degree.

Sprains. A sprain is a stretch, tear, or complete rupture of a ligament. Like strains, sprains are classified according to severity: first, second, or third degree.

Bruise/contusion. A bruise, or a "contusion" as it is known medically, is bleeding in the muscle fibers caused by a direct blow to a muscle. If the impact is particularly severe, or if a bruise is aggravated by continued vigorous use of the muscle, it can worsen into a condition known as a *hematoma*, which is a dramatic pooling of blood in the area of the bruise.

Dislocations/Subluxations. A dislocation is where the ball of a joint is forced out of its socket, or when the ends of two bones that meet at a joint are forced apart (the latter is sometimes called a "separation"). A subluxation occurs when the ball of the joint pops out of its socket, then immediately pops back in.

Acute Compartment Syndrome. Acute compartment syndrome occurs when sudden, massive bleeding takes place in the muscles, causing them to swell within their encasements. This can occur when a bone gets fractured, a muscle completely ruptures, or the muscle gets severely bruised. Though less common than overuse compartment syndromes (see page 163), when they occur, acute compartment syndromes are a medical emergency, and require immediate surgery.

Overuse Injuries

Tendonitis. Tendonitis refers to microtears in the tendon fibers caused by repetitive stretching. This overuse condition is especially prevalent in athletes with tight or weak tendons. Tendonitis is most frequently seen in the Achilles tendon (heel), rotator cuff (shoulder), biceps, and around the kneecap.

Stress Fractures. Stress fractures are tiny cracks in the bone's surface caused by rhythmic, repetitive overloading. One of the most common causes of stress fractures is the pounding of the feet in running, dance, and aerobics, which can cause stress fractures in the foot and shinbone. These injuries are especially common among female athletes (see "The Female Athlete Triad," page 166).

Neuritis. Neuritis is an irritation or inflammation of nerves caused when they are repetitively stretched or trapped against a bony surface.

Osteochondritis (Loose Bodies in the Joint). Loose bodies in the joint are created by the repetitive bumping and grinding of the ends of the bones, which may in turn cause tiny pieces of the bone and cartilage to become loose. Sometimes, the piece of bone dislodges and falls into the joint, at which time it is colloquially known as a "joint mouse" because it is small, looks white on X rays, and causes havoc.

Bursitis. Bursitis occurs due to repetitive "microtrauma" to a bursa sac, usually from the adjoining tendon. In response to these forces, the bursa sac fills with synovial fluid and becomes swollen. The bursa most frequently affected are those in the shoulder, elbow, and knee.

Overuse Compartment Syndrome. A compartment syndrome occurs when certain muscles become too large for the walls that encase them, perhaps as a result of intensive training. At rest, there is no problem, but when the athlete exercises, the muscles swell with blood causing pressure in the compartment to increase. This pressure compresses the muscles and nerves within the compartment, and therefore causes tightness, numbness, and muscle weakness. Compartment syndromes usually occur in the lower leg. For reasons unknown to sports-medicine experts, young female athletes suffer from compartment syndromes more often than their male counterparts.

Adapted from The Sports Medicine Bible for Young Athletes *by Dr. Lyle Micheli with Mark Jenkins. Reprinted with permission.*

Sports Injuries and the Young Female Athlete

Whether girls sustain more injuries than boys because they are anatomically different is controversial. Evidence suggests that girls *do* get injured more than boys, but not because of physical or physiological differences.

Overuse injuries in particular may be more common among female athletes, according to Dr. Lyle Micheli. "Female athletes are especially susceptible to overuse injuries for two main reasons," says Dr. Micheli. "First, they often lack long-term preparation for vigorous sports training, and secondly, they may start intensive sports training at the height of their growth spurt—between the ages of eleven and thirteen—when their muscles are tighter than normal."

Three overuse injuries are especially prevalent in young female athletes. These are stress fractures, kneecap disorders, and compartment syndromes.

Stress fractures are a series of tiny cracks ("microfractures") that don't heal because of the frequency or intensity of an athlete's training schedule. Usually these occur in the feet and shins due to running or dancing.

Kneecap disorders are aching pains caused by the kneecaps being pulled out of alignment by muscle-tendon imbalances.

Compartment syndromes are swelling of the muscles inside their membraneous casings. Usually this occurs in the muscles in the front of the lower leg and is commonly known as "shin splints."

As for acute injuries, sports-medicine doctors are becoming aware that girls who play sports are at a higher risk of anterior cruciate ligament ("ACL") knee injuries. This injury involves a partial or complete tear of the main ligaments that join the thigh and shinbones in the center of the joint like "guy wires." ACL injuries are most often seen in sports such as soccer, basketball, field hockey, and lacrosse that involve powerful direction changes when running ("cutting").

A recent study of young athletes who had suffered knee injuries showed that girls are much more likely than boys to sustain an ACL tear. In basketball, girls are five times more likely to tear their ACL, and twice as likely to be injured this way in soccer. The total number of girls who sustain ACL injuries is still relatively low—less than 2 percent of the total number of female athletes. According to Dr. Micheli, the reason girls are more likely than boys to sustain ACL injuries probably has less to do with anatomical

Sports Injury Prevention

These are some general recommendations for preventing injuries:

- Conditioning should be as important a part of training sessions as skill development.
- Practices should include warm-up and cool-down periods.
- Stretching should be mandatory for young athletes, especially during rapid growth phases when muscles can be very tight.
- Coaches must stress playing within the rules.
- Strength training with weights, done with *knowledgeable instruction and adequate supervision*, is not only safe for adolescents and children as young as nine, but can also help prevent injury.
- Coaches and other adults in charge must be knowledgeable about game rules, safety equipment, and healthy sports behaviors.
- Coaches need to monitor the intensity of training and the duration of training.
- Coaches at all levels should be certified.
- Parents should be supportive of and positive toward their daughters' athletic endeavors without applying excessive pressure on them to win.
- Parents need to make sure that their children use appropriate protective equipment and that the playing equipment their children use is also safe.

differences—although some sports-medicine experts believe these differences *are* to blame—than the fact that their leg strength and cutting skills aren't as well developed as boys'.

What can we do to prevent our daughters from sustaining ACL injuries? Much of what I've encouraged you to do in this book will work—especially improving motor skills and leg strength by participating in sports from a young age. If your daughter plays a sport where there are a lot of cutting-type motions, experts suggest that you encourage her to strengthen the muscles around her knees (especially the hamstring muscles in back of the thigh) and practice cutting maneuvers. For younger kids, a simple game of tag where a child has to dodge her parents' attempts to tag her is a straightforward example of how we can help our daughters practice such motor skills.

The Female Athlete Triad

One of the most troubling issues facing parents of young female athletes is something called the "female athlete triad." This condition refers to three separate but interrelated conditions that are seen in young female athletes: stress fractures, excessive thinness, and menstrual abnormalities. What happens is that girls whose body-fat levels drop below a certain point due to dieting or an intensive training schedule (or both) tend to experience menstrual abnormalities—teenage girls may not start menstruating and girls who have reached puberty may stop having menstrual periods or get them irregularly. When menstrual periods don't start or become irregular, a girl's body doesn't produce enough estrogen and her bones get weaker. In turn, this predisposes her to stress fractures if she participates in intensive sports or dance training.

The third aspect of the female athlete triad, excessive thinness, may be a sign of an eating disorder, as we discussed in the previous chapter.

If your daughter exercises frequently and has stopped menstruating, she is at high risk of sustaining stress fractures. If this is the case, speak as soon as possible with your family doctor about getting a referral to someone experienced in treating the female athlete triad. The main goal will be to get her to start menstruating regularly again so her bones will restrengthen. Often this is as straightforward as getting the athlete to reduce her training regimen and increase how much she eats. Unfortunately, the highly competitive athlete may resist suggestions to do either, in which case it may be advisable to involve a multidisciplinary approach involving a sports psychologist.

Acute Injuries

If your daughter suffers an acute injury while she is playing sports, or at any time, the adults supervising should know standard first-aid treatments and apply them immediately. As a parent, it is also important to know what signs to look for that require immediate medical attention.

The Importance of RICE

"RICE" stands for Rest, Ice, Compression, and Elevation. If your daughter plays sports, chances are that at some point you'll need to know how to use RICE, which is the first line of defense for any number of injuries, especially sprains, strains, and bruises.

RICE reduces inflammation and swelling. The more inflammation and swelling are controlled early on, the sooner motion and recovery can take place.

RICE should begin as soon as an injury occurs or as soon as symptoms are felt. "If you start RICE within fifteen to twenty minutes of an injury occurring, you can make a huge difference in recovery time," says Dr. Micheli. "Use of RICE within the first twenty-four hours after injury can reduce how long an athlete is out of action by 50 to 70 percent." Sometimes it can take a while to get seen by a doctor in an emergency room, or to get an appointment with your family doctor, so if your daughter gets injured, don't wait to be seen by a health professional before starting RICE.

When Immediate Medical Attention Is Necessary

Any child who has the following symptoms should be taken to the nearest hospital emergency room:

- Neck pain
- Unconsciousness
- Seizure
- Deep cut
- Unequal pupil size
- Breathing problems
- Eye injury
- Grogginess and disorientation
- Vomiting
- Obvious bone deformity

This is how Dr. Micheli suggests you apply RICE if your daughter gets injured.

Rest/"Relative rest." Stop playing! Continuing will only cause the injury to worsen and result in even longer layoffs. During the first twenty-four to seventy-two hours (depending on the severity of the injury), complete immobilization is necessary to properly ice, compress, and elevate the injury.

After initial immobilization, rest does not mean total inactivity until the injury has healed. This will only cause muscles to get weak, joints to stiffen, and endurance to decline. An athlete with a stress fracture of the foot caused by running or dance should be encouraged to swim or row to maintain endurance. A swimmer who develops a shoulder problem can in-line skate or walk to stay in shape. This is known as "relative rest."

Ice. Cooling the injury decreases swelling, bleeding, pain, and inflammation. The most effective way to do this is to apply ice to the injury. To get the full benefit, ice needs to be applied within ten to fifteen minutes of the injury occurring.

Normal sensations experienced when using ice are cold, a burning sensation, then aching, and finally numbness.

The most common method of icing an injury is to cover the injured area with a *wet* towel and place a plastic bag full of ice over it.

"Ice massage" can be even more effective. This is done by freezing water in a polystyrene coffee cup, then tearing off the upper edge of the cup. This leaves the base as an insulated grip, allowing the athlete to massage the injured area with slow, circular strokes. Ice massage combines two elements of RICE—icing and compression. Ice massage is especially effective for treating the symptoms of overuse injuries around the joints. If your kids are active in sports, it doesn't hurt to have some cups of ice in the freezer in case an ice massage is needed.

Intermittent icing may be beneficial for up to seven days, particularly for severe bruises. The first seventy-two hours are especially important, and icing should be done as much as possible during this period. Minor injuries may need only twenty-four hours of icing.

Ice the injury for ten to thirty minutes at a time at intervals of thirty to forty-five minutes.

Safety Tips for In-Line Skating

Sometimes known by the brand name "Rollerblading," in-line skating is incredibly popular among kids. Falls and collisions can cause injuries, however, so it is well worth reviewing some safety precautions.

If your daughter plans to take up in-line skating, make sure she receives instruction. Often, the same places that sell equipment also offer lessons. A certified instructor will know the importance of teaching balance, braking, safe skating, and how to fall without getting hurt. Kids as young as four can learn to skate.

It's important that your daughter wear protective equipment, including a helmet, wrist guards, knee pads, and elbow pads. When renting skates, do so only from outlets that also offer package deals that include protective gear. Make sure when buying skates for your daughter that she is taught to maintain her skates, and especially to monitor the condition of the brake pads.

Supervise your daughter until she has adequate skills to skate safely on her own. It's especially important she learns how to use her heel brake, which should be a fundamental part of her instruction.

Remind your daughter of the other lessons she should have been taught—that she should skate with her weight over the balls of her feet, and not to lean backward. This makes it easier to skate, and also provides that if she falls, she falls forward in a controlled fashion, not backwards so that she might hit her head.

Many cities and towns have created in-line skating paths as they do bike paths, and maintain them for the use of those wishing to engage in such healthful activities. Parents should take their children to such areas whenever possible so they can skate in safety. If your locality doesn't provide such an area, talk to your municipal department of parks and recreation. It may be possible for them to designate a multiuse space or area for in-line skating.

The duration of each icing session depends on the type of injury, and how deep it is. Because they are closer to the skin's surface, injured ankle and knee ligaments require less icing time for cooling to take place than thigh or biceps muscles.

Compression. To reduce swelling, gentle but firm pressure should be applied to the injury to minimize swelling. Compression can be performed while icing is being done, and also when it is not.

During icing, perform simultaneous compression by doing ice massage using the previously explained "coffee cup method." Alternatively, an elastic bandage can be wrapped over the ice pack and limb. When icing is not being done, an elastic bandage should be used for compression.

Elevation. Keeping the injury elevated is necessary to stop blood and fluids from pooling in the injury area, where they create swelling and inflammation.

If possible, raise the injury above heart level. For example, an athlete with an ankle, knee, or thigh injury should lie on a couch or bed and use a pillow to keep the injury elevated. During the first twenty-four to seventy-two hours, the injury should be kept elevated as much as possible.

During the first twenty-four to forty-eight hours, do not apply heat to the injured area (avoid hot showers and baths, liniments, etc.); massage the injury; or exercise. All can *increase* swelling and bleeding in the injured area.

Remember, RICE is only a first-aid measure. If your daughter is still experiencing pain after twenty-four to forty-eight hours, make an appointment with your family doctor.

It is important to note that sports-related injuries are a risk of sports participation, but the risks of an inactive lifestyle are much greater. Don't allow fear of injury to stop you from encouraging your daughter to be active and enjoy all the benefits that sports have to offer her.

chapter 13

Why Sports Need Girls

● ● ●

This book began by explaining why girls need sports. From my perspective as a network sportscaster and mother, I firmly believe that *sports* need *girls* as well! And I am not alone.

When covering the WNBA Championship in 2001, I interviewed the coach of the champion L.A. Sparks, Michael Cooper, who had won several NBA titles as a player with the Lakers. He said that his WNBA Championship meant more than any he won in the NBA because of the determination and dedication of his players. At courtside sat Derek Fisher, a member of that year's championship Lakers team. He explained to me that he attended all of the women's games while rehabbing from a difficult injury because the women served as an inspiration to him with their hard work and love of the game. Even the legendary John Wooten has often extolled the virtues of women's basketball, saying that they play the game the way it was "meant to be played," below the rim. I encounter comments like these all of the time, across every sport. Women are good for sports because they play the same game, but do it differently than men. Just as female sportscasters bring a different perspective to what we see on TV, female athletes bring a fresh perspective to competition. Along with this, there are a number of practical ways in which women are good for sports as a whole.

Brain Power

Women hold many important positions in sports. The presidents of the U.S. Olympic Committee, the American College of Sports Medicine, and the American Alliance for Health, Physical Education, Recreation, and Dance (AAHPERD) are all women. Until recently, all these organizations were headed by men. The growing number of women with athletic backgrounds means that sports now have at their disposal millions of women who can offer their intellect and experience to the field of sports. Women aren't necessarily smarter than men, but they definitely bring different perspectives and ideas to the table. For example, AAHPERD president Joanne Owens-Naustler is in the process of trying to organize a national "Walk Off Day," when every American shuts down the computers or lays down the tools to go for a brisk, fifteen-minute walk. American College of Sports Medicine president Angela Smith is forging strong relationships between the ACSM and other national and multinational sports-medicine organizations.

Strength in Numbers

The very fact that more girls are playing sports gives sports programs additional advocacy muscle. For instance, your local Parks and Recreation Department is more likely to maintain its fields and provide better facilities when it knows it's catering to a thousand boys *and* girls, not just five hundred boys. With not just sons playing sports but daughters, too, more parents are likely to push for improvement of sports programs and greater allocation of public funds for school and community sports programs. Public swimming pools, bike and in-line skating paths, and tennis courts, to name a few—these are more likely to receive support when *everyone*, not just the male gender, has an interest in sports.

Money Matters

The more that girls play sports, the bigger the sports industry "pie." The fact that growing numbers of girls and women are playing soccer and basketball means that sales of soccer cleats and basketball shoes are going up, more tickets are being sold to pro soccer and basketball (men's and women's), and more people are signing up to watch these events on cable and satellite television. Sporting-goods manufacturers, pro sports teams, and media outlets are marketing their products to the female segment of the market because they know it means financial windfalls for them at the cash registers.

Let's Hear It for the Girls...*from* the Girls!

While I was writing this book, I spoke with several prominent female athletes and coaches about the influence of girls and women on our sports culture. Their comments helped seal many of the opinions I have about sports and girls.

My friend and NBC colleague Chris Evert observes that the increased participation of women in sports has changed the sports landscape for the good. "Sports today are a more inclusive environment for everyone," says the legendary tennis player, "and this is due in large part to women being more involved in more areas of sports."

Reiterating that theme, all-time leading soccer goal-scorer Mia Hamm— a standout on the world championship U.S. women's soccer team—made the point that women athletes welcome the chance to "give back" to sports. "Women athletes tend to view this as an important opportunity to make a difference in the lives of others," says Mia.

Of all the people I contacted to talk about the impact of girls and women on sports, coach Pat Summit of the University of Tennessee provided some of the most eye-opening insights. The most successful women's basketball coach working today, Pat points out that girls who have a positive sports experience are much more likely to raise their own kids to love sports. As Pat points out, "this is the ultimate way of giving back."

I started to think about Pat's comments. How right she is! The love of a mother for sports and the desire to pass on this love to her daughters is what inspired this book. The fact that I am raising my daughters to be athletes can only benefit sports. My daughters will be players, spectators, coaches, and eventually, perhaps, sports parents themselves. Just as important, they'll know how to be *responsible* athletes. I want them to have the proper perspective where it comes to competition—to know that there is something very valuable about learning to accept defeat with grace and win with humility.

If everyone who reads this book passes these lessons on to their daughters, it will be impossible for sports *not* to benefit!

chapter 14

Sports 101

● ● ●

With all the sports available now for young girls to play, it can be a challenge trying to decide in which direction to steer your daughter. Ultimately, the decision is hers, but you can try to provide some guidance. In order to help your daughter make the best choice for her, it is important to be familiar with the ins and outs of the sports that are most popular with girls.

The following pages provide information about a variety of sports, including historical information, how the sports are played, and the opportunities for young, female athletes to play, learn, and excel in the sports. For each sport, I also provide tips on whether it might suit girls with certain personality traits or sets of skills. Remember that these are guidelines only— you know your daughter better than anyone else, and are best qualified to decide which programs she should explore.

Another reason that I provide a lot of background information is because it is a huge boost for our kids when they know we've made an effort to find out something about the sports they're playing. The information in these pages might yield a few facts that you can share with your daughter. Descriptions of the basics of the sports will enable you to be a more educated viewer of sports, some of which before may have seemed quite mysterious to you. This sports in this section are arranged starting with ones that children can begin at a young age and moving to the sports that girls start later in life.

The following pages won't tell you *everything* you need to know, but it is a collection of the information I found most interesting—and that I think you will, too!

Sports 101 Contents

Gymnastics

If your daughter always seems to be hurling herself around the house and backyard, and is as flexible as a cat while as strong as an ox, then gymnastics might be the right sport for her. The same applies if she has shown an interest in tumbling and has shown promise in this activity.

Gymnastics is an excellent sport for girls to develop strength, coordination, and flexibility. Rather like figure skating, gymnastics demands an enormous commitment from its participants and the competition can be fierce. The prospects for long-term participation in this sport are quite limited, though the benefits of the athletic skills gained are immeasurable. A girl who has demonstrated a facility for this demanding sport could quite easily turn her hand to learning other activities later on.

The Basics

Gymnastics have existed in one form or another since civilization began. Competitive gymnastics has developed as a sport over one hundred years, with women first competing in Olympic gymnastics in 1936. Girls' interest in gymnastics has always been strong, but thanks to the dazzling performances by female gymnasts at the Olympic games, the demand is even higher today. Scores of girls have been driven to the gym by the memorable Olympic performances of Nadia Comaneci, Mary Lou Retton, Olga Korbul, and Kerri Strug.

What makes gymnastics such a special sport is that it requires both strength and grace, and therefore combines all of the elements of athleticism more completely than any other sport. The routines are physically demanding, but must be performed smoothly as well as successfully in order to score the most points.

How to Play

Women's gymnastics is a unique sport in that it is an individual and a team sport at the same time. The gymnasts participate in four events: vault, balance beam, uneven bars, and floor exercise. The performances are scored by a single judge or panel of judges, depending on the level of competition, on a scale from zero to ten, with ten being the highest possible score. Each gymnast starts an event with a point value (the value increases with the difficulty of the routine being attempted), and deductions are taken from that for every error that the judge sees in the routine. Bonus points can be given for superior execution of a move, but this is much more common in the elite levels of gymnastics.

The score is given to the individual gymnast, and also added to the entire team's score in the event. Therefore, a gymnast from one team could earn the best individual score on the vault while another team wins for best total team score. This system helps to make sure that every aspect of this multifaceted sport is celebrated, and also makes it much more likely that your daughter will proudly come home with a medal or ribbon.

The following is a brief explanation of the four events in women's gymnastics. For a more detailed version of the rules and scoring criteria, consult your local youth gymnastics governing body, or visit www.usa-gymnastics.org.

Vault

In the vault, the gymnast runs across a platform and launches off of a springboard, with the goal of pushing off of an obstacle called a "horse" and landing on a mat without taking a step or falling. The gymnast can increase the difficulty of doing this by adding twists, turns, and flips to the vault. The judges score the event based on the height and distance of the vault, as well as the gymnast's hand, leg, and body position during the vault's jump, push, and flips. The more straight together the gymnast's legs are and the more centered her body is, the fewer deductions the judge will take off of her score. It is also important for the gymnast to land on the mat with as few extra steps as possible. Every foot movement after the landing can lead to a deduction. In this event, the gymnasts are allowed two attempts, and receive the highest of the two scores.

Balance Beam

The balance beam is the event in which the gymnast performs her routines atop a beam 120 cm high, 500 cm long, and a mere 10 cm wide. Because of the thinness of the board, the balance beam event is the one of the most difficult to perform and thrilling to watch in all of sports. Each routine lasts between seventy and ninety seconds, and begins with a mount, in which the gymnast moves from the floor to the top of the beam. Once on the beam, she must perform a series of maneuvers that display athleticism and grace. The types of maneuvers that are required or performed vary with the level of competition, and range from simple turns to no-handed cartwheels to flips. The routine ends with a dismount, in which the gymnast jumps from the beam back to the floor, adding twists and flips to increase the difficulty. As with the vault, the gymnast should take as few steps as possible when landing.

The judges score the event based on the difficulty of the maneuvers, as well as how perfectly they are performed. While falling off of the beam is the most noticeable reason for a deduction, the judges also can take off points for bent knees during cartwheels, slips of the foot, and other minor mistakes. The judges also score the event based on the grace with which the routine is performed.

Uneven Bars

One of the most memorable images of women's gymnastics is of gymnasts flying and spinning between the uneven bars. In this event, the gymnast must perform her routine by leaping between and spinning around two bars set at, not surprisingly, uneven heights. As with the balance beam, the routine is started with a mount, in which the gymnast jumps and grasps onto one of the bars. From there, she moves between the two bars, adding spins, twists, and various releases, ending with a dismount to the mat below. The event is again judged based on how well the gymnast executes her maneuvers. The other consideration in the uneven bars is the consistent flow with which the routine is performed. The moves should be crisp and quick, and the gymnast should move between the bars without any slips, falls, or stops.

Floor Exercise

This exercise takes place on a square carpeted floor space, where the gymnast performs a routine set to music. Of all the exercises, the floor routine focuses the most on the elements of dance. The gymnast performs by mixing a choreographed dance with a series of acrobatic moves and tumbling passes. The tumbling passes are the highlights of the routine. In a tumbling exercise, the gymnast runs and executes a series of somersaults, cartwheels, flips, and twists. Although they do not have to, most gymnasts start their tumbling passes from one corner of the square and finish at the opposite corner, because this path provides the longest distance across the square. The floor exercise is judged based on the difficulty and execution of the tumbling maneuvers performed, and the artistry of the choreographed dance moves. The gymnast must also stay within the square, marked by a white line. Any step outside of the square will cause a deduction.

Get Her in the Game!

For young children, gymnastics is one of the most widely available sports. Gymnastics and tumbling classes for children as young as four are provided by gyms and local athletic organizations such as the YWCA and the Boys and Girls Club. Toddlers can get into the mix almost as soon as they can walk, through Gymboree classes and other beginning tumbling classes.

Organized gymnastics is most often taught through local gymnastics facilities, or clubs, which are businesses that offer training and competition for girls interested in the sport. These clubs have instructors certified by USA Gymnastics (USAG), the national governing body for the sport, and run practices and competitions on various levels of skill. Most competitions are arranged by the clubs, and are USAG certified with USAG judges. These clubs and competitions not only offer young gymnasts the chance to learn and develop in the sport, but also the only real chance at making gymnastics their life's pursuit. It is through these competitions that the elite national gymnasts rise, soaring through the levels quickly and becoming groomed for the Olympic team at a very young age.

The sport of gymnastics provides many opportunities for girls as they advance into the school years. While the number of high schools that offer gymnastics as a sport are small compared to other sports, the interest is growing, and more schools are picking it up each year. Competing for the high-school team can be a wonderful experience for girls who have done well without excelling to elite status at the club level. Currently, eighty-eight colleges and universities offer gymnastics, with scholarships available in seventy-two of the schools. While competitive gymnastics careers very rarely continue after the college years, if your daughter truly loves the sport she may consider becoming a coach, trainer, or club operator. For more information, consult the USAG at www.usag.org.

Swimming

If you can never seem to get your daughter out of the tub, and she's always begging to go to the beach or town pool, then swimming might be the sport for her. Swimming is one of the best sports for building all-around athleticism. It provides a good heart/lung workout while working the legs, arms, chest, back, and abdominals. The term "swimmer's body" refers to the lean, muscular physique that swimmers build over time. Swimming also relies on quickness and endurance, so it is a great sport for girls who run around the house all day without ever seeming to tire out!

The Basics

The sport of swimming is one of the oldest and traditional in existence, and competitions have been held in every modern Olympics. Swimming is similar to gymnastics in that it is a sport that has traditionally been run through clubs, but is slowly making its way into the school athletic systems. Swimming gains its largest audience during the Summer Olympic games, when the attention of the world focuses on athletes trying to shatter world records and bring home the gold. U.S. swim stars such as Amy Van Dyken, Janet Evans, and Misty Hyman have made the sport one of the most popular for high-school girls.

How to Play

There are four basic strokes that are used in competitive swimming: freestyle, backstroke, breaststroke, and butterfly. *Freestyle*, also commonly called the "crawl," is perhaps the simplest of the four. It consists of the swimmer pulling her body through the water one arm at a time, using the "flutter" kick to propel herself forward. The swimmer turns her head to the side every few strokes in order to breathe. The *backstroke* is similar to freestyle in pull and kick, the major difference being that the swimmer is facing skyward with her face out of the water.

Breaststroke and *butterfly* are more advanced strokes in both style and execution. The breaststroke consists of the swimmer pulling herself forward using both arms at the same time, parting the water in front of her as if she were opening a set of curtains, with the swimmer coming up for breath with each stroke. The breaststroke kick, often called the "frog kick," is used when a swimmer opens and closes her legs in a scissor-like fashion. Butterfly is perhaps the most difficult of the strokes to learn. In butterfly, both arms are lifted out of the water in an arc and the swimmer pulls them back simultaneously to her sides. Typically, the swimmer will lift her head to breathe every two or three strokes. The "dolphin kick" is the dominant force of the butterfly, in which the swimmer keeps her legs held together and kicks with the whole of her legs from the waist.

The race begins with a signal, usually a tone or firing of a starter pistol, and the racers jump from a platform into the pool except in backstroke races, in which the racer starts the race in the water. Each swimmer advances down the length of the pool while staying within her own lane, which is designated by a floating, plastic barrier line. Races vary in length, anywhere from 50 to 1,500 meters. Depending on the size of the pool and the length of the race, the swimmers might be required to make one or several turns. For example, if a one hundred–meter race takes place in a pool fifty meters long, the swimmer must touch the wall upon reaching the end of the pool, turn around, and swim back to the other end to complete the required one hundred meters. There are different kinds of turns used with various strokes. The breaststroke and butterfly require that the racer touch the wall with two hands at a turn, while freestyle and backstoke turns require the swimmer to flip in the water and push off the wall with her legs. The swimmer must touch the wall to finish the race, and the first contestant to do so wins.

There are five different individual races. There is one race for each style of swimming (freestyle, breaststroke, butterfly, and backstroke), and a medley race, in which the swimmer uses all four styles equally over the course of the race (e.g., a two hundred–meter medley would require the swimmer to use the freestyle, breaststroke, butterfly, and backstroke for fifty meters each).

Relays are team races in which four swimmers work together to complete one race. In a relay race, each team member swims for the same distance (e.g., fifty meters each for a two hundred–meter relay). One teammate races at a time, and the next teammate may not enter the water until the previous racer has touched the wall. The race ends when the fourth teammate touches the wall, and the first team to do so wins. Relays can be either freestyle or medley. In a freestyle relay, all four swimmers swim according to freestyle rules. In a medley relay, all four styles are used in this order: the first swimmer uses the backstroke, the second uses the breaststroke, the third swims the butterfly, and the fourth finishes the race with the freestyle.

Get Her in the Game!

Your daughter's first exposure to the sport of swimming will be through swimming classes, which can start as young as six months, although the American Academy of Pediatrics recommends that children do not take swimming lessons until the age of four. Swimming lessons are offered through most Parks and Recreation Departments, as well as YMCAs, YWCAs, and Boys and Girls Clubs, as well as in school PE programs if the school is fortunate enough to have a pool. Here your daughter can progress from basic floating and treading water to learning the freestyle, breaststroke, butterfly, and backstroke.

As with gymnastics and tennis, most competitive youth swimming is run through the sport's national governing body, USA Swimming. By joining a local swim club that is a member of USA Swimming, your child can participate in competitions that can give her the chance to learn about and excel in her sport, and perhaps even earn a national ranking. Events are run on a local, national, and international basis, so the opportunities are endless. To find out more about these programs or to find one in your area, contact USA Swimming at www.usswim.org.

Swimming is also a favorite sport for high-school girls, with over 130,000 participants swimming in state-run meets each year. Because of the popularity of this sport, many high schools are building pools, and even schools that don't have pools are scheduling practice times at other schools or the town aquatic center. Swimming is also one of the top female collegiate sports, with over 450 colleges and universities sponsoring teams, and just over half of those schools offering scholarships to talented swimmers. While there is not much opportunity for professional swimming, extremely talented swimmers may be chosen to compete in national competitions such the Pan America games or the Olympics.

T-ball, Baseball, and Softball

Batter up! Softball, baseball, and T-ball are the three sports that make up the baseball "family," and are played by millions of children each year. These sports not only require athletic skill, but are fundamental in building the teamwork and strategic skills that athletes will carry with them into other sports, or higher levels of the game. These sports are great for any girl who enjoys playing with others, and using her brain as much as she uses her feet.

The Basics

Baseball is often referred to as America's "national pastime," and the nickname is well deserved. Legend has the sport being invented in 1839 by Abner Doubleday. Regardless of how or when it was invented, the variation of the popular British game cricket took America by storm, with the first official game being played in 1846. Baseball soon became the most widely played and traditional sport in the United States. Local baseball programs are popular with many kids, and thousands of girls are exposed to the sport through Little League programs in their towns.

Softball was invented in the late 1800s as an indoor version of baseball. It became popular as a competitive sport, and now ranks as one of the top sports played by young female athletes. Women's softball made its debut in the 1996 Olympics, and the U.S. team defended its gold medal in 2000, due to the talent of players such as Dot Richardson and Lisa Fernandez.

How to Play

The three sports of the baseball family are similar, but with slight variations. I will begin by describing the basic rules of T-ball, as this is the sport most girls begin with, and then explain the variations to the sport that make baseball and softball unique.

T-ball

Most children play T-ball from the ages of four to eight. In the game of T-ball, as in baseball, the field is arranged around four bases shaped in a diamond extended from home plate around first base, second base, and third base. This area is called the infield. Beyond the infield lies the outfield, which is an area extending from the infield to the home-run fence.

Each team bats once per inning. The team that is on offense sends a player "up to bat," and she stands in the batter's box near home plate. The other team is on defense, and all nine players are on the field in nine positions. All members of the defense must stand behind an imaginary line (or real line, if you chose you mark one) that runs between the first and third bases until the ball is hit. The defensive positions are as follows:

- Infield. The infield positions are played by four positions: first base, second base, and third base (each player positioning themselves near the named base), and shortstop, who covers the gap between second and third base.
- Outfield. The outfielders each cover a portion of the outfield area, sometimes indicated by the names of the positions (e.g., left field, center field, and right field).

Play begins with a ball set upon a tee at home plate. The batter may take swings at the ball until she hits the ball fair. If the batter hits the ball but it lands outside either of the foul lines (the lines that extends from home plate, through first base and third base, and extend to the home run fence), the ball is called foul and she is given another chance. If the player hits the ball onto the field (in T-ball, the ball must be hit at least ten feet), the ball is in "fair territory," and she attempts to advance to first base. The player will be called out if a defensive player catches the ball before it hits the ground; or if a player tags the base while holding the ball or tags the batter with the ball before she reaches the base. If the batter reaches base without being called out, she is "safe" and may not be tagged out as long as she remains on the base. The baserunner's goal is to score a run by making it back to home plate. To do this, she must advance through first, second, and third bases before returning home. She may advance as many bases at a time as possible, as long as she tags the bases and is not called out in the process.

When a player is on base, she can be called out in one of two ways. She can be tagged out, meaning that a defensive player touches her with the ball while she is off of a base. She can also be forced out. A player is forced out if the defensive player who has caught the ball steps on the bag she is advancing to and there are no open bases for her to retreat to. For example, if there are runners at first and second base and the ball is hit, the runners are forced to run to second and third base, respectively, in order to free first base for the batter. In this case, the fielder with the ball simply needs to step on third base before the runner gets there in order to "force" her out. However, if the runners were on second and third base, they do not have to advance on a hit, because first base is already open. Therefore, these runners cannot be forced out and must be tagged.

Each team continues batting until every player on the team has hit once. When this happens, the batting team takes their positions on the field and plays defense while the other team bats. When both teams have finished batting, the inning is over and a new inning begins. When the four innings have ended, the team with the most runs wins. If the teams are tied at the end of the game, the game remains a tie.

Little League Baseball

After the age of eight, many girls begin playing baseball through coed Little League teams. (Some towns do provide youth softball leagues as an alternative to Little League) In the game of baseball, nine players on each team play in an attempt to score the most runs over the course of nine "innings." (Nine is the official amount for professional games. The amount of innings played is determined by the age of the players.) The field is arranged in the same way as a T-ball field, except that there is no line between first and third behind which the players must stand. The main difference between T-ball and baseball is that, in baseball, the player does not hit the ball off of a tee, but must attempt to hit a pitch thrown by the other team's pitcher. As described later, a player may be called out if she is not able to hit the pitches after a certain number of tries.

The defensive positions in baseball are as follows:
- Pitcher (1). The pitcher stands on the pitcher's mound and pitches the ball to the batter.
- Catcher (1). The catcher stands crouches behind home plate and catches any pitch not hit into the infield by the batter.
- Infield (4). The infield positions are played by four positions: first base, second base, and third base (each player positioning

themselves near the named base), and shortstop, who covers the gap between second and third base.

- Outfield (3). The outfielders each cover one third of the outfield area, as indicated by the names of the positions: left field, center field, and right field.

The play begins when the pitcher pitches the ball to the batter. If the player does not hit the ball, the umpire may make one of two calls: 1) strike, indicating that the ball has crossed through the "strike zone," the imaginary region above home plate between the batter's knees and chest; or 2) ball, indicating that the pitch did not pass through the strike zone. If three strikes are called on the batter, she is out and her turn at bat is over. If four balls are called, the batter has been "walked," and proceeds to first base.

If the batter hits the ball, but it lands outside either of the foul lines (the lines that extends from home plate, through first base and third base, and extend to the home-run fence), the ball is called foul and the batter receives a strike. The only exception to this is that a player cannot strike out as a result of a foul ball. Therefore, if a batter has two strikes and hits a foul ball, it does not count as a strike.

If the player hits the ball onto the field in "fair territory," she attempts to advance through the bases in the same way as she would in T-ball. If the batter hits the ball over the home-run fence in fair territory, she has hit a "home run" and is allowed free passage around the bases, scoring a run for herself and any other players already on base.

Each team continues batting until it gets three outs. When this happens, the batting team takes their positions on the field and plays defense while the other team bats. When both teams have finished batting, the inning is over and a new inning begins. Professional baseball teams play nine innings, high-school softball teams play seven innings, and the number decreases in youth play. When the agreed-upon number of innings have ended, the team with the most runs wins. If the teams are tied at the end of the game, they play "extra" innings until one team ends an inning with more runs than the other. (For younger children, a tie game should simply be called a tie.)

Because baseball is such a strategic sport and has been in existence for so many years, the rules of the sport are numerous, fascinating, and cover almost every possible scenario that can happen on the baseball field. For a complete listing of the rules of baseball, consult www.mlb.com/NAS-App/mlb/mlb/baseball_basics/mlb_basics_foreward.jsp.

Softball

After they advance beyond Little League play, usually during junior high, softball becomes the "baseball family" sport of choice for young girls. Softball is played much like baseball with some key differences. Softball is played not with a nine-inch ball like baseball, but with a twelve- or sixteen-inch ball. Softball teams are made up of ten players instead of nine, with the extra player covering an area of the outfield. Each softball game is made up of seven innings instead of nine (again, this number can be reduced for younger players). Another key factor is that a softball field is smaller than a baseball field. A softball field has bases placed sixty-five feet apart as opposed to ninety feet in baseball, and the pitcher's mound is fifty feet away from home plate, as opposed to 60.5 in baseball. In the youth leagues, every field is smaller than regulation, and it is likely that baseball and softball games will be played on the same field. Finally, in softball, the pitcher must pitch with an underhand motion, as opposed to the overhand motion used in baseball. While this results in slower pitching than can be found in the elite leagues of baseball, talented softball pitchers can still fire the ball across the plate at impressive speeds.

Get Her in the Game!

Most girls begin their baseball/softball "career" by playing T-ball, and then advancing to baseball through Little League play. These leagues are normally run by a town's Parks and Recreation Department, and provide kids with a fun environment in which to learn the basics of this complex sport. T-ball and Little League teams are usually coed, but some larger towns may have single-sex leagues. If your town participates in the PONY (Protecting Our Nation's Youth) program, your daughter may have the opportunity to play softball as young as six years old. (To find out more about the PONY program, visit www.pony.org.) If this is an option, you can decide together which sport she would rather play at this young age.

Upon reaching middle school, most girls begin playing softball, as offered through their school's athletic program. Most junior high schools and high schools do not have baseball teams for girls, but if your daughter wishes to play baseball instead of softball, encourage her to try out for the boys' team. If she does want to play softball, the options should be numerous. Fast-pitch softball is the fourth most popular girls' sport in high school, with more than 325,000 girls playing the game each year, according to the National Federation of State High School Associations. If your daughter has her eye toward playing in college, she'll be glad to know that softball is one of the most popular female collegiate sports. Softball is sponsored by almost nine hundred colleges and universities, and over five hundred of those schools offer softball scholarships. Professional leagues, such as the Women's Professional Softball League and the American Women's Baseball League, offer career opportunities for the country's best female softball and baseball players.

Softball is also one of the most popular adult recreational activities, and amateur softball leagues are run almost year-round across the country. If your daughter's love for the sport sticks throughout her life, she will have plenty of opportunity to play as an adult, even if its not in front of a crowd of thousands.

Figure Skating

Figure skating is an extremely popular sport among young girls. Figure skating was the first sport that I ever pursued. I began in the fourth grade and still love it today; but I always skated purely for fun, not for competition. Girls who enjoy and find success in figure skating tend to be determined and focused, and able to put up with stress. If your daughter is interested in figure skating, and you can afford it (rink time and lessons can be very costly!), help her pursue her interest. The sport of figure skating builds strength and discipline, as well as excellent balance. Devotees can skate well into old age and enjoy all the health benefits that it offers.

The Basics

The "birth" of modern competitive figure skating goes back to Jackson Haines, an American who lived during the Civil War era and revolutionized the sport by adding elements of dance, music, and expression. Although it took many years, Haines's new style took hold, and figure skating made its debut in the Olympics in 1908. Like gymnastics, figure skating combines elements of strength and artistry as the participants glide, dance, jump, and spin across the ice.

Also like gymnastics, figure skating draws most of its popularity from the success of its Olympic stars, such as Peggy Fleming, Dorothy Hamill, Kristi Yamaguchi, Tara Lipinski, and Michelle Kwan, most of whom go on to star professionally in tours and made-for-TV events. The World Figure Skating Championships are another high-profile event that capture worldwide attention and help set the stage for the skating fever that takes over during the Olympics. Figure skating ranks as the female sport with the highest-rated television viewership, and this popularity encourage thousands of girls to lace up a pair of skates and take a shot at landing a flawless double axel!

How to Play

There are two common types of figure skating competitions: singles and pairs events. Both types provide a lot of opportunity to develop skill. We will begin by looking at the singles event.

Singles

A singles figure-skating competition is divided into two programs, a short program and a long program, in which the skater performs a routine set to music. In the short program, the skater must perform a series of required maneuvers that include jumps, spins, and footwork moves known as "steps." The various moves have exotic names such as axel, camel, lutz, and salchow. (For a further explanation of these and other figure-skating terms, consult www.hickoksports.com/glossary/gfigurs.shtml.) The performance is scored by a judge or panel of judges on a scale of zero to six, with six being the highest. Each performance receives two scores: a technical score based on how well and controlled the jumps, spins, and other maneuvers are executed, and a presentation score, which focuses on how fluent, choreographed, and expressive the routine is.

The long program, often known the "free skate," allows the skater to choose the elements that they include in the program. The long program is scored with the same system as the short program, but more attention is paid to the presentation portion of the routine, including its originality. The long program is traditionally the more popular of the two programs because it allows the skater more artistic expression, and usually includes maneuvers that are more complicated than those performed in the short program.

Pairs

In pairs skating, the female skater is paired with a male skater, and the two perform a routine together. The key to this competition is for the two skaters to present a routine that seems smooth and unified, even when the two skaters are performing different maneuvers. As with singles skating, the pairs competition features jumps, spins, and steps, most often done simultaneously by the two skaters. The main difference is the joint maneuvers, in which the two partners work together to create one maneuver. The most common of these are the lift, in which the male skater lifts the female skater off of the ice, and an assisted jump, in which the male skater helps the female skater jump higher in the air to perform more complicated spins than she could on her own. Pairs skating competitions include short and long programs similar to singles competitions, except that the judges pay special attention to the harmony between the two skaters over the course of the routine.

For more information on how figure-skating competitions are run, consult the United States Figure Skating Association (USFSA) at www.usfsa.com.

Get Her in the Game!

Ice skating can be an enjoyable family activity all year round if you live near an indoor rink with public skating hours. The easiest way to start is to go to the rink during these hours, put yourself and your little one into a pair of skates, and hold her as you both glide around the rink. With a little practice, your daughter will soon let go of your grasp and take off on her own. If you've never learned to skate, join your daughter for a few group lessons. If you find that your family enjoys this activity, you can look into the expense of season passes and owning your own skates. Some sports stores that operate inside the rink will allow you to buy used skates and trade in children's skates as they grow.

If your daughter is interested in competitive figure skating, it is important to know that this can be one of the most demanding of sports. Like gymnastics, most of the training is expensive, time consuming, and difficult to find unless you live in an urban or suburban area. Unlike gymnastics, there is rarely an opportunity to participate in figure skating through school-sponsored programs.

Figure-skating lessons and competitions are available mainly through local ice rinks or figure-skating clubs. Ice rinks offer lessons and competitions through the Ice Skating Institute (ISI). ISI competitions are recreational in nature, and open to anyone who wishes to participate, regardless of skill. These competitions are ideal for girls who are more interested in the sport as a hobby or recreational activity, and aren't as competitive.

Girls who demonstrate talent and a love for the sport, and wish to compete on a more elite level, do so through competitions sanctioned by the United States Figure Skating Association (USFSA). USFSA competitions are club based, meaning that the competitors are drawn from figure-skating clubs that operate as teams, requiring commitment to the club from its members. So while the sport can be demanding and expensive on an elite level, figure skating offers a wealth of opportunity for young women, and is a worthwhile activity even just for fun.

Soccer

Soccer is a wonderful sport for girls who love to be active and enjoy working in groups—with eleven players on a team soccer is the ultimate team sport! Your daughter is more likely to enjoy soccer if she enjoys being outside and doesn't mind getting hot, sweaty, and dirty! Soccer is an excellent way to build heart/lung endurance and helps girls develop the type of strategic and analytic skills that are necessary in all team sports.

Soccer is a physically demanding game that is also a lot of fun for its participants because all the players get to participate equally. More and more opportunities are becoming available for women to play soccer after they have graduated from high school and college. Recreational leagues—both coed and single-sex—are springing up around the United States.

The Basics

Soccer, known as football in countries outside of the United States, is the world's most popular sport, and is one of the most popular youth sports in the United States. The American Youth Soccer Organization reports that over 650,000 children are currently playing soccer. Modern soccer was developed in Great Britain, and established itself in the United States due largely to the success of youth soccer programs.

While soccer has always been a popular sport for girls because of the wide availability of its programs, interest in the sport has boomed in recent years thanks to the thrilling success of the U.S. Women's Soccer team. In 1999, the U.S. Women's team, led by Mia Hamm and Brandi Chastain, captured the attention of their country as they advanced through the World Cup tournament. On July 10, an estimated forty million viewers tuned in to see Chastain score a game-winning goal to defeat China and give the U.S. Women's team its second-ever World Cup title. The event not only made stars of the U.S. players and generated an upsurge in soccer participation, but it is regarded by some as one of the most important moments in U.S. women's sports history.

How to Play

Soccer is played on an outdoor, rectangular grass field that varies in length based on the age group of the players. A goal is located at each end of the field, and the objective of the players is to move the ball into their opponent's goal. The defining aspect of soccer is that the players, with the exception of the goalkeeper (also known as the goalie), are not allowed to touch the ball with their hands. They must move the ball up the field using their feet, and may also hit the ball with their chest or head if desired. The goalie is allowed to use her hands to stop the ball and return it to play, as long as she is within the goal area, which is defined by a white line known as the goal line. The only time that a player besides the goalie may use her hands is if she is throwing the ball back onto the field after it has been knocked out of bounds.

Each team fields players in the following positions: defenders, midfielders, forwards, and one goalie. The goalie's duty is to protect the goal and try to stop the ball from entering. The goalie usually wears a differently colored shirt from the rest of the team to distinguish her position. The defenders mostly remain on the same side of the field as their own goal, and focus on trying to stop the opposing team from scoring on their goal. The midfields are positioned in the middle of the field, and assist the offensive or defensive end, depending on where the ball is on the field. The forwards mostly remain on the opposing side of the field and focus on trying to score points by kicking or heading the ball into the opposing goal. Each goal is worth one point.

Penalties are given in soccer for rules violations such as tripping, running into an opponent, or touching the ball with your hands. If a player is penalized, the opposing team is given either a free kick or an indirect free kick, depending on the severity of the penalty. In either case, the opposing players must stay ten yards away from the kicker until the ball has been touched. In a free kick, the kicker may attempt to score a goal, while in an indirect kick, the ball must be fielded by another player after the kick before a goal can be attempted.

Soccer games are played in two halves, and the team with the highest score at the end of the time limit wins. Each half lasts anywhere from twenty to sixty minutes, depending on the age and skill level of the players. If the teams are tied when the time ends, an overtime period may be played, or the game may be declared a tie. Various factors of the game such as field length and width, number of players on the field, use of goalies, and the height and width of the goal can be modified to best suit the age of the players. While each local league will most likely apply their own set of standards, a set of guidelines has been issued by the American Youth Soccer Organization, and can be found at their website at www.soccer.org.

Get Her in the Game!

Soccer is one of the first sports that children play, starting as young as age four, through youth soccer programs that are widely available through from Parks and Recreation Departments. These leagues offer numerous options and opportunities for young girls interested in sports. Starting with beginner leagues and moving through to high school, girls have the chance to play soccer almost all year-round, with Parks and Recreation leagues and town-sponsored, "advanced," traveling teams. Girls can even head off to soccer camps, where they can hone their skills while making great friends and having lots of fun. The American Youth Soccer Organization (AYSO) is one of the nation's largest supporters of youth soccer, and promotes leagues and camps across the country. For more information about the soccer teams in your area, contact your local Parks and Recreations Department, or the AYSO at www.soccer.org.

Older girls become focused on their school's soccer team. Soccer is the fifth most popular high school sport for girls, with almost 275,000 participants each year. Competitions are run by the state through regional conferences, with the ultimate goal of capturing the state title. As she moves on to college, your daughter will find that there are over 850 colleges and universities sponsoring women's soccer teams, with scholarships available at 480 of the schools. For the elite soccer star, the WUSA, a women's professional soccer league, held its inaugural season in 2001. And of course, she can try to for a spot on the U.S. women's team for a chance to take home a gold medal and inspire a whole new generation of female soccer players.

Bowling

Everyone grab your favorite bowling shirt and hit the lanes! If your daughter is interested in sports but is intimidated because she's not as athletic as her peers, then bowling can provide a great alternative to traditional competitive sports. Bowling is a game that takes strategic skills and relies heavily on hand-eye coordination. Bowling leagues are common across the country, and many schools offer this sport as an afterschool activity.

The Basics

Although there are professional leagues for men and women, most girls are more familiar with bowling because of its popularity as a recreational activity. Bowling is a common way for families to get out of the house and spend some time together. Many adults participate in amateur bowling leagues, sharing their enthusiasm with their children. With the invention of "bumper bowling," in which bumpers are placed in the gutters so that any ball veering off of the lane is knocked back toward the pins, even young children can get into the action and knock down a strike!

How to Play

In the game of bowling, the player rolls a ball down a hardwood lane in an attempt to knock down ten pins set up at the end of the lane. The lane is sixty feet long and coated with a thin layer of oil to reduce traction as the ball travels toward the pins. Each game is played over ten "frames." At the start of each frame, the bowler rolls the ball down the lane, attempting to knock down the pins located at the end of the lane. If the ball stays on the lane for its entire length, it will connect with one or more of the pins, and knock them over. If the ball does not stay on the lane, it rolls into the "gutter," a smoothed-out trench that carries the ball past the pins without knocking them down. If the bowler does not knock down all of the pins of the first throw, she is given a second roll at the remaining pins. After the second shot, the frame is over.

The bowler receives one point for each pin knocked down in the frame. If the bowler knocks down all of the pins on the first roll of the frame, it is called a "strike," indicated by an "X" on the scoring sheet, and her frame is over. When a player gets a strike, she receives ten points for the frame plus however many points she scores in the next frame. So, if she rolls a strike in the first frame and knocks down eight pins in the second frame, she receives eighteen points for the first frame and eight points for the second frame, for a total of twenty-six. If the bowler does not knock down all of the pins on the first throw, but does knock down all of the remaining pins on the second throw, it is called a "spare," indicated by a "/" on the scoring sheet. When the bowler gets a spare, she gets ten points for the frame plus however many points are scored on the *first* throw of the next frame. For example, if she rolls a spare in the first frame and a nine in the second frame, five on the first throw and four on the second, she receives fifteen points for the first frame and nine points for the second frame, for a total of twenty-four.

Whew! Now that you have that down, there is little else to understand about bowling. The bowlers play for ten frames. On the tenth frame, if the bowler rolls a strike, she is given two extra throws, and if she rolls a spare she is given one extra throw. When all the frames are complete, the player with the highest score wins. The highest possible score is 300, known as a "perfect game," but it takes years of practice to achieve such an honor.

Get Her in the Game!

Bowling is a fun and inexpensive sport to get your daughter involved in. Almost every community has a local bowling alley, or one close by. Bowling is a popular activity for every youth program, so young girls get a lot of unorganized exposure to the sport. If she's interested in competitive play, her best option is to join a youth league. Youth bowling leagues are run much like adult bowling leagues: competitive but friendly, and organized by the bowling alley or town recreation department. Lessons are offered through the league or through bowling professionals. Contact your local bowling alley to find out more about the options available to you in your area.

While most junior highs and high schools do not offer bowling as a sponsored team sport, many run bowling clubs as a recreational, after-school activity. The opportunities for collegiate play are also not great for female bowlers—only thirty-nine colleges and universities sponsor teams (but thirty-eight do offer scholarships). If your daughter excels in bowling and is thinking of going pro, she should consider joining the Professional Women's Bowling Association (PWBA). Members must maintain a 180 (190 for national play) average and pay an annual membership fee to join. Joining the PWBA allows her to try to qualify for and win professional bowling tournaments. For more information, visit www.pwba.com.

Martial Arts

The martial arts require speed, agility, and mental sharpness. They provide a great way to develop the body and mind, emphasizing confidence, concentration, and self-discipline. The martial arts also promote athleticism, and many girls who participate in these sports count the philosophies and character-building traits of the sport as a major part of their interest. Girls of any age, size, or shape can excel in the martial arts, so they are a great option for young girls or older girls who have had less success with other sports. However, the martial arts require a lot of practice to master, so the athlete must be dedicated and patient. While the martial arts do offer competitions, the emphasis is on mind-body development, not winning a match.

The Basics

The martial arts originated in Asian countries, such as Japan and Korea, as self-defense and meditation systems. They involve kicking, punching, and tossing an opponent using a variety of fascinating motions. The martial arts remain an important cultural and traditional part of these countries, and are practiced by millions of people around the world. The martial arts slowly made their way into the United States, but truly boomed in interest after the release of the popular *Karate Kid* movies. These movies drove hundreds of kids to the local YMCA or training facility to try to learn to kick and move like the Karate Kid, and the interest has remained as strong, if not as feverish, up to today. While some high schools and colleges offer competitive martial arts, these sports are mostly run through local recreational programs or training facilities—businesses that specifically operate to run martial arts lessons and leagues.

As children progress in their training, they test for and earn different-colored belts. Many programs start with a white belt and progress to the famed black belt, although the actual colors of the belts may differ depending on the training facility your child goes to or the type of martial art that your child participates in. Each level of belt requires the child to learn different kicks, blocks, and forms (a series of movements performed together). Advancing in her belts can be highly motivating and exciting for your daughter.

How to Play

The two most common martial arts are tae kwon do and karate. The following section gives a brief explanation of each of these arts and how their competitions are run.

Tae Kwon Do

In tae kwon do, the object is to score points by making controlled kicks or punches to certain spots on the opponent's body, such as the midsection or face. The disciplined punches and spinning kicks are the highlight of this sport. Competitions involve two contestants of the same weight class. The two contestants start in the middle of a twelve-meter by twelve-meter mat, and begin at the referee's signal. They attempt to score points on their opponent while stopping the opponent's attempts to score point on them. Penalties can be assessed for illegal hits or unsportsmanlike behavior. At the end of a predetermined time limit, the match is ended and the contestant with the most points wins.

Karate

Karate competitions consist of two different types: kumite and kata. A kumite competition is much like a tae kwon do competition, in that two contestants try to score points by making controlled punches and kicks to certain parts of their opponent's body. In karate, the goal is to score a *sanbon* (six points) by scoring a combination of *ippons* (single points) and *waza-ari* (half-points). Ippons and waza-ari are given by the referee based on how well the moves are executed. The first contestant to reach sanbon wins. If no contestant has reached sanbon by the end of the time limit, the one with the most points wins the match. In kata competitions, the contestants perform a series of moves by themselves, displaying the techniques as if they were actually in combat. This competition is judged based on the execution of the moves performed.

Get Her in the Game!

For a young girl who wants to learn a roundhouse kick, her main option is to take lessons at a martial arts training facility. Training facilities can be found in most towns, and if there is not one in your town there is most likely one a neighboring town or county. However, martial arts lessons can be expensive, and children can be known to lose interest after the fees have been paid. Some Parks and Recreation Departments have martial arts classes that run for a limited time and only cover a certain set of skills. If this option is available, I suggest that you enroll your daughter in one or several Parks and Recreation classes first to gauge her interest. If she enjoys the martial arts and wants to continue her training, you can then make the commitment to enroll her at the local training facility.

While competition is not the main focus of the martial arts, competitions are often offered by training facilities through local associations and clubs. Your local training facility can provide more information on the tournaments and types of competitions available in your area. The Amateur Athletic Union also offers regional, national, and Junior Olympic tournaments for karate, tae kwon do, and other martial arts. To find out more about these competitions, log on to www.aau.org.

Golf

Golf is the perfect sport for a girl who is patient, dedicated, and who prefers a slower pace. As golf is for the most part an individual sport, it is also a great activity for girls who are are independent or prefer working by themselves.

Golf can be costly, as the equipment, course fees, and lessons can be quite expensive. The time commitment is also considerable—an eighteen-hole round of golf can take up to five hours to play. However, if your daughter is truly motivated to take up this sport, the investment is well worth it. Since golf is a sport that can be played by people of any age or size, the golf clubs you buy her today can open the door to a sport she can play for life. In fact, you may want to get the whole family on the course for some real quality time away from the phone or TV.

The Basics

Although golf began as a sport played mainly in Scotland, its popularity has swept the world, and you can now find people playing golf in almost every country. While high schools and colleges provide excellent golf programs, the sport gets most of its recognition from the two major professional leagues, the PGA and the LPGA. The LPGA was established in 1950, and continues as one of the most successful professional women's sports leagues today. Although Tiger Woods has clearly been a major golf role model for both genders , top female stars like Nancy Lopez, Karrie Webb, and Annika Sorenstam inspire many girls to take up the sport.

Girls' interest in golf is also encouraged by the fact that so many adults play the sport in their free time. If you enjoy playing golf, you can start your daughter off by taking her with you to the course and showing her how to play. If you don't know how to play, now is the time to learn! Becoming a golf enthusiast can be something that you and your daughter share.

How to Play

The object of golf is to strike a small ball over a certain distance, getting the ball into a hole in the ground with as few swings as possible. You strike the ball by hitting it with a golf club, which has a long handle reaching to the ground and is capped off by a striking surface, called the "head" of the club. Golfers carry a variety of clubs with them, each of which is designed to hit the ball for certain distances. *Woods* are clubs with a large head that hit the ball for long distances. *Irons* are clubs with a thin head that hit the ball for less distance than woods, but make more accurate shots. The higher the number on the club, the less distance it will hit the ball (e.g., a 3-iron will hit the ball farther than a 7-iron).

You strike the ball by swinging the club at it and launching the ball into the air and down the course. The mechanics of a good swing is a subject far too detailed to go into here, and something with which every golfer will struggle throughout her life. Many books on golf technique can be found at your local library or bookstore.

Each hole starts with a tee box and ends with a cup placed somewhere in the surface of the putting green. The tee box is the designated area from which the golfer must take her first shot. The putting green is an area of closely cut grass surrounding the cup (hole) that allows the golfer to make smaller, more accurate hits of the ball with a putter. The distance from the tee box to the hole location is most often different at each hole, and the hole is assigned a "par" value depending on its length. Par refers to how many strokes it should take to put the ball into the cup, assuming that two strokes are taken on the putting green. The longer the distance from the tee box to the green, the higher the par. Putting the ball in the cup in one less stroke than par is known as a "birdie" and doing so in one more stroke than par is called a "bogey." If you put the ball in the cup on the first shot (tee shot), you have scored a hole-in-one, although usually only the luckiest or most skilled of golfers ever get to experience that thrill.

There are different surfaces or obstacles that the golfer can encounter on the way from the tee box to the putting green. The most pleasant of these is the fairway, which is a mown section of grass from which it is easiest to make a shot. Surrounding the fairway is the rough, which has higher grass that is harder to hit out of, and sometimes trees that can get in the way of the shot. Sand traps, also know as bunkers, are patches of sand that slow down the impact of the club on the ball. The most daunting of golf obstacles are the water hazards—lakes or streams placed on the course. If a player hits their ball into a water hazard, they receive a one-stroke penalty and must hit the ball again from a spot behind the water hazard.

A round of golf commonly consists of eighteen holes, although younger children will need to play less. The game is scored in one of two ways: stroke play or match play. In stroke play, the player who took the least number of strokes over the course of the round wins the game. In match play, the person who scores the lowest score on each hole receives one point, and the person who has the most points at the end of the round wins the game, regardless of how many total strokes were played.

There are many intricate and fascinating rules of golf, and someone could make a hobby just out of trying to learn all of them! For more information on how to play golf, consult your local golf professional or www.lpga.com.

Get Her in the Game!

Getting your daughter involved in golf at a young age is fairly easy—taking for granted that you have one or several public golf courses in your area. If not, then it may be very difficult for your daughter to be able to practice the necessary amount (although, she can always work on her swing at a driving range or her putting on a practice putting green). But if you do have access to a golf course, all you need to do is get hold of a set of clubs, take her to the course, and either get her lessons or teach her yourself. Golf is a unique sport because it is an individual game, and therefore, for the most part, self-competitive. Most golfers play the game with the eternal goal of improving their own score, not to come out ahead of a competitor. Therefore, your daughter can play for years without any need of a league or team to join. Be aware that golf equipment and greens fees are very expensive; and you must make sure that her clubs are the appropriate length and weight for your child, which may mean repeated purchases of new equipment as she grows. The more that your daughter becomes involved in golf, the more expensive it will be for you.

Sometimes competition can help drive your golfer, especially if she is excelling in the sport and is looking for other players to challenge and motivate her to improve. There are a great number of youth golf programs available. Visit www.juniorlinks.com to learn more about youth golf programs and to search for programs in your community. Some high schools do offer golf programs, but golfers who wish to compete for a school team will have their most luck on the collegiate level, where over four hundred colleges and universities field female golf teams, and about three hundred of them offer golf athletic scholarships. Around 120 golf scholarships for women went unclaimed in 1998, so this is an area with a great deal of opportunity. To pursue these scholarships, contact the colleges and universities that you are interested in to see if they offer them, or call the NCAA for a complete listing of all schools that offer women's golf scholarships.

When people think of professional golfers, they most often think of the pro tournaments. However, many golf professionals earn their living not on "the tour," but in the town. Golf professionals work at golf courses across the country, promoting the game and giving lessons to help amateur golfers improve their game. So, even if your daughter doesn't win the U.S. Open, her love of golf might lead her to a successful and rewarding career as a golf pro.

Tennis

Learning tennis can teach your daughter good footwork as well as throwing and striking skills. Because tennis isn't a team sport (though most community programs are done in groups), tennis might be an option if your daughter is quite independent. Learning tennis can be a challenge because it is a subtle combination of skill and power, but your daughter might find it easy to pick up this sport if she is patient and has some mastery of basic motor skills such as throwing and striking. My kids are still small, but they like trying to hit the tennis ball with a racquetball racquet (make sure little kids use a youth racquet!).

Remember that no matter what caliber a tennis player your daughter is, she can get plenty of fun and fitness benefits out of this sport all her life.

The Basics

Tennis is one of the oldest sports, dating back before Renaissance times. (Tennis balls even play a prominent role in the plot of Shakespeare's *Henry V*!) The first women's tennis championship, the Lawn Tennis Championships, was held in 1884 at the All England Croquet and Lawn Tennis Club. This tournament is known today as the Wimbledon Championships, and is the most prestigious of tennis tournaments. Today, tennis is one of the most prolific women's sports, and is played on every level, from youth to professional leagues.

Professional women's tennis is rare in that it is the sport in which the women's competition is as popular and respected as the men's. From Billie Jean King's defeat of Bobbie Riggs in the "Battle of the Sexes" to top tennis stars such as Chris Evert, Jennifer Capriati, and Venus and Serena Williams, female tennis players have proven countless times through the years that the sport of women's tennis is one of the most exciting to watch.

How to Play

The game of tennis is played in two versions: singles and doubles. For the sake of clarity, I will describe how tennis is played in terms of the singles game, and then briefly describe how the rules of the doubles version vary significantly from the singles version.

Tennis is usually played on a cement court seventy-eight feet long by twenty-seven feet wide. (Some tennis courts are also made of grass or clay, but this is somewhat rare and is not something your daughter is likely to encounter outside of the elite levels.) Across the center of the court, a net is suspended that is thirty-six inches high at the center. Each player stands on opposite sides of the net, and attempts to hit the ball with their racquet onto their opponent's side of the court without the ball being returned.

The ball is put into play by a serve. The player who is serving stands behind the baseline of their side of the court and attempts to hit the ball over the net into a box created by the lengthwise center of the court and the service line, a line that extends twenty-one feet from the net. The server must alternate from which side of the court they hit the ball, and serve into the box on the opponent's opposite side.

If the serve is successful, the ball is in play and is hit back and forth between the players until one player either hits the ball out of bounds or fails to return the ball legally to their opponent's side of the court. When this occurs, the opponent receives a point, and play is continued with another serve.

If the server fails to serve the ball into the box, or breaks one of the rules through an infraction such as stepping over the baseline, it is called a "fault," and the server must try again. If the server faults twice, the opponent receives a point and a new serving set begins. If the server hits the net on the serve but the ball still goes into the correct box, it is called a "let" and is not counted as a serve or a fault.

Each game is scored by a system of points. The point system is quite different from normal scoring, and although there are many theories, no one knows quite for sure where it originated. Each player starts with zero, known as "love," from the French word *l'oeuf* for "egg." The next point is fifteen, followed by thirty, then forty. If a player scores a point when they have forty, they have won "game point," and therefore won the game. The only exception to this rule is if both players have forty. In tennis, you must win by two points, and therefore when both players have forty they are said to be at "deuce." From deuce, a player must win two consecutive points to win the game. Whoever wins the first point is at "advantage." If they win the next point they win the game; if not, the players return to deuce and try again. It sounds complicated, but you get the hang of it after watching just a few games!

Yet, winning a game is not enough to seal a victory. Tennis is played in a series of sets. For adults, a set is won by being the first player to win at least six games and by a two-game margin. If a set is tied at six-six, then a tiebreaker game is played in which a player wins by being the first to score at least seven points while holding a two-point margin. The first player to win two sets wins the match. For younger players, the amount of games that must be won to win a set or the amount of sets that are played may be reduced. The length of the game will be determined by the club or competition in which your daughter is playing.

In doubles tennis, two players play as a team against two other players. For doubles play, the court is widened to thirty-six feet and the teammates alternate serving. However, teammates do not have to alternate hitting the ball once it is in play.

Get Her in the Game!

If your daughter wants to serve up some aces or develop her backhand, there are many opportunities for her to learn the game of tennis. Most town Parks and Recreation Departments offer introductory tennis lessons, where your daughter can try her hand at the sport and see if it is right for her. If she really enjoys the sport and wants to continue playing at a higher level, the cost of lessons increases and it may become more difficult to find a qualified coach. The Untied States Tennis Association (USTA) is the major governing body for tennis in the United States, and runs youth programs that include competitions and national ranking systems. Elite tennis athletes can gain national exposure through this system. By contacting the USTA at www.usta.com, you can find out more information about certified coaches and programs in your area.

Tennis is also a traditional favorite for school-age girls. Ranking sixth, just below soccer, among the most popular girls' sports in high school, tennis draws over 160,000 participants each year, according to the National Federation of State High School Associations. Just under nine hundred colleges and universities offer women's tennis as a collegiate sport, with scholarships available at over five hundred of the schools. Most colleges and universities that don't sponsor tennis programs do offer it as a club sport. Professional tennis players are ranked by the World Tennis Association (WTA), and play in a tournament season that includes such major championships such as the U.S. Open, Wimbledon, and the Australian Open.

Catching the tennis bug can give your daughter a fulfilling activity for life. The USTA program called USA League Tennis runs adult recreational leagues across the country, and even hosts regional and national championships. In fact, as your daughter picks up this great sport, perhaps you can get into the game yourself!

Track & Field/Cross-Country

Track & field is an excellent sport for any girl who is quick, strong and agile, or has bottomless endurance. This sport builds excellent heart/lung endurance and develops strong, toned muscles. Track & field works to create and celebrate the all-around athlete, so any girl interested in sports would benefit by taking a run around the track or tossing the discus down the field. Cross-country, track & field's tough-minded cousin, is a perfect fit for girls who prefer to run long distances.

The Basics

Track & field events have been around since the earliest days of sports. These events made up most of the original Olympic games, and are based on the fundamental athletic skills: running, jumping, and throwing. Track & field gains its greatest recognition during the Olympics, producing such stars as Florence Griffith-Joyner and Marion Jones. The World Championships are also a big draw, and set the stage for the Summer Olympics. Track & field is also popular because of its wide availability in school athletic programs. Most schools offer competitive track teams starting as young as junior high, with excellent programs in high schools. As a result, girls start running at a young age, and therefore track & field and cross-country running have become two of the most popular sports for young female athletes.

How to Play—Track & Field

To best describe the sport of track & field, let's look at its two components separately.

Track

Track events involve races in which the contestants run for a certain distance, with the best time winning the race. Races for distances less than four hundred meters are called sprints. In sprints, the focus of the runner is on running as quickly as possible for the entire race. Sprints are best suited for quick and powerful runners. Races over four hundred meters are called long-distance races. Long-distance races call for the runners to be quick, but also to set a proper pace so as not to tire out too early in the race. Long-distance races are run from eight hundred meters up to two miles.

Races are also run in team format, know as relays. In a relay, four runners form a team that works together to complete a race, with each one covering one-fourth of the total distance. The first runner begins the race holding a baton. She runs down the track toward the spot where the second runner is positioned. Once she reaches her, the first runner must pass the baton to the second runner before the new runner can continue the race. This method is continued until the last runner has the baton and races to the finish line.

One of the most interesting track events is the hurdles. In the hurdles, obstacles are placed on the track over which the runners must jump while racing toward the finish line. The runners must jump over the hurdle, but are not penalized for unintentionally knocking one over. Hurdle races may be run as singles or relay events. Steeplechase events have hurdles and water jumps, but these races are not commonly run at the high school level or below.

Field

Field events are a collection of competitions that involve either throwing or jumping. The following is a brief explanation of the different field events:

- High Jump. In the high jump, the contestant tries to jump over a bar placed at a specific height, landing on a mat on the other side. The contestant who clears the highest setting of the bar without knocking it off wins.
- Long Jump. In this event, the long jumper runs toward a sand pit, and must jump from behind a board and try to land in the pit as far from the board as possible. Her landing point is marked by the impression that she leaves in the sand. The jumper who jumps the longest distance wins.
- Triple Jump. This event is similar to the long jump, except that instead of one long jump, the triple jumper makes three landings. After jumping from the board, she must land on the same foot from which she jumped, take a step with her other foot, and then jump

for one final time. The final landing point is marked and the jumper with the farthest final distance wins.

- Pole Vault. The pole vault is similar to the high jump in that the contestant is attempting to clear a bar set at a certain height without knocking it over. However, unlike the high jump, the pole vaulter runs toward the bar and springs herself up into the air by bending the pole and using its force to reach great heights. The pole vaulter who clears the highest setting wins.
- Shot Put. A shot putter starts off within a circled area holding a metal ball weighing 8.8 pounds. She must start with the ball in her hand atop her shoulder. She then tosses the shot onto the field as far as possible. The farthest throw wins.
- Discus. The discus event is much like the shot put except that instead of a metal ball, the contestant throws a discus (shaped somewhat like a frisbee). Most discus throwers will spin their body as they throw to maximize the force they generate.

How to Play—Cross-Country

Cross-country involves a running race, but is run on an outdoor, natural-terrain course as opposed to a track. All of the contestants run in the same race, with a distance longer than that of track events. For high school girls, the distance is usually just over two miles, but it varies depending on the terrain of the course. The order in which each runner finishes (places) is worth a certain number of points, and the point totals of the members of each team are added up to determine the team total. The team with the highest score at the end of the race wins the meet.

Get Her in the Game!

Running is something that comes naturally to children, and any parent can attest that you don't have to teach your daughter how to scamper around the house all day. However, she will probably not be exposed to organized track & field or cross-country until she reaches the junior high level. From there, though, her opportunities mushroom. Track & field and cross-country are offered at almost every junior high school, high school, college, and university. Track & field is the second most popular girls' high school sport, with over 400,000 girls lacing up their track shoes each year, and cross-country ranks seventh on the list, drawing more than 150,000 girls out for all-terrain races. Track & field scholarships are offered at six hundred colleges and universities, with scholarships available at more than four hundred of them. Cross-country is sponsored by more than nine hundred colleges, with scholarships available at more than half of those schools.

If your daughter excels in the sport at a young age, or is looking for a field of competition outside of school, then you should look into the competitions run by USA Track & Field. USA Track & Field is the national governing body for track & field, long-distance running, and race walking, and is the organization that runs the Olympic team. USA Track & Field sanctions track & field and cross-country events across the country, and runs a national competition known as the Junior Olympics. This is a great opportunity for any girl who loves the sport and wants to take her participation beyond the traditional path. While options for professional running are limited, they are available through this organization. So, if your daughter is an elite runner, then USA Track & Field competitions may put her on the road to a successful athletic career. (You can contact USA Track & Field through their website at www.usatf.org.) And who knows, maybe some day she'll bring home the gold!

Basketball

Basketball is widely available for girls of all ages starting around eight years old. Your daughter might be suited to basketball if she loves to run and enjoys team activities. This sport provides excellent coordination development and a vigorous heart/lung workout, and teaches girls to work in a team environment with their peers. Basketball is an inexpensive sport to get your daughter involved in—even if you *do* end up paying for a pair of those super-expensive basketball shoes!

The Basics

Basketball was invented in 1891 by Dr. James Naismith, an athletic instructor at a Massachusetts YMCA, as an indoor sport for his students to play during the winter months. Soon after, the game was adapted for women by Sendra Berenson Abbott, a teacher at Smith College. Today, women's basketball is played at almost every level, from junior high to the professional leagues.

While basketball has always been a prominent women's sport, its popularity has skyrocketed in recent years, due in large part to the increased media attention earned by today's top female basketball stars. The U.S. women's Olympic basketball team won Olympic gold in 1984, 1988, 1996, and 2000 and captured the hearts of America's sports fans. The attendance of NCAA women's basketball games surpassed six million in the 2000–2001 season, and the NCAA championship tournament draws major national attention and TV coverage.

One of the most important events in the recent rise of women's basketball was the formation of the Women's National Basketball Association (known as the WNBA) in 1996. The WNBA used its partnership with the NBA to quickly become the most recognizable and influential women's professional sports league, broadcasting games on major television networks during each of its summer seasons. During the WNBA's first season, thousands of people flocked to the arenas to see the games live, and fifty million television viewers watched the new teams shine. As a result, the WNBA's talented players have become valuable role models for girls who wish to participate and succeed in sports. If your daughter is a basketball fan, she probably has her own favorite WNBA star!

How to Play

The object of basketball is to shoot the ball into the opposing team's basket while preventing them from getting the ball into your own. The game is played on a rectangular court that is ninety-two feet long and fifty-two feet wide. The baskets are located at each end of the court, and suspended at exactly ten feet high by a pole. Behind the basket is a backboard, which serves to rebound missed shots back onto the court, and off of which the players can try to bank a shot into the basket. Professional and college teams play two twenty-minute halves. Most high schools play four twelve-minute quarters, and game lengths vary for young players.

The team that has possession of the ball is said to be on "offense," and their goal is to score points by shooting the ball into the opposing team's basket. Each team has five players on the court at all times. The players can move the ball in three ways: 1) bouncing, known as dribbling, the ball down the court with their hands; 2) passing the ball to another teammate; and 3) shooting the ball toward the basket. A player can never touch the ball with her feet. A shot that successfully goes through the basket is worth two points. A shot made from behind the three-point line, a curved line that extends 19′9″ from the basket at all points, is worth, of course, three points. Once a basket is made, possession of the ball is given to the opposing team, and they "take over on offense" and try to score.

When a team does not have the ball, they are said to be on defense, and their job is to prevent the offensive team from scoring. They do this by trying to regain possession of the ball, either by blocking a shot or "stealing" the ball from the offensive player. When trying to steal the ball or block a shot, the defensive player is not allowed to make contact with the offensive player.

Players commit a "foul" when they violate one of the rules of the game. If a player is fouled (touched) in the act of shooting, they are given two "free throws." A free throw is a shot during which no player may try to block it. It is taken from behind the foul line, which is located fifteen feet from the basket. Each free throw is worth one point. Each team is allowed a certain number of fouls per half (the amount varies depending on the league). When this occurs, the team is said to be "over the limit," and the opposing team receives free throws after each foul, regardless of whether it was committed in the act of shooting the ball.

For more detailed information about the rules of basketball, consult www.wnba.com, www.ncaa.org, or your local school's athletic department.

Get Her in the Game!

If your daughter is interested in playing basketball, her options are almost limitless. For girls below the junior-high level, consult your local YMCA or YWCA, Boys and Girls Club, or Parks and Recreation Department. Many of these organizations have programs designed to teach young girls about the game and how to develop their skills. Beginning in junior high and continuing through high school, girls' basketball programs are offered through your daughter's school athletic program. These programs are extremely popular, with almost half a million girls playing in state-run high school systems. In fact, basketball is the most popular girls' high school sport, according to the National Federation of State High School Associations. In most schools, a girl must simply be willing to attend practices and games to join the team. Some larger high schools do have selective tryouts to make the team. For alternative or off-seasons options, the Amateur Athletic Union Girls' Basketball website (www.auugirlsbasketball.org), organizes basketball for girls from ten through eighteen.

Thanks to Title IX, there any many scholarships available for women to play sports in college. Of all sports, basketball provides the greatest opportunities for girls entering the elite levels of college and beyond. According to the NCAA, over one thousand colleges and universities offer women's basketball programs, with scholarships available at over six hundred of the schools. While the competition is more intense at this level, it is a great opportunity if your daughter is talented and loves the sport. Beyond the collegiate levels come the professional leagues. If your daughter is one of the .02 percent of female high school basketball players who will make it to the professional leagues, her most desirable option would be the prestigious WNBA. Barring that, there are various leagues in Europe and Japan where women can have great careers playing for loyal and enthusiastic crowds.

Volleyball

Volleyball is a fast-moving, highly enjoyable sport that can be played for fun and competition by people of all ages. If your daughter has well-developed motor skills and is good at throwing or striking activities, she will probably find success in volleyball. Athletes skilled in sports as varied as tennis and softball have taken easily to this sport.

Volleyball is an extremely popular game among girls in junior high and high school.

The Basics

Volleyball was invented in 1895 by William Morgan, who, much like James Naismith, the inventor of basketball, created the sport at a Massachusetts YMCA to fill the need for indoor sports. The game made its debut at the Olympics in 1964, and the U.S. women's team gained prominence in the eighties, taking the gold medal in 1984 and 1988, and capturing the bronze in 1992.

Women's indoor volleyball has its greatest recognition through its collegiate players, whose games are broadcast regularly on cable sports networks such as ESPN2. While indoor volleyball draws a lot of fans, much of the current interest in volleyball for women has been driven by the emergence of outdoor, or "beach," volleyball. Beach volleyball stars such as Gabrielle Reece and the sport's entrance into the Olympics at the 1996 Atlanta games (the USA won gold in the 2000 in Sydney) have made beach volleyball a key sport for girls interested in playing and excelling in sports.

How to Play

While beach volleyball is becoming more popular, programs for this version of the sport are far less common than for indoor volleyball, especially since schools are not in session during the summer months when the beach volleyball season hits its peak. Therefore, I will focus on the rules of indoor volleyball to give you a basic understanding of the game. To learn more about beach volleyball, visit www.usavolleyball.org.

Indoor Volleyball

Much like tennis, volleyball is played on a rectangular court divided by a mesh net. Unlike tennis, the net does not touch the ground and rise a few feet above it, but is instead suspended in the air above the court by two poles. The height of the net varies with the age group of the players (2.2 meters high by international standards). Also like tennis, the ball is put into play by a serve, and the object is to hit the ball over the net into the opposing team's court area without the ball being returned. But this is where the similarities end.

Each team has six players, three in the front court close to the net, and three in the back court. Once the ball is served, either by an overhead, open-handed hit or an underhand, closed-fist hit, it is in play and a "volley" has begun. Volleyball players can only move the ball with their hands or arms, and must always keep the ball in the air. If a team allows the ball to touch the ground, the volley is awarded to the opposing team. If the serving team wins the volley, they score a point. If the nonserving team wins the volley, they score no points, but they serve the next volley and get the chance to score points. Each side is allowed to touch the ball three times before sending the ball over the net. If they touch the ball a fourth time, the play is ruled dead and the opposing team wins the volley. The final way for a team to lose a volley is if the same player touches the ball twice in a row. On of the common misconceptions about volleyball is that the play ends if the ball hits the net. This is not true. If the ball hits the net without going over, the team may continue to play the ball as long as they have not used all three of their hits. Also, if a team hits the ball out of bounds on their own side of the court, they may go of of bounds and continue to play as long as the ball does not cross over to the other side of the court while out of bounds.

The most common ways for the players to move the ball are the bump, set, and hit (commonly know as a spike). The player bumps the ball by folding her arms together and hitting the ball with her arms. This motion is normally done to pass the ball to one of her teammates, although it can also be used to send the ball back over the net. A set is accomplished when the player places herself underneath the ball and knocks it back into the air with her fingertips. This must be done as a fluid motion, as no player is allowed to hold the ball at any time. The purpose of a set is to send the ball up high and close to the net so that another teammate can deliver a hit. A hit is when a player smacks the ball with a open hand, using the top part of her palm. This sends the ball onto the other side of the court at a high speed, the goal being to make it hard to return the ball. Since each team is allowed three hits, the most effective play is the bump-set-spike, in which the ball is first bumped in the air to a teammate who sets the ball near the net to another teammate waiting to deliver a monstrous spike.

On defense, a player may attempt to block a hit by jumping and placing their hands open and together above the net, without crossing over the top of the net. If the block is successful, the ball will fall back on the opponent's side. However, if the ball still crosses the net, the attempted block is not counted as a touch, and the team still has three hits to return the ball to the other side.

Most volleyball games are played to a score of fifteen, although the final score can be reduced for younger players. A game must be won by two points, so play continues until one team has fifteen or more points and a two-point advantage. A match normally consists of a best-of-three-games or best-of-five-games series, but again this may vary depending on the age group of the players.

For more information about the rules of volleyball, consult your local league or check out www.usavolleyball.org.

Get Her in the Game!

Although many young children get exposed to volleyball because it is a favorite picnic and beach sport, there are few opportunities for children to play volleyball before they reach junior-high age. Volleyball becomes a more promising options once your young female athlete has developed the strength and coordination to get the ball over the net on a consistent and controlled basis, and this does not usually happen until she matures. However, if your little one loves to play, you can always check to see what programs are available in your area, or head out the park or backyard and teach her yourself. Once she reaches junior high, many schools teach girls volleyball in their physical education programs, and a good number run competitive teams.

High school and college competitions are usually the highlight of the volleyball player's career. Volleyball is the third most popular sport among high school girls, with programs in almost every school and close to four hundred thousand participants each year. If your daughter is hoping to take her athletic skills to the college level, volleyball ranks second only to basketball among university-sponsored female sports—offered at almost one thousand schools with scholarships available at almost six hundred of them.

After college, the options for professional play are few and highly selective. Most competitions are run for beach volleyball, through the Association of Volleyball Professionals. However, volleyball is one of the most popular adult recreation sports. Thousands of amateur leagues, both indoor and outdoor, are run across the country each year, giving girls the opportunity to hone their skills during the off season or continue their play after their school years are over.

Field Hockey

If your daughter enjoys team activities and doesn't have a problem with getting hot and sweaty, then field hockey may be the sport for her. Field hockey has characteristics that are similar to soccer and lacrosse, so any girl interested in those sports might want to give this traditional favorite a try. Field hockey is a terrific way for young girls to build heart/lung endurance and learn how to work with other girls in a team setting. Opportunities for adult recreational play are growing as more and more girls who played field hockey at high school and college seek to continue participating in this high-endurance, exhilarating sport.

The Basics

Field hockey is one of the most common and traditional women's sports in the United States—you can probably remember running around with that funny curved stick during your PE classes back in your school days. The modern sport of field hockey was developed in England in the 1860s, and spread throughout Europe and the United Kingdom. The first field hockey organization specifically for women, called the International Federation of Women's Hockey Associations, was formed in 1927. However, it was not until 1980 that women's field hockey was introduced at the Olympic games.

Although field hockey does not receive the widespread media attention that other women's sports such as gymnastics, basketball, and figure skating do, its understated appeal draws many girls to the sport each year. Almost any girl can play, and this appeals to many girls who are looking for an alternative sport as they enter the high school years.

How to Play

Field hockey is played on a field one hundred yards long by sixty feet wide. As with soccer, there is a goal at each end of the field into which the players try to shoot the ball. However, unlike soccer, the players advance the ball with sticks instead of their feet, and the ball is small and plastic, and can rocket across the field after a solid smack. Each team fields eleven players, and once the ball is in play the teams try to gain possession of the ball and score by shooting it into the opposing team's goal. The goalkeeper guards the goal and tries to prevent the ball from entering it.

The players move the ball with a field-hockey stick, which has a curved head and is rounded on one side and flat on the other. The players can only hit the ball with the flat side of the stick. Once a player has possession of the ball, they can push it up the field or pass it to another teammate, but they cannot use their body or the stick to keep other players from trying to take the ball. Therefore, speed is a vital part of the game, as the athlete must keep the ball moving to avoid it getting stolen by the defense. A shot on the goal can only be made from within the striking circle, a semi-circle that surrounds the goal from exactly sixteen yards at all points. Each goal is worth one point.

If a team receives a foul, the other team may be awarded a free hit, penalty corner, or penalty stroke, depending on the severity of the foul and where it took place. A free hit allows a player to hit the ball with every other player five yards away; a penalty corner reduces the number of defenders allowed in the striking circle for an initial hit by the attackers, and a penalty stroke gives the attacker a free shot at the goal from seven yards away with no one but the goaltender defending.

The game ends if one team is ahead in points when the time limit has expired. College teams play two thirty-five-minute halves, while most high schools play thirty-minute halves. If the teams are tied when time expires, they then play two sudden-death overtime periods, in which the first team to score wins the game. If the game is still tied after the overtime periods, the game is decided by a shootout, in which five players from each team get the chance to go one-on-one with the goalie, and the team that score the most points wins.

There is also an indoor version of field hockey, with rules variations that accompany the smaller and more fast-paced court. To learn more detail about the rules of field hockey and indoor field hockey, visit www.usfieldhockey.org.

Get Her in the Game!

Girls usually start playing field hockey through one of two ways: school-sponsored teams or club play. Field-hockey clubs across the country run programs for adults and children interested in learning the game and playing in recreational competition. Field-hockey clubs provide a place to play for girls whose schools do not offer the sport, or for girls interested in playing the game at a young age. Some Parks and Recreation departments run field-hockey leagues, but they are not as popular as other sports.

Field hockey is largely available through high school play, and ranks tenth among the most popular sports for high school girls, according to the National Federation of State High School Associations. More than 250 colleges and universities have women's field hockey teams, and more than one hundred of those schools offer field hockey scholarships. If your daughter is very talented in field hockey, she could chase the dream of joining the U.S. National Team, which competes in the Olympic games. To encourage the development of its elite teams, the U.S. Field Hockey Association fields elite youth teams in many age brackets. Visit www.usfieldhockey.org for more information about getting your daughter into these programs.

Lacrosse

Lacrosse is a fast-paced, strategic sport that should appeal to any girl who is agile and quick footed. Because the action rarely stops in this game, lacrosse players must have strong endurance. Lacrosse builds good cardiovascular fitness and develops excellent strategic and throwing skills.

Lacrosse uses many of the same skills as soccer (except for kicking!) and field hockey, and will therefore most likely be of interest to girls who already play these sports. Lacrosse is not widely available for girls until the high school level. But if your daughter does catch on to this exciting sport at this time, there are many opportunities to continue playing into college and adulthood.

The Basics

Lacrosse was invented and played by Native Americans long before Europeans came to the New World, and was played on fields that could extend for over ten miles. The modern game of lacrosse has developed into one of the few American home-grown phenomena. US Lacrosse estimates that over 200,000 people currently play lacrosse in the United States, and there are two professional lacrosse leagues: National Lacrosse League and Major League Lacrosse. Most of competitive lacrosse's support is drawn from high schools and colleges. The NCAA lacrosse championships rank second only to the famous NCAA basketball tournament in terms of attendance drawn.

Women's lacrosse is similar in play to men's lacrosse, but has a few key rule differences. Physical contact between players is limited in women's lacrosse, eliminating the checking that is common in the men's game. While men play on a field 110 yards long by 60 yards wide, there are no boundaries in the women's game.

How to Play

The game of lacrosse is played with a small rubber ball, and each player carries a "crosse"—a stick consisting of a long handle attached to a head that contains a netted pocket, in which the ball may be carried. The lacrosse field is comprised of two goals facing each other, about ninety meters apart. The goal is six feet wide and six feet high, with a net suspended from the goal to the ground so that a shot can only enter the goal from the side facing the other goal. Each goal is surrounded by a goal circle about five meters in diameter, and only the goalkeeper may be in the goal circle at any time. Directly between the two goals is the center circle, which is about eighteen meters in diameter.

The game start with a "draw" in the center circle, in which a player from each team meet in the middle and place their crosses together so that the backs of the heads are touching. The umpire sets the ball on top of the two crosses and blows a whistle. When the whistle is blown, the players must swing their crosses up above their head before attempting to retrieve the ball.

A player gains possession of the ball when it is in the head of her crosse. Once she has possession of the ball, she may run with it, pass it to another teammate who attempts to catch it in their crosse, or shoot the ball at the goal. The defensive players try to gain possession of the ball by either intercepting a pass or using their crosse to knock the ball out of the offensive player's crosse, knocking the ball to the ground. Once the ball is loose, any player may take possession of it by scooping it off of the ground with her crosse.

If the player sends a shot into the goal, she scores a point for her team. A goal can only be scored by a shot made with the crosse. If the ball does not go into the goal, or is stopped by the goalkeeper, the goalkeeper must send the ball out of the goal circle within ten seconds of when it entered. The goalkeeper's crosse has a larger head than the other players' to aid in guarding the goal.

Lacrosse is normally played in two twenty-five-minute halves, although the time can be reduced depending on the age of the participants. At the end of the game, the team that has scored the most goals wins.

Get Her in the Game!

Lacrosse, like rugby, is a sport that most girls do not get involved in until the high school or college years. Because this sport is not as popular as basketball or softball, most girls do not even hear about the sport until they have reached the higher levels of schooling, when girls' interest in alternative sports grows and branches out to lacrosse. However, your daughter may take a liking to the sport at a young age if she is exposed to it. For young children, lacrosse can be learned and played through youth lacrosse organizations. While membership may vary in your area, most of these organizations are run through association with US Lacrosse, the national governing body of men's and women's lacrosse. By visiting www.uslacrosse.org, you can find out the name of your regional lacrosse chapter, which you can contact to find out about youth lacrosse programs in your area. Be aware that because lacrosse teams are not as numerous as other sports, if your daughter joins a youth league it might mean a large time commitment for both of you. As she enters adulthood, your daughter can play in one of many amateur lacrosse leagues run in association with US Lacrosse. Visit www.uslacrosse.org to find an adult team in your area.

Lacrosse is also like rugby in that it is very popular on college campuses. Currently, 250 colleges and universities sponsor women's lacrosse teams, and more than one hundred of those schools offer scholarships to play the sport. This is a great incentive to get your daughter started in lacrosse early. If she does not happen to attend a college where lacrosse is sponsored by the school, it is highly probable that she will find a competitive women's lacrosse club on campus, where she can play games and develop her skills. And if there is no club, perhaps she can start one herself!

Rugby

Is your daughter a rough-and-tumble type who loves to run and isn't afraid to get bruised or banged up? Then you may have a future rugby star in the family! Rugby union, or "rugby" as it is commonly called, is a fast-paced, tough game that features strength, speed, agility, and throwing skills. Because rugby combines elements of soccer and football, it is a great alternative for any girl who wishes to play football but can't find a program for girls in her area, or for soccer players looking for a different sport to play.

Because of the rough nature of the sport, rugby is better suited for older girls. Programs and clubs for women's rugby can be found at most colleges, and the sport is even making its way into the high school ranks.

The Basics

As legend has it, the sport of rugby emerged at Rugby School in England during a game of soccer in 1823, when William Webb Ellis, perhaps tired of using only his feet, picked up the ball and ran with it into the goal. Although he was breaking the rules of soccer, the act was so exciting for the players and fans that it inspired an entire new sport to be invented. The new sport was first played at Cambridge University, and after some resistance, soon gained acceptance among England's colleges and universities.

Today, rugby is one of the world's most popular games, especially among the countries of the United Kingdom. Rugby players are most recognizable for their colored, striped shirts and the oddly shaped ball that the sport uses. Although professional rugby is played in the United States, its foundation in the country is based in hundreds of amateur rugby clubs, many of which build women's teams. Colleges and universities are also a great breeding ground for rugby players, where experienced and new players alike find it easy to persuade others to get a game together.

How to Play

Rugby is played on an outdoor, rectangular grass field. The field is divided in the center by a halfway line, and each end of the field contains an in-goal area, which is the area between a goal line and the end of the field, known as the dead-ball line. A goal post is placed at the center of each goal line. Between the halfway line and the goal line are the ten-meter line (located ten meters from the halfway line) and the twenty-two meter line (located twenty-two meters from the goal line). The game is played with an oval ball that is larger in size than a football.

The object of the game is to score more points than the other team before the time limit expires. The players may run with the ball or kick it down the field. They are allowed to pass the ball to a teammate, but not in a forward direction. The team with the ball attempts to score points by getting either a "try" or a "goal." A try occurs when a team enters their opponent's in-goal area and touches the ball to the ground. A goal is scored when a player kicks the ball through the opponents' goalpost. A try is worth five points, and a goal is worth three points. After a team scores a try, they are given the chance to kick a goal, called a conversion. If the conversion is successful, it is worth two points.

The game is played in two halves, the length of which varies depending on the league or skill level of the players. It begins with a kickoff, in which one team kicks the ball from the halfway line across their opponents' ten-meter line, behind which the opponents must stand. Once the ball is in play, the player that has it tries to move the ball down the field, and the members of the other team try to stop her by tackling her. Once a player is tackled, she must immediately give up possession of the ball. When this happens, a member of either team can pick up the ball and put it back into play.

One of the unique features of rugby is the "scrum." A scrum occurs after a stoppage of play to reintroduce the ball to play. Players from each team lock arms in two lines, and the ball is dropped in the middle. The players in the scrum may only use their feet to grab the ball, and when they do they attempt to pass the ball to a teammate outside of the scrum, who recovers the ball and puts it back into play. There are two other variations of this: the ruck, where one or more players converge on a ball that is already loose; and the maul, in which one or more players surround the person carrying the ball and attempt to recover it.

This is a very basic understanding of rugby, as the rules of the sport are intricate and take experience playing the game to master. For a complete listing of the "Laws of Rugby Union," visit www.irb.org/irblaws.htm.

Get Her in the Game!

Because rugby is such a rough game, most girls do not begin playing it until the high school or college years. Unfortunately, very few high schools and colleges sponsor rugby teams. However, a good number do offer the sport as a club or afterschool activity. Rugby is especially popular on college campuses. Your daughter will most likely be able to find a girls' rugby club among the college's or university's official list of organizations. Adult amateur rugby clubs are also very popular, and organizations can be found across the country.

Finding a rugby club in your area can sometimes be difficult. I suggest that you contact USA Rugby, the U.S. wing of the International Rugby Union. By visiting www.usarugby.org, you can find out the names and locations of rugby clubs in your area, and contact information on how to get your daughter involved. By going to the "Youth Rugby" section of the website, you can download information on how to properly teach rugby to young players, how to develop their skills in the game, and how to set up a rugby camp. If your town does not have a rugby club, you can start one yourself.

Extreme Sports

While traditional sports continue to be popular with girls, the presence of "extreme" sports has experienced an enormous growth over the last ten years. Extreme sports are, for the most part, individual sports, and are characterized by a higher degree of showmanship and risk of injury than in traditional sports. While extreme-sport competitions are available, the focus of these sports is usually on developing skill and interacting socially with peers as opposed to winning or losing.

For parents with daughters involved in extreme sports, the most important things to be alert about are safety and equipment. Providing your daughter with the proper protective gear and safe equipment will help ensure that she is able to experience the thrills of these sports without jeopardizing her health.

There are many different types of extreme sports, almost too many to mention. The following is a brief explanation of the extreme sports that your daughter is most likely to get involved in:

- **Skateboarding.** Skateboarders jump using ramps, jumps, rails, and platforms to perform a series of "tricks"—maneuvers such as spins, twists, flips, and inverts—while riding on their skateboards. Another popular arena for skateboarders to perform is a half-pipe, which is a U-shaped ramp that allows the skater to go back and forth between each open end of the ramp.

- **Snowboarding.** Snowboarding is considered by some to be "skateboarding on snow." The description is actually quite accurate, as snowboarders perform tricks off of the jumps and half-pipes on downhill ski slopes in a manner that is very similar to skateboarding. While skiers also can perform tricks, snowboarding has soared in popularity among youth because it allows for better trick maneuvering than skiing does.

- **In-line skating.** While in-line skating, or "Rollerblading" as it is sometimes branded, is for the most part a recreational sport, many in-line skaters are also using the jumps, rails, ramps, and platforms at skateboarding parks to perform "extreme" tricks.

- **Mountain biking/BMX.** These two extreme forms of bicycling provide an alternative to simply riding around the neighborhood.

BMX biking allows bicyclers to compete either by performing tricks as in skateboarding, or by racing in a motorcross-type event, where contestants race to the finish line on a course filled with jumps and hills. Mountain biking involves riding a bicycle up and down the rough terrain of a mountain trail. While mountain biking is not normally a competitive sport, its difficult nature classifies it as an extreme sport.

• **Surfing.** Surfers ride a flat, oblong surfboard along an ocean wave, performing tricks while trying to keep riding the wave without falling or getting caught in the wave's current. Surfing is only available on certain ocean coasts, but is very popular with the local youth where it is an option.

chapter 15

Post-game Chat

● ● ●

As we have seen, encouraging your daughter to be active and involved in sports offers her benefits that last a lifetime. Even if you weren't athletic yourself as a child—even if you aren't athletic now—there is much we as parents can do to support our daughters in reaping these benefits. We can teach our toddlers the "alphabet of movement"—running, kicking, throwing, catching, and other skills—that will get them off to a good start in physical fitness. When our daughters are ready for team sports, we can seek out local programs that are well-run and emphasize fun over competition. We can support local programs in training coaches, or even become coaches ourselves. At all ages, we can teach our daughters good sportsmanship and encourage them by attending games, telling them we're proud of them, and taking them to see exciting live sports events. If we do enjoy sports ourselves, we can share our enjoyment with our daughters, including them in our activities. And as they grow older, we can support our daughters in sticking with the sports of their choice—or trying out new ones. Let us never forget that sports offer unique opportunities for bonding with our daughters, and are a wonderful source of fun and enjoyment, for daughters and parents alike!

Title IX Compliance

● ● ●

The following program will help you determine if your daughter's school is complying with Title IX, and show you how to fix any problems that exist. It was developed by the Women's Sports Foundation, and is reprinted here by permission.

Title IX Compliance Program

First Half: Get Prepared!
Step One: Grade Your School
Complete the checklist (which follows on page 239) to see exactly how your school is measuring up to the requirements of the law. Share the results with anyone you talk to about your concerns—your daughter and her teammates, other parents, or school administrators.

Step Two: Put the Power to the Pen

Once you are certain the school is violating Title IX, jot down a list of specific concerns. Make sure your list includes every valid discrepancy. Carry this list along with you to meetings and enclose a copy in any correspondence in which you voice your concerns.

Step Three: Rally a Strong Team

If the school isn't complying with Title IX, chances are that you're not the only one feeling shortchanged. Gather the support of other parents, your daughter, and her teammates, and anyone else who is willing to get involved—sons and fathers, too! Share information with these folks and make sure they know what Title IX requires. Get as much support as possible. There is strength in numbers!

Step Four: You Tell 'Em!

It's hard to believe that school administrators don't know about the law. Make sure they do by printing out and distributing several copies of *Playing Fair*, an excellent Women's Sports Foundation publication that explains the essentials of Title IX. You can find this free resource in downloadable form on the worldwide web at www.womenssportsfoundation.org/binary-data/WSF_ARTICLE/pdf_file/195.pdf. Multiple copies are also available from the Women's Sports Foundation headquarters. Always have *Playing Fair* handy when you talk to people about your concerns—it will back up your concerns with cold, hard facts.

Step Five: Make a Paper Trail

Leave your list of concerns, *Playing Fair*, and a copy of the school's graded Title IX checklist at every meeting. Even if you don't feel very appreciated, follow up with a thank-you letter that repeats what your concerns are and anything that was decided or promised to you during your meeting. Keep copies of everything, so you have a record of what attempts you've made.

Second Half: Talk to the Right People!

You're prepared and ready to go. It's time to approach the school's decision makers and convince them that it's only right to abide by the law. If possible, include in your meetings other team parents, your daughter and her teammates, teachers, and other supporters. Be polite, concentrate on the facts, and always assume that the administrators you meet with want to do the right thing.

Step Six: Meet with the Athletic Director

Start by meeting with the school's athletic director to share your list of concerns. After the meeting, follow up with a thank-you letter reiterating your concerns. Be sure you "cc:" the school principal and athletic director, especially if you are unhappy with the outcome of the meeting.

Step Seven: Meet with the Principal

If you are unsuccessful in your meeting with the athletic director, work your way up the administration ladder and schedule a meeting with the principal. During the meeting, be sure to review your meeting with the athletic director and why it was unsuccessful. Bring your paperwork and be forthright about sharing your concerns.

Step Eight: Search Out the School's Title IX Compliance Officer

If the athletic director and principal are both unresponsive, your next step is to call the principal's office and ask for the name, address, and phone number of the Title IX compliance officer (the law requires that every school have one). Call the compliance officer and investigate the procedure for filing an official Title IX complaint. If things get too technical for you at this point, call the Women's Sports Foundation (1-800-227-3988), where advisors can help you through the process.

Overtime: Let People Know What's Going On!

What happens if trying to educate school administrators didn't work? Sometimes it's hard for people to change. You probably need to go beyond the school administrators to make the right things happen. Remember…don't get angry! Be matter-of-fact. Tell people your story. Ask them to be fair, to comply with the law, and to do the right thing.

Step Nine: Take a Stand!

If you are sure of your facts and disappointed at the lack of responsiveness of your school officials, you may wish to consider taking the following steps. Consult with the other team parents, your daughter and her teammates, teachers, and/or coaches. You will benefit from their help and advice. Email (wosportre1@aol.com) or call (1-800-227-3988) the Women's Sports Foundation to discuss your situation and what might be the best next steps.

Step Ten: Write to Your School Board

Call the office of the superintendent of your school district and ask that a list of the names and mailing addresses for each member of the board be mailed to you. Send a letter with a list of your concerns to the chair of the board, detailing whom you have met with and asking them to investigate your concerns. Have as many athletes and parents as possible sign the letter. Send a copy of that letter to each board member. Ask for an opportunity to meet with the chair to state your case. Ask the Women's Sports Foundation to write to each board member on your behalf.

Step Eleven: Tell Your Local Newspaper, Radio, and TV!

Find the names of your local newspapers, radio stations, and television stations and email or mail the editor, general manager, or sports department head. Send them all the same email or letter.

Step Twelve: Write to Your Legislators

Ask your legislators to help…both state and federal representatives. Helping voters is important to them. After you sign the letter, have your daughter and her teammates sign the letter. Also mail a copy of your email via regular mail to be sure it's been received.

Appeal The Call: What to Do If All Else Fails!

Everything that has been suggested to this point has been political, in other words, to persuade them to do the right thing. Sometimes none of this works, and you may wish to consider reporting your case to a federal agency like the Office for Civil Rights, or even bringing a lawsuit. Give the Women's Sports Foundation a call, and they will help you think through the pros and cons of these actions as well as the "How To's." Remember, it's important to stand up for the rights of your daughter.

Step Thirteen: The Title IX Complaint

A complaint to the Office for Civil Rights (OCR) is not a lawsuit. It is an administrative complaint that can be filed by anyone: a parent, an athlete, a team, or even an outsider. All that is required is a letter to the OCR. The complaint should be filed with one of the ten OCR regional offices (listings can be found in appendix A of *Playing Fair*). In a specific instance of discrimination, the complaint must be filed within 180 days or 60 days after the last action of the school's internal grievance procedure. Within fifteen days of receipt of the complaint, OCR must notify the institution involved, and an investigation will be initiated.

Step Fourteen: A Title IX Lawsuit

No one likes going to court, but you may decide to pursue this avenue. A lawsuit must be filed by someone who is directly affected by the discrimination, which in your case would be your daughter. You will need an attorney. The Women's Sports Foundation will help you identify an attorney who in some cases work *pro bono* (at no cost to the client).

Title IX Checklist

Use this two-part checklist to see exactly how your daughter's school is measuring up to the requirements of the law. It is excerpted from the Women's Sports Foundation pamphlet, "Check It Out," and is reprinted by permission. A free downloadable version of this 24-page pamphlet is available on the web at http://www.womenssportsfoundation.org/binary-data/WSF_ARTICLE/pdf_file/782.pdf or by writing the Women's Sports Foundation at Eisenhower Park, East Meadow, NY 11554.

Part I. Does Your Daughter's School Offer Girls Equal Opportunities to Play Sports?

There are three ways to answer to this question. A "yes" to any of the following three questions means that your daughter's school is providing female students with equal opportunities to play sports:

1) Are the percentages of male and female athletes about the same as the percentages of male and female students enrolled at the school?
   ❏Yes   ❏No

NOTE: When you're counting the total number of athletes, you should only include those athletes who a) receive school support in the form of coaching, equipment, etc. on a regular basis during a sport's season; b) regularly participate in organized practice sessions and team meetings; and c) are listed on a team's squad list. Most often this will mean that you count only varsity and possibly junior varsity athletes, and do not count club or intramural athletes.

CHECK IT OUT: Compare the percentages of male and female athletes to the percentages of male and female students enrolled. Check "Yes" in the box above if they are about equal and go to Part II. If not, check "No" and go to question 2.

2. Does your daughter's school have a history and a continuing practice of expanding athletic opportunities for female students? ❑Yes ❑No

Unsure? Schools must make good-faith efforts to increase athletic participation opportunities for students who previously have been denied opportunities, usually girls, either through the addition of teams or the addition of athletes to existing teams. These opportunities must be added in response to female students' developing interests and abilities. If a school can only show that it increased opportunities during the early years of its girl's program, but has stopped doing so, then the answer is "No." Also, if your school just keeps making promises to increase opportunities for female students in the future, but fails to follow through, the answer is "No." Finally, cutting or capping male teams does not count as increasing opportunities for females.

CHECK IT OUT: If your daughter's school has added new teams over the years for girls, then check "Yes." If, on the other hand, your school has dropped female teams, hasn't responded to female students' requests to add more sports, has no plans to add girls' sports, or isn't fair when it comes to deciding whether sports should be added, check "No" and go to question 3.

3. Does your daughter's school provide interested female students with the opportunity to compete? ❑Yes ❑No

Unsure? Your daughter's school should provide female students with opportunities that match their interests and abilities.

CHECK IT OUT: If female students have asked their school to add any sport(s), or there is evidence that female students have the interest and ability to play any sport(s) currently not offered, and the school has added the sport(s), then check "Yes" in the box above. If, on the other hand, the school has refused requests to add any girls' sport(s), or the school has not found out what female students are interested in playing, then check "No."

Part II. Are Male and Female Athletes at Your Daughter's School Given Equal Benefits and Services?

Across the board, schools must provide male and female athletes with equal benefits and services. However, schools don't have to spend the same amount of money on their male and female athletes, nor do their opportunities have to be identical. The key question in this area is, overall, are male and female athletes treated equally?

The fact that a school spends more on boys' uniforms than on girls' uniforms may not be unfair if the boys' uniforms simply cost more than the girls'. But if the school spends more on boys' uniforms because they are top-of-the-line, and the girls' uniforms are inferior, then the school is not treating male and female athletes equally. Or if the school provides half of the male athletes with top-of-the-line uniforms, but only one-fourth of the female athletes with similar quality uniforms, then the school is not treating girls fairly.

To find out whether your daughter's school really is being fair requires looking at a variety of areas, such as the following:

Overall Support

1. Are overall budgets for the male and female programs (including income from booster clubs, concession-stand profits, and fundraisers) equitable? ❏Yes ❏No
2. Are school-sponsored athletic banquets and social events for male and female athletes equal? ❏Yes ❏No

Equipment and Supplies

1. Does your school provide athletic paraphernalia (gym bags, towels,

jackets, travel bags, sweaters, rings, etc.) of similar quality and quantity for female and male athletes? ❑Yes   ❑No

2. Does your school provide practice and competitive uniforms of similar quality and quantity for male and female athletes? ❑Yes   ❑No

3. Are uniforms and equipment paid for in the same way for both male and female athletes? ❑Yes   ❑No

4. Are the replacement schedules for equipment and uniforms the same for male and female athletes? ❑Yes   ❑No

Scheduling of Games and Practice Times

1. Do male and female athletes have equal amounts of practice time (hours of practice, days per week)? ❑Yes   ❑No

2. Are the numbers of competitive events for male and female teams equal? ❑Yes   ❑No

3. Are practice and competition times equally desirable for both male and female athletes (e.g., scheduling boys' games for Friday nights and girls' games for Tuesday mornings would not be equally desirable)? ❑Yes   ❑No

4. Do male and female athletes lose similar amounts of academic time due to practices and games? ❑Yes   ❑No

5. Do the competitive schedules for male and female teams provide equal quality competition (e.g., do male and female athletes have opportunities to compete at the same division levels)? ❑Yes   ❑No

6. Are post-season, league championship, etc. opportunities equal for male and female teams? ❑Yes   ❑No

7. Are the seasons (time of year) of competition the same for male and female teams (e.g., do both boys and girls play basketball in the traditional, winter season)? ❑Yes   ❑No

Travel and Related Expenses

1. When male and female athletes travel to games, do they get meals at similar places (e.g., if boys eat at nice restaurants, while girls eat at fast-food spots, check "No")? ❑Yes   ❑No

2. Are pre-game meals, snacks, etc., provided equally to male and female athletes? ❑Yes   ❑No

3. Do male and female athletes have similar modes of transportation to away games (e.g., if coaches or athletes drive female athletes in cars or vans, while professionals drive male athletes in buses, check "No")? ❑Yes ❑No

4. When extensive travel is required, are provisions for overnight stays equal for male and female athletes (quality of motels, number per room, etc.)? ❑Yes ❑No

5. Does your school provide equal amounts of money for food to male and female athletes when they travel? ❑Yes ❑No

Availability of Coaches and Their Compensation

1. Are the numbers of athletes seen by coaches of male and female teams equivalent? ❑Yes ❑No

2. Does your daughter's school provide the same quality coaches for male and female athletes? ❑Yes ❑No

3. Do coaches of male and female teams receive equal salaries for equal work? ❑Yes ❑No

4. Do coaches of male and female teams have equal "other duties" (e.g., teaching versus full-time coaching)?❑Yes ❑No

5. Do coaches of male and female teams have equal support staff and office resources to handle paperwork, hire officials, line fields, set up the gym, etc? ❑Yes ❑No

6. Are quality officials (referees, umpires, linespeople, etc.) provided equally to male and female teams? ❑Yes ❑No

7. Are assistant coaches equally available to male and female teams? ❑Yes ❑No

Locker Rooms, Practice, and Competitive Facilities

1. Are practice and competitive facilities equally available to male and female teams at desirable times? ❑Yes ❑No

2. Are practice and competitive facilities maintained equally for male and female teams? ❑Yes ❑No

3. Do male and female athletes have locker rooms of equivalent quality and size? ❑Yes ❑No

4. Are spectator seating and scoreboards provided equally to male and

female teams? ❑Yes   ❑No

5. Are the conditions of playing fields, courts, and pools for male and female teams equal? ❑Yes   ❑No

Medical and Training Services

1. Are weight training and conditioning facilities equally available and of equal quality for male and female athletes? ❑Yes   ❑No

2. Are medical personnel provided equally for male and female athletes' physicals and at games? ❑Yes   ❑No

3. Are qualified athletic trainers or auxiliary coaches (strength, sports psychology, etc.) provided equally to male and female athletes? ❑Yes ❑No

4. Is health, accident, or injury insurance equally available? ❑Yes   ❑No

Publicity

1. Is coverage in the school's paper and media of female and male athletes equal? ❑Yes   ❑No

2. Is the school's sports publicity personnel equally available to male and female teams? ❑Yes   ❑No

3. Are cheerleaders, pep bands, drill teams, etc. equally provided for female and male teams? ❑Yes   ❑No

4. Are athletic awards and recognition equal for male and female athletes? ❑Yes   ❑No

5. Are the quantity and quality of press guides, press releases, game programs, etc., equal? ❑Yes   ❑No

Now take a look at the answers to your questions and formulate an action plan.

Strength and Flexibility Training Programs

● ● ●

The following strength and training programs are adapted from ones designed by Drs. Wayne Westcott and Avery Faigenbaum in their book *Strength and Power for Young Athletes* (available online at www.humankinetics.com), and are reprinted by permission.

Strength Training

First of all, parents need to know how often their kids should lift weights and how many repetitions ("reps") and sets they should do. Here are the basics:

- Girls aged 7–9: twice a week, do one set of ten to fifteen repetitions of each exercise
- Girls aged 10–12: two or three times a week, do one or two sets of ten to fifteen repetitions of each exercise
- Girls aged 13–15: two or three times a week, do one or two sets of eight to twelve repetitions of each exercise

The weights should be heavy enough that the set is challenging but not so heavy that your daughter can't maintain correct technique. Increase the size of the weight once your daughter can do the maximum number of recommended repetitions while still maintaining correct technique. However, when she moves to a heavier weight, reduce the number of repetitions down to the minimum number and steadily build back up again over the next week or so. So let's say your ten-year-old started off doing two sets of ten biceps curls using a three-pound weight. The next time she works out she should attempt two sets of eleven biceps curls using the three-pound weight. Once she can do two sets of fifteen repetitions using the three-pound weight, she should start using a five-pound weight but drop down to ten repetitions and gradually build back up to fifteen repetitions, and so on.

Tips on Technique for Young Strength Trainers

Secondly, children learning to train with weights should under no circumstances attempt maximum lifts (lifting the most weight you possibly can). These are some other tips on technique:

- Your daughter must always have total control over the weights being lifted. If she can't control them at all times, they are too heavy.
- She should breathe in when lifting the weights, and breathe out when returning them to the starting position.
- Never allow her to twist or contort her body when lifting.
- She must focus on what she's doing and not let anyone distract her.
- She should use a "spotter" whenever free weights are used (a spotter is a person who helps guide the weights into their proper position).

Lower-Body Exercises
Dumbbell Squat
Muscles
Quadriceps (front of the thigh), hamstrings (back of the thigh), gluteals (buttocks)

Procedure
1. Have your daughter begin by grasping a dumbbell in each hand, and standing erect with feet about hip-width apart and toes pointing slightly outward. She should hold the dumbbells so they hang straight down at the sides of her body.

2. She should slowly bend her ankles, knees, and hips until her thighs are parallel to the floor, keeping her back flat, head up, and eyes fixed straight ahead.
3. She returns to the starting position by slowly straightening her knees and hips.

Technique Tips

- The knees should follow a slightly outward pattern of the feet. Do not let the knees cave in.
- Inhale during the downward phase of the exercise and exhale during the upward phase.
- Avoid bouncing out of the bottom position.
- Concentrate on keeping the head up and chest out. Avoid excessive forward lean.
- Beginners may find it easier to learn this exercise by positioning their upper back and buttocks against a wall for support (i.e., slide up and down a wall).
- This exercise can also be performed with a barbell, as long as skilled instruction and supervision are available.
- It is important that an adult spotter be nearby to provide assistance if needed.

Barbell Squat

Muscles

Quadriceps (front of the thigh), hamstrings (back of the thigh), gluteals (buttocks)

Procedure

1. Have your daughter grasp the barbell with an overhand grip while it is on the rack.
2. Her hands should be wider than shoulder-width apart, and the barbell should rest on her shoulders and upper trapezius muscle, not on her neck.
3. Have her lift the bar off of the rack, keeping her back straight, eyes looking forward, and feet slightly wider than shoulder-width apart.

4. She should slowly bend her knees and hips until her thighs are parallel to the floor, keeping her heels in contact with the floor.
5. She returns to the starting position by straightening her knees and hips.
6. When she has completed the desired number of repetitions, she should walk the barbell back to the rack.

Technique Tips

- Inhale during the lowering phase and exhale during the lifting phase.
- The back should remain upright during this exercise. Excessive forward lean places undue stress on the lower back and may result in an injury.
- A spotter should stand directly behind the lifter during this exercise.

Dumbbell Lunge

Muscles

Quadriceps (front of the thigh), hamstrings (back of the thigh), gluteals (buttocks)

Procedure

1. Have your daughter begin by grasping a dumbbell in each hand. She should stand erect with feet about hip-width apart, and hold the dumbbells so they hang straight down at the sides of her body, and she should be looking straight ahead.
2. She takes a long step forward with her right leg; bending the knee of the right leg and lowering her body. The thigh of the right leg should be parallel to the floor, and the right knee should be over the ankle of the right foot. The left knee bends slightly.
3. She returns to the starting position by pushing off the floor with her right leg, then taking one or two steps backward to the starting position. Have her repeat with the opposite leg.
4. Be sure she keeps her head up, back upright, and shoulders over the hips.

Technique Tips

- This exercise requires balance and coordination. Begin with just body weight to learn proper form.
- Keep the head up, back upright, and shoulders over the hips.
- Inhale during the forward phase of the exercise and exhale during the return phase.
- Avoid using upper-torso momentum to return to the starting position. Concentrate on keeping the back upright throughout the exercise.

Dumbbell Side Lunge

Muscles

Quadriceps (front of the thigh), hamstrings (back of the thigh), gluteals (buttocks), hip abductors and adductors (groin and outer hip)

Procedure

1. Have your daughter begin by grasping a dumbbell in each hand. She should stand erect with her feet about shoulder-width apart, and hold the dumbbells in front of her body. She should look straight ahead.
2. She lunges to the side of her body with one leg while holding the dumbbells in front of her body.
3. Have her point her toes slightly to the side as she steps out.
4. Have her bend her knee until her thigh is parallel to the floor.
5. Then she should push herself to the starting position.
6. Have her repeat with the opposite leg.

Technique Tips

- Inhale while lunging to the side and exhale while returning to the starting position.
- Keep the head up and facing forward during this exercise.
- This exercise requires balance and coordination. Begin with just body weight to learn the proper form.

Dumbbell Step-Up
Muscles
Quadriceps (front of the thigh), gluteals (buttocks), hip extensors (muscles in front of the hip)

Procedure
1. Your daughter begins by grasping a dumbbell in each hand, and standing erect with feet about hip-width apart. She should hold the dumbbells so they hang straight down at the sides of her body. Have her look straight ahead.
2. Beginning with her right leg, she now steps onto a bench that is about knee height. Have her lift her body with her right leg and bring the knee of her left leg up.
3. She then slowly lowers her body by stepping back down to the starting position, and repeats with the opposite leg.

Technique Tips
- This exercise requires balance and coordination. Begin with just body weight to learn proper form.
- Exhale during the upward phase of the exercise and inhale during the downward phase.
- Concentrate on keeping the torso upright during this exercise.
- Before starting, check to be sure the bench is stable and secure.

Dumbbell Heel Raise
Muscles
Gastrocnemius, soleus (calf area)

Procedure
1. Your daughter begins by grasping a dumbbell in the right hand. Placing the full ball of the right foot on a board or stepping with the heel off the surface, she wraps the left foot behind the right ankle. She can use the free left hand for balance by holding onto the wall or bench.

2. She rises up onto the right toe as high as possible; then slowly lowers the heel as far as comfortable. Have her complete the assigned number of repetitions, and repeat with the opposite leg.

Technique Tips

- Inhale during the lowering phase and exhale during the lifting phase.
- Concentrate on keeping the torso and knees straight to avoid upper-leg involvement.

Barbell Heel Raise

Muscles

Gastrocnemius, soleus (calf area)

Procedure

1. Your daughter should grasp barbell with a wider than shoulder-width grip, and position barbell across her shoulders and upper trapezius, not on her neck.
2. Standing erect with her feet about shoulder-width apart, she keeps her torso and knees straight.
3. She slowly rises up on the toes as high as possible; then returns to the starting position.

Technique Tips

- Exhale while lifting the weight and inhale on the return movement.
- To increase the range of motion, stand with the balls of the feet on a board about one to two inches high.
- A spotter should stand behind the lifter in case the lifter needs assistance.

Toe Raise
Muscles
Tibialis anterior (outer shin area)

Procedure
1. Your daughter should sit on the edge of a high bench with her legs hanging straight down. Attach one end of a looped rope near the toe and ball area of one foot. Attach a light weight to the other end of the rope, and let the weight hang freely.
2. She lowers the toe and ball area on her foot as far as possible.
3. She lifts the weight by raising the toe and ball of her foot as high as possible.
4. Have her pause briefly, then slowly lower the weight to the starting position.

Technique Tips
- Exhale on lifting the weight and inhale on lowering it.
- Only a light weight is needed for this exercise because these are small muscles.
- Note that the foot cannot be raised much farther than the horizontal position. Thus it is important to lower the toe and ball area of the foot as much as possible to perform this exercise through the maximum range of motion.

Upper-Body Exercises
Dumbbell Chest Press
Muscles
Pectoralis major (chest), anterior deltoid (front of the shoulder), triceps (back of the upper arm)

Procedure
1. Have your daughter grasp a dumbbell in each hand. She lies on her back on a bench with her feet flat on the floor. If her feet don't reach the floor, use a stable board to accommodate her size. Have her hold

the dumbbells at arm's length over the chest area with palms facing away from her body.

2. She slowly bends her elbows and lowers the dumbbells to the outside of the chest area.

3. Then she presses the dumbbells upward until she fully extends both arms.

Technique Tips

- Inhale during the lowering phase of the exercise and exhale during the upward phase.
- Keep the head, shoulders, and buttocks in contact with the bench during this exercise. Do not twist or arch the body.
- Keep the dumbbells above the chest and not above the face.
- It is important that a spotter is nearby to provide assistance if needed. A spotter can place his or her hands on the child's wrists to teach proper dumbbell exercise technique or complete a repetition.
- This exercise can also be performed with a barbell, providing skilled instruction and supervision are available. If performed with a barbell, an adult spotter must be nearby to provide assistance if necessary.

Dumbbell Incline Press

This exercise is the same as the dumbbell chest press except that your daughter performs it on an inclined bench, typically angled between 30 to 45 degrees. She starts with the dumbbells above her chin and finishes with the dumbbells just above the upper chest.

Barbell Bench Press

Muscles

Pectoralis major (chest), anterior deltoid (front of the shoulder), triceps (back of the upper arm)

Procedure

1. Your daughter lies flat on her back with her feet flat on the floor, grasping the barbell with a wider than shoulder-width grip. She

should hold the barbell at arm's length above her upper-chest area.

2. Have her slowly lower the barbell to the middle of her chest, pause briefly, then press the barbell to the starting position. During the movement, the upper arms should be about 45 to 60 degrees from the torso.

Technique Tips

- Inhale on lowering the weight and exhale on lifting it.
- A spotter should be behind the lifter's head and should assist the lifter with getting the barbell into the starting position and returning the barbell to the rack when finished. Impress on young weight trainers the importance of a spotter during the exercise because the bar is pressed over the lifter's face, neck, and chest.
- This exercise should be learned with an unloaded barbell or long stick.
- The barbell should never be bounced off the chest.
- The buttocks should not lift off the bench during this exercise.
- Avoid hitting the upright supports by positioning the body about three inches from the supports before starting.

Dumbbell Chest Fly

Muscles

Pectoralis major (chest), anterior deltoid (front of the shoulder)

Procedure

1. Have your daughter grasp a dumbbell in each hand and lie on her back on a bench with her feet flat on the floor. If her feet don't reach the floor, use a stable lift to accommodate her size. She should hold the dumbbells at arm's length over the chest area with her palms facing each other and arms slightly bent.
2. She slowly lowers the dumbbells until her upper arms are parallel to the floor. She should feel a gentle stretch across her chest.
3. Have her lift the dumbbells to the starting position, keeping her elbows slightly bent.

Technique Tips

- Inhale during the lowering phase of the exercise and exhale during the upward phase.
- Keep head, shoulders, and buttocks in contact with the bench during this exercise. Do not twist or arch the body.
- Keep the dumbbells above the chest and not above the face.
- It is important that a spotter is nearby to provide assistance if needed. A spotter can place his or her hands on the child's wrists to teach proper exercise technique or complete a repetition.

Dumbbell One-Arm Row

Muscles

Latissimus dorsi (sides of the mid-back), biceps (front of the upper arm)

Procedure

1. Have your daughter grasp a dumbbell in her right hand with the palm facing the side of the body, and place her left hand and left knee on the bench. She should bend over at the waist so the upper body and lower back are parallel (flat) to the floor. Have her support the body on the bench, and keep the back flat from the shoulders to the hips. She lowers the dumbbell toward the floor so she fully extends the right arm.
2. She slowly pulls the dumbbell upward until it reaches the side of the chest area, then lowers the dumbbell back to the straight-arm position. She performs the assigned number of repetitions; then switches the supporting posture and exercises her left side.

Technique Tips

- Exhale during the pulling phase of the exercise and inhale during the lowering phase.
- The legs and nonexercising arm should remain stationary during the exercise. The lower back should not rotate during this exercise.
- For variation, this exercise can be performed with the elbow pointing away from the body (palm toward feet) during the lifting motion.

Dumbbell Pullover

Muscles

Latissimus dorsi (sides of the mid-back)

Procedure

1. Grasping one dumbbell with both hands, have your daughter lie on a flat bench with her arms extended over her chest area. She can secure her grip by cupping both hands around one end of the dumbbell.
2. She slowly lowers the dumbbell behind her head toward the floor as far as comfortable, maintaining a slight bend in the elbows. Then she slowly returns to the starting position.

Technique Tips

- Inhale on lowering the weight and exhale on lifting it.
- A spotter should kneel directly behind the lifter's head during this exercise and provide assistance if necessary.
- Because the dumbbell is over the head of the lifter, begin with a light weight and gradually increase the load. A solid dumbbell (rather than a dumbbell with plates and collars) is recommended for this exercise.

Dumbbell Upright Row

Muscles

Deltoids (shoulder), upper trapezius (middle of upper back), biceps (front of upper arm)

Procedure

1. Your daughter begins by grasping a dumbbell in each hand, and standing erect with feet about hip-width apart. She should hold the dumbbells so they hang straight down in front of her body with her palms facing her body. The dumbbells should be closer than shoulder-width apart.
2. She slowly pulls both dumbbells upward to the height of the upper chest; then lowers them to the starting position.

Technique Tips

- Exhale during the lifting phase of the exercise and inhale during the lowering phase.
- Stand erect and keep the dumbbells close to the body during this exercise.
- At the top of the movement the elbows should be higher than the shoulders.
- This exercise can also be performed with a barbell, providing skilled instruction and supervision are available.

Dumbbell Overhead Press

Muscles

Deltoids (shoulder), upper trapezius (middle of upper back), biceps (front of upper arm)

Procedure

1. Have your daughter begin by grasping a dumbbell in each hand, and standing erect with feet about hip-width apart. She should hold the dumbbells at shoulder height with her palms facing away from her body.
2. She slowly pushes both dumbbells upward until she fully extends both arms over the shoulders; then she lowers the dumbbells to the starting position.

Technique Tips

This exercise requires balance and coordination. Begin with a light weight to learn proper form.

- Exhale during the lifting phase of the exercise and inhale during the lowering phase.
- Stand erect and keep the lower back straight by contracting the abdominal and lower-back muscles.
- This exercise can also be performed while sitting on an adjustable incline bench or chair, which can provide back support and stability.
- This exercise can also be performed with a barbell, providing skilled instruction and supervision are available.

- It is important that a spotter is nearby to provide assistance if needed. A spotter can place his or her hands on the child's wrists to teach proper exercise technique or complete a repetition.

Dumbbell Lateral Raise
Muscles
Deltoids (shoulder)

Procedure
1. Have your daughter begin by grasping a dumbbell in each hand, and standing erect with her hands extended at her sides and palms facing her outer thighs. Her elbows should be slightly bent, and her feet should be about hip-width apart.
2. She slowly lifts both dumbbells upward and sideward until her arms are level with her shoulders (arms parallel to floor). Have her keep her elbows slightly bent, and return to the starting position.

Technique Tips
- Exhale during the lifting phase of the exercise and inhale during the lowering phase.
- Stand erect and keep the lower back straight by contracting the abdominal and lower-back muscles.
- Don't raise the arms higher than parallel to the floor.

Dumbbell Shrug
Muscles
Upper trapezius (upper part of mid-back)

Procedure
1. Have your daughter begin by grasping a dumbbell in each hand, and standing erect with her arms extended at her sides and palms facing her outer thighs. Her arms should be fully extended, and her feet should be about hip-width apart.
2. She should slowly elevate (shrug) both shoulders toward the ears as high as possible; then lower both dumbbells to the starting position.

Technique Tips
- Exhale during the lifting phase of the exercise and inhale during the lowering phase.
- Stand erect and keep the lower back straight by contracting the abdominal and lower-back muscles.
- Don't bend the elbows while lifting the weights.

Dumbbell Shoulder External Rotation
Muscles
Rotator cuff musculature (inside the shoulder)

Procedure
1. Your daughter lies on her side in a comfortable position, holding a light dumbbell with the top hand, and maintaining the elbow in a 90-degree angle. She should hold the upper arm against the side of her body and use her other arm to support her head.
2. She now rotates her forearm out and up without letting her elbow move away from her body. Then she slowly returns to the starting position.

Technique Tips
- Exhale on lifting the weight and inhale on lowering it.
- This is a lightweight exercise. Start with a two- or three-pound dumbbell and increase in one-pound increments.
- Keep the arm pressed against the body during this exercise.
- This exercise can also be performed in the standing position by using rubber tubing attached to a sturdy object or a cable attached to appropriate resistance.

Dumbbell Shoulder Internal Rotation
Muscles
Rotator cuff musculature (inside the shoulder)

Procedure

1. Your daughter lies on her side in a comfortable position, holding a light dumbbell with one hand, and maintaining the elbow in a 90-degree angle. She holds her upper arm on the floor against the side of her body and her forearm perpendicular to the floor.
2. She slowly lowers the dumbbell toward the floor by rotating her shoulder, then returns to the starting position.

Technique Tips

- Inhale on lowering the weight and exhale on lifting it.
- This is a lightweight exercise. Start with a two- or three-pound dumbbell, and increase in one-pound increments.
- Keep the elbow pressed against the body during this exercise.
- This exercise can also be performed in the standing position by using rubber tubing attached to a sturdy object or a cable attached to appropriate resistance.

Dumbbell Biceps Curl

Muscles

Biceps (front of the upper arm)

Procedure

1. Your daughter begins by grasping a dumbbell in each hand, and standing erect with her arms extended at her sides and palms facing forward. She fully extends her arms, and places her feet about hip-width apart.
2. She slowly curls both dumbbells upward toward her shoulders until her palms face the chest. Then she lowers both dumbbells to the starting position.

Technique Tips

Exhale during the lifting phase of the exercise and inhale during the lower phase.

- Stand erect and keep the lower back straight by contracting the abdominal and lower-back muscles.

- If necessary, stand with the back against a wall to prevent upper-body torso movement.
- This exercise can also be performed while sitting on an adjustable incline bench, which can provide back support and stability.
- This exercise can also be performed with a barbell, providing skilled instruction and supervision are available.

Dumbbell Incline Biceps Curl

This exercise is the same as the dumbbell biceps curl, except that your daughter performs it on an inclined bench, typically angled between 45 to 60 degrees.

Dumbbell Triceps Kickback

Muscles

Triceps (behind the upper arm)

Procedure

1. Your daughter grasps a dumbbell in the right hand with the palm facing the side of the body, and places the left hand and left knee on the bench. She bends over at the waist so that the upper body and lower back are parallel (flat) to the floor, bending the right elbow to 90 degrees so the right forearm is perpendicular to the floor. She should support the body on the bench, and keep the back flat from the shoulders to the hips.
2. She slowly straightens the right arm until it is fully extended; then returns to the starting position. Have her perform the assigned number of repetitions; then switch her supporting posture and exercise her left arm.

Technique Tips

- Exhale during the lifting phase of the exercise and inhale during the lowering phase.
- Only the elbow and forearm should move during this exercise. The legs and nonexercising arm should remain stationary and the lower back should not rotate.

Dumbbell Triceps Overhead Extension
Muscles
Triceps (behind the upper arm)

Procedure
1. Have your daughter grasp one dumbbell with both hands and extend her arms overhead, interlacing her fingers under the dumbbell. She should keep her torso erect and eyes facing forward. Her upper arms remain perpendicular to the floor during this exercise.
2. She slowly bends her elbows and lowers the dumbbell behind her head, pauses briefly, then returns to the starting position.

Technique Tips
- Inhale during the lowering phase and exhale during the lifting phase.
- Maintain an erect posture during this exercise Avoid leaning forward or backward. Keep the elbows pointing upward while lowering and raising the dumbbell.

Dumbbell Wrist Curl
Muscles
Wrist flexors (inner side of the forearm)

Procedure
1. Have your daughter begin by kneeling on the floor with the forearms resting on a bench. She should grasp a dumbbell in each hand in a palms-up position so the wrists just hang over the bench.
2. She slowly flexes the fingers and the wrists as high as possible while keeping the forearms flat on the bench; then returns to the starting position.

Technique Tips
- The entire forearm should remain in contact with the bench during this exercise. Only the fingers and wrists should move.

- This exercise can also be performed with one dumbbell at a time or with a barbell, providing skilled instruction and supervision are available.

Dumbbell Wrist Extension
Muscles
Wrist extensors (inner side of the forearm)

Procedure
1. Your daughter begins by kneeling on the floor with the forearms resting on a bench. She grasps a dumbbell in each hand in a palms-down position, and places the palm side of the forearms on the bench so that the wrists just hang over the bench.
2. She slowly lifts the fingers and the wrists as high as possible while keeping the forearms flat on the bench; then returns to the starting position.

Technique Tips
- The entire forearm should remain in contact with the bench during this exercise. Only the fingers and wrists should move.
- Because this muscle group is weak, begin with a light weight.
- This exercise can also be performed with one dumbbell at a time or with a barbell, providing skilled instruction and supervision are available.

Wrist Roller
Muscles
Wrist flexors and extensors (inner/outer sides of the forearm)

Procedure
1. Your daughter should grasp the handle of the wrist roller with her palms facing downward. She stands erect with her elbows bent slightly.
2. Have her roll up the string on the bar until the weight reaches the uppermost part. Then she slowly unrolls the string.

Flexibility Program

The stretching exercises in this section can be done at home or, if your daughter is old enough to join, at a health club. Use your own judgment as to whether your daughter is mature enough to do them by herself or whether you need to supervise. If your daughter can't hold a particular stretch for the length of time given, that's OK—she can rest for a moment, or where appropriate, switch to the other limb. Your daughter should do the stretch as many times as is necessary to reach the recommended stretch time.

Chest Stretch

Have your daughter interlock her fingers behind her head and gently move her elbows backward.

Triceps and Lat Stretch

Your daughter should reach one arm behind her head as if she were trying to scratch her back. Have her gently pull the elbow toward the midline of her body. Repeat on the other side.

Upper-Back Stretch

Your daughter reaches across her body with one arm and places the hand on the opposite shoulder, gently pressing the elbow across her body. Repeat on the other side.

Hamstring Stretch

Have your daughter sit upright with one leg straight in front of her body and the other knee bent with the heel against the inner thigh of the extended leg. She should bend at the hip and gently lean forward while keeping the extended leg straight. Repeat on the other side.

Low-Back and Hip Stretch

Your daughter sits upright on the floor with both legs straight in front of her body. She crosses one leg over the other and places the opposite arm against the bent knee to assist with torso rotation. Repeat on the other side.

Inner-Thigh Stretch

Have your daughter sit upright with her knees bent and the soles of her feet touching. She should grasp her ankles and gently press her elbows against her knees.

Quadriceps Stretch

Your daughter should lie on her side and bend one knee toward her buttocks. She grasps the ankle with one hand and gently pulls her heel toward her buttocks. Repeat on the other side.

Calf Stretch

With her arms extended in front of her body, your daughter should place both hands against a wall for support. She bends the knee of the front leg and keeps the back leg straight with the heel on the floor. Repeat on the other side.

Resources

● ● ●

Sports Organization Websites

- American Academy of Pediatrics: www.aap.org
- American Alliance for Health, Physical Education Recreation and Dance
- (AAHPERD): www.aahperd.org
- American Council on Exercise: www.acefitness.org
- American Dietetic Association: www.eatright.org
- Boys and Girls Clubs of America : www.bgca.org
- The Female Athlete: www.thefemaleathlete.com
- Girl Power!: www.health.org/gpower
- Girl Scouts of America: www.girlscouts.org
- Healthy People 2010: www.health.gov/healthypeople
- Iglow—For Girls Who Play: www.iglow.com
- Ladies Professional Golf Association: www.lpga.com
- The Melpomene Institute: www.melpomene.org
- National Association of Girls and Women in Sport:
  www.aahperd.org/nagws
- National Athletic Trainers´ Association (NATA): www.nata.org
- National Bone Health Campaign: www.cdc.gov/powerfulbones
- National Osteoporosis Foundation (NOF): www.nof.org

- Office of the Surgeon General: www.surgeongeneral.gov
- Shape Up America!: www.shapeup.org
- Sports Illustrated for Kids: www.sikids.com
- The Tucker Center for Research on Girls & Women in Sport: www.coled.umn.edu/tuckercenter
- United States Olympic Committee (USOC): www.olympic-usa.org
- US Public Health Services Office on Women's Health: www.4women.org
- USA Hockey, Inc.: www.usahockey.com
- Women's National Basketball Association (WNBA): www.wnba.com
- Women's Sports Foundation: www.womenssportsfoundation.org
- YMCA of the USA: www.ymca.net
- YWCA of the USA : www.ywca.org

Books

The Beautiful Game: Sixteen Girls and the Soccer Season That Changed Everything by Jonathan Littman. Harperperennial Library: 2000.

Game and the Glory by Michelle Akers and Gregg Lewis. Zondervan Publishing House: 2000.

Games Girls Play: Understanding and Guiding Young Female Athletes by Caroline Silby PhD, and Shelley Smith. St. Martin's Press: 2000.

Get With It, Girls! Life Is Competition by Teri Clemens and Tom Wheatley. Diamond Communications: 2001.

Girls Got Game: Sports Stories and Poems, edited by Sue Macy. Henry Holt & Company: 2001.

The Girls of Summer: The U.S. Women's Soccer Team and How It Changed the World by Jere Longman. HarperCollins: 2000.

Go for the Goal: A Champion's Guide to Winning in Soccer and Life by Mia Hamm and Aaron Heifetz. Quill: 2000.

A History of Basketball for Girls and Women: From Bloomers to Big Leagues by Joanne Lannin. Lerner Pub Group: 2000.

In These Girls, Hope Is a Muscle by Madeleine Blais. Warner Books: 1996.

Little Girls in Pretty Boxes: The Making and Breaking of Elite Gymnasts and Figure Skaters by Joan Ryan. Warner Books: 2000.

Nike Is a Goddess: The History of Women in Sports edited by Lissa Smith. Atlantic Monthly Press: 1998.

Play Like a Girl: A Celebration of Women in Sports edited by Sue Macy and Jane Gottesman. Henry Holt & Company: 1999.
See How She Runs: Marion Jones & the Making of a Champion by Ron Rappaport. Amistad Press: 2001.

The Sports Medicine Bible for Young Athletes by Lyle J. Micheli with Mark Jenkins. Sourcebooks: 2001.

Winning Ways: A Photohistory of American Women in Sports by Sue Macy. Henry Holt & Company: 1996.

Reports

U.S. Department of Health and Human Services. The Surgeon General's call to action to prevent and decrease overweight and obesity. .Rockville, MD: U.S. Department of Health and Human Services, Public Health Service, Office of the Surgeon General; Available from: US GPO, Washington. 2001.

The President's Council on Physical Fitness and Sports Report - Physical Activity & Sport in the Lives of Young Girls: Physical & Mental Health Dimensions from an Interdisciplinary Approach. Washington DC: President's Council on Physical Fitness and Sports. 1997.

Miller Lite Report on Women in Sports. East Meadow, NY: Women's Sports Foundation. 1985.

Miller Lite Report on Sports & Fitness in the Lives of Working Women. East Meadow, NY: Women's Sports Foundation. 1993.

Index

About the Authors

Hannah Storm is the nation's top female sportscaster. She moderates NBC's *NBA Showtime* and co-hosts the Olympics. She has hosted coverage of four Olympic Games, Notre Dame football, the World Series, Wimbledon, the WNBA championships, the NBA playoffs, and the NBA Finals. She is a two-time Emmy nominee, and the winner of the Grace Allen Award for Outstanding Achievement. She has reported on the NBA, women's golf, college football, the NFL, Major League Baseball, and NASCAR, among other sports. She is married to fellow NBC sportscaster Dan Hicks and they live in Connecticut with their three daughters. *Go Girl!* is her first book.

Mark Jenkins is the coauthor of several highly regarded books on sports health, including the definitive book in its field, *The Sports Medicine Bible*. As a consultant at the Sports Medicine Division at Boston Children's Hospital, Mark's expertise on the sports-health concerns of young athletes is well established. Mark also has plenty of personal experience in the area of youth sports—he has coached and refereed girls soccer and plays stepdad to his fiancée's two sports-mad kids, who play organized hockey, basketball, golf, baseball, and football. Living on the island of Martha's Vineyard, Mark still finds time to work out, bike, and play competitive soccer and tennis.